W9-CES-353

JUL

Fell's
Official Know-It-All
Guide™

FELL'S OFFICIAL KNOW-IT-ALL GUIDE™

TO CASINO GAMBLING

CASINO
GAMBLING

Fell's Official Know-It-All Guide™

FELL'S OFFICIAL KNOW-IT-ALL GUIDE™ TO CASINO GAMBLING

CASINO GAMBLING

Your Absolute, Quintessential,
All You Wanted to Know, Complete Guide

DENNIS HARRISON

Frederick Fell Publishers, Inc.

Fell's Official Know-It-All Guide to Casino Gambling
FREDERICK FELL PUBLISHERS, INC.

2131 Hollywood Boulevard
Hollywood, Florida 33020
800-771-3355
e-mail: fellpub@aol.com

Visit our web site at www.fellpub.com

Reproduction, translation, or use in any form by any means of any part of this work beyond that permitted by Section 107 or 108 of the 1976 United States Copyright Act without the permission of the copyright owner is unlawful. Requests for permission or further information should be addressed to the Permissions Department, Frederick Fell Publishers, Inc., 2131 Hollywood Boulevard, Hollywood, FL 33020.

This publication is designed to provide accurate and authoritative information in regard to the subject matter covered. It is sold with the understanding that the publisher is not engaged in rendering legal, accounting, or other professional service. If legal advice or other assistance is required, the services of a competent professional person should be sought. From A Declaration of Principles jointly adopted by a Committee of the American Bar Association and a Committee of Publishers.

Library of Congress Cataloging-in-Publication Data
Harrison, Dennis R.
       Casino gambling / Dennis R. Harrison
              p.   cm. -- (Fell's official know-it-all guide)
       ISBN 0-88391-013-6
       1. Gambling 2. Casinos   I. Title II. Title. III. Series.
       GV1301 .H277 2000
       895--dc21

                                                                99-086835

10 9 8 7 6 5 4 3 2 1

Copyright © 2000. All rights reserved.
Interior Design by Vicki Heil

BELLEVILLE PUBLIC LIBRARY

Table of Contents

Introduction:
Building a Foundation

 am going to make an assumption. I'm going to assume that you want to learn how to win. If you don't, I'm wrong and this chapter will probably prove to be, at best, mildly interesting. But if my assumption is correct you need to start you off with something so basic it should be engraved in both your conscious and unconscious beings. Something which is absolutely vital to your future success. Each of the forthcoming chapters will reveal money management ideas and strategies, but we're going to start with something more elemental than what you'll read later. I'm now asking that you do two things. Here's the first:

I believe that you and I can agree it's important that you study the games, learn about the odds, etc. Fine. Now let's go one step further. In addition to learning about all of the games, I want you to select one to which you will devote the lion's share of your time. I would prefer that you pick a game which can actually be beaten, but for right now the game is not important. What is important is that you study that particular game until you become so proficient you can rightfully be termed an expert. Doing so is to your benefit.

This, like everything else in this book, is directed at helping you have more fun because you're winning, or losing less, or at least know what's going on.

Okay. Why is it important to become expert in one of the games? Why can't you simple walk into a casino and throw your money at whatever strikes your fancy at that particular moment? My answer is that some games of chance provide a better chance of winning than others. Yet, those "others" can be interesting and fun to play. But you shouldn't want to spend the majority of your time playing the "others," because to do so is to add infection to the wound at a time when you should be cleansing it.

It is not reasonable to believe that you can become "expert" in all the games. You lead a busy life. You have other interests. Fine. I am not asking that you give up everything else and study nothing but casino gambling. I am merely requesting that you consider studying one game . . .the choice is yours . . .long enough and well enough so that you "know" how to play as well as anyone. You may prefer Craps or Roulette, Baccarat or Blackjack. Take your pick. Regardless of the game, the point is that you must study your choice. This book will teach you the basics of all the major games and either give you tips on how to win or tips on how not to lose. After reading this book you still might lose, but you won't lose as much as most people, and you'll be able to avoid disaster. So, I strongly suggest that you choose one of the games as your specialty. That's my first request. Here comes the second.

Is it reasonable to assume that you will play only your specialty, to the exclusion of all the other games, for your entire trip, or for the weekend, or for the day that you gamble? Can you avoid the temptation to pop a few coins in a Slot Machine, control the urge to wager on your favorite number at Roulette? Can you ignore those joyful cries emanating from the Craps tables? I doubt it. Even if you know that you'll lose, you'll still want to test your luck. But it is how you play the games that will determinewhether you leave town with winnings of losses. So, please do this:

After you determine the size of your gambling bankroll, divide it into two groups. Doesn't make any difference whether your gambling will be for several days, half a day, or just a few hours. Group A should be at least eighty percent of the bankroll, and is to be used only on the game you have mastered. Group B, the other twenty percent or less, can then be used to experiment with the other games, to test your luck, or to help pass time between your serious gambling sessions. Group A contains your "serious" gambling money. Group B contains your "fun" gambling money. Plan on playing seriously with at least eighty percent of your funds and using the rest on whatever strikes your fancy.

If your bankroll is $1,000 for the trip, you would gamble with $800, toy with $200. Who knows what may happen? Perhaps while playing with your fun money you'll win a jackpot playing Video Poker or hit your lucky number five times in succession at Roulette. If that happens, great! But don't count on it. If you're only going for a day and your bankroll is $400, $320 should be for serious gambling, $80 for fun. If you're only going for a few hours and you only have $60 in your pocket, you may want to avoid all other games entirely and concentrate on your specialty. But under no circumstances should you ever use any of your serious money to supplement the loss of fun money.

If you think my request foolish, at least grasp the basic idea. Is 80% too much for the serious fund? Provide a percent of your own. The point is not the amount, it's the fact that you are doing something to help provide control while you're in the casino.

Two requests, neither outrageous. Two parts of a foundation. The first two steps on the ladder. Call them what you may, but the more solid the flooring the easier it is to walk.

1

American Poker/ Casino Style

kay, let's start this with a disclaimer. You could read my chapter on Blackjack, memorize most of it, and become a really good Blackjack player. You could read my chapter on Craps, memorize most of it, and become a pretty darn tough Craps player. However, in this chapter it is not my intent to help make you a great Poker player, or even a better Poker player. The purpose of this chapter is to explain the differences between how Poker is played in casinos versus how it is played in the normal, friendly (all right, sometimes maybe not so friendly) game you are accustomed to playing in New York, or Nebraska, or wherever you happen to live. The idea here is that after reading this chapter you should have an easier time of it should you decide to play Poker in Tunica, Mississippi, or Black Hawk, Colorado, or even Las Vegas . . .that town in Southern Nevada.

As to why you might want to play Poker in a casino, the answers are simple. Unlike virtually all of the other casino games, you are not fighting a fixed percentage disadvantage. You are not competing against the house. You are now testing your skill and luck against other gamblers. No one has you at a fixed percentage disadvantage.

Yet, even though the reasons stated above are true, I firmly believe that the real reason people enjoy Casino Style Poker is that it gives them a chance to test their skill against some of the best Poker players in the world. You will not be playing against your Uncle Ernie, who couldn't care less if he loses, or your Aunt Donna, who still can't remember that she should not fold when all her cards are of the same suit, or your pals Jimmy and Dutch Boy who can both be bluffed consistently by anyone who raises more than a quarter. You will now be playing with people who, for the most part, really know how to play. Granted, I've seen players in casino Poker games who couldn't pass muster in a penny ante game, let alone a Vegas casino, but these folks are the exception and not the rule. Whether you decide to play in a $1-3 game, or for "no limit," the vast majority of the players at your table will be better than the people you play against at home. And though there is always the chance that you may sit in at a game somewhere and encounter a few slick locals playing as a team, that would definitely be the exception and not the rule. It is true, nonetheless, that you will be sitting in on a number of games where virtually all of the other players appear to know each other. There are casinos all over the country in which the Poker games have been inhabited by the same ten of fifteen players for years and years. Does this mean the new player is at a disadvantage? Depends on your viewpoint. One way to look at it is that none of the "regulars" know how you play. The way to look at it is that the "regulars" only need to figure out one style of play . . . yours. You, on the other hand, need to figure out the style of every other person at the table.

On the low end, most Poker games will fall into the $1- $3 category. On the high end, the sky is the limit. Obviously, you should only play in games you can tolerate financially. No matter how good you think you are, I wouldn't

POKER VIGORISH

The amount of vig you are fighting when you play Poker can only be determined by your level of play. Top of the class? No vig. Playing like a rookie? The vig might be as high as 100%; it's up to you.

2

suggest that you tackle the top seven finishers in last years' World Series of Poker until you've tested your skill at a lower level.

BASIC TERMINOLOGY

This is common stuff you should know.

THE POT:

This is where all the money goes. This is what you are playing to win. Every time you make a bet the chips need to go somewhere. In some games all the chips and money are shoved into the center of the table. In others it is permissible to merely nudge your bets out in front of your player position. Regardless of where you put them, they will be collected at the end of the hand and distributed to the winners.

ANTE:

This would be the minimum requirement in chips to get the game going and is tossed or placed into the Pot. This is also a way to build the Pot.

3

BLIND or BLIND BET:

The bet made by the first player in certain games. A forced bet. A bet made regardless of the value of the cards in your hand. Another way to build the Pot.

 Act only when it is your turn. You are no longer at home. You can no longer bet out of turn, or call out of turn, or check or fold out of turn, even in jest. Make no move and take no action until it is your turn to do so. This is one of those "do it again and you'll wind up on a cold slab" type of rules.

CALL or SEE:

Somebody makes a bet. If you want to stay in the game you must match that bet. In Poker lingo you "call" or "see" the bet. In most casino games, there is no need to "call" or "see" because you can speak using only your chips.

CHECK:

If no bet has been made, and it's your turn to wager, you can stay in the game without making a bet. You simple "check" or "check the bet," which means you are still in the game but you do not want to initiate the betting for that round.

FOLD:

No checking here. To fold is to give it up, toss in your cards, get out of the game, not call any bets. But even though you are giving up, do so only when it is your turn. To fold, either toss your cards, face down, onto the center of the table or lay them out, face down, above your player position.

RAISE:

You have a good hand. You want to build the pot. Somebody makes a bet. You "raise," which means you call the previous bet and also add on another bet. In your home games you might say something like "I'll call the $5 and raise it another $5."

4   At the casino you don't even need to speak. If the bet is $5 to you and you want to kick (raise) it up to $10, simply place twin $5 chips on the table. If you want to raise from $5 to $15, and it's allowed, you would nudge out one $5 chip alongside a stack of twin $5 chips. The dealer will acknowledge your action and make any announcements which may be necessary.

CHECK and RAISE:

Here's something which is ostracized in most "friendly" games, but is common in the casinos. Imagine that you're one of the first bettors. You have a strong hand, but you want to test the waters. You want to see if anyone else at the table is proud of their cards. So, you check. Then, after somebody else initiates the betting you come back with a raise. This is like laying in the weeds, or sneaking up on somebody, and is often considered too dishonorable for neighborhood games. Yet it is a part of Poker you must deal with on this level.

BLUFF:

You don't got anything but you bet like you do. This is an attempt to "fake out" or deceive your fellow gamblers. All it takes is money and the ability to conceal your feelings . . .the ability to look like you've got a million dollars when you can't afford to feed the dog. This is a move often utilized to test the waters, or drive weak players out of the game.

HIGH:

Normally refers to the fact that only high hands can win. In other words, winners are determined by the highest Poker hands based on rank. The Ace is the highest card in the game. There are no splits for Low hands.

LOW:

Exactly the opposite of High. The Ace is now the lowest card in the deck,and winners are determined by who has the lowest ranked hand. A perfect low? Ace + 2 + 3 + 4 + 5. Also, Low hands are usually called by the highest two cards. If you held Ace + 3 + 4 + 5 + 7, your hand would be dubbed a seventy-five, which means that your highest card is a seven and the second highest is a five. Low is also commonly called Lowball. In casinos, it is possible to play a low hand to conclusion and not have a winner. The reason? There is normally a minimum requirement for winning low hands. If it is not achieved there is no winner. The money stays in the Pot and the game begins anew.

5

HIGH-LOW SPLIT:

A description which tells you that there may be more than one winner in this game. There will be the winner who produces the highest Poker hand, and another winner who produces the lowest hand. Two winners. But not always. And that's because it is possible to achieve both on the same hand. Also, like most all Low hands, there may not be a winner for the Low hand due to the minimum qualifications. Which means that even though it's a High-Low split game the entire Pot could go to the High hand.

BUTTON:

The small and usually plastic device which identifies the imaginary dealer. It's simply a small disc which rotates around the table, moving one player at a time after each game, so that the initial bettor is different every game. Another way to think of it is that the button identifies the "pretend" dealer. Since the deal does not rotate, the button does.

BASIC DIFFERENCES

Types of Games Played

You will not find any "wild" or "wild card" games being dealt in the casinos. You know what I'm talking about. Games like Baseball, Low Hole-Card Wild, Dime Store, or Black Mariah. The fare is basic. Seven Card Stud (both high, low, and high-low split), Texas Hold'em (high only), Omaha (high, and high-low split), and Five Card Draw. Hold'em is, by far, the most popular of these and also the most important because it's the game played by the big boys. So, if you want to prove your worth as a Poker player, it's the game you must learn to play. Or, actually, if you want to add your name to the honor rolls of Poker greats, it's the game you must learn to play better than 99% of the rest of the Poker players currently inhabiting this particular planet.

In Seven Card Stud, players who stay until the end will have a total of seven cards. After making the ante bet, players receive two cards face down and one face up to start out. You bet. You're dealt another card, face up. You bet. You're dealt another card, face up. You bet. You're dealt another card, face up. You bet. You're dealt another card, face up. You bet. The last card is dealt face down. You bet for the last time. High hand usually wins. Or, the lowest hand could win. Or, the pot could be split between the highest and lowest hands. Depends on which version of Seven Card Stud you are playing.

In Five Card Draw you ante, then receive five cards, all of which are dealt face

> ### HERE'S A DEFINITE NO-NO
> Don't even think about touching the "Flop" cards. This is true in Texas Hold'em and Omaha. The fact that you can use the common cards in your hand does not mean they are actually yours. They belong to the table, and only the table can touch them. The table, that is, and the dealer. Yes, this is another one of those "Don't do it again unless you want to lose your arm" kind of rules.

6

down. You bet. You then discard any unwanted cards, receive replacements, and bet again for the final time.

Hold'em is quite a bit different from the two previously mentioned. Due to the fact that so few cards are dealt, it is a game which can accommodate a larger number of players. Each player receives two cards down, you bet, there is a "flop," face up, of three cards in the center of the table. These three cards are played as though they were actually in your hand. Of course, they can be used by everyone else, too. You bet. There is another face up flop of one card. You bet. There is a final face up flop of one card. You bet, and someone wins. If you stay for all the cards, you'll have

What's a Flop? Think Hold'em and Omaha. After the first round of betting, the dealer will burn cards off the top of the deck, then peel off the next round of cards and drop them all at the same time in the center of the table. This is usually done with a certain amount of flair and emphasis, thus meeting at least one of the official dictionary definitions of the word "flop". I know not from where it came, but it is certainly appropriate terminology.

7

two in your hand, and five "common" flop cards out in the middle of the table. You must use the two cards in your hand and three of the cards from the flop (the common cards) to make up your five-card hand.

In terms of card distribution and the ability to serve large tables of players, Omaha is similar to Hold'em. Everyone receives four cards face down. The flop is the same: three, one, and one. You bet between all the intervals. This is usually a high-low split game. And even though you have four cards in your possession, and a total of nine cards when the "common" cards are included, you can only play five at a time, two of which must be from your four concealed cards. That's right, you must play two from your hand and three from the common cards laying out there in the center of the table. Yes, you can play two of your four cards for low and the other two for high. Or, you can play the same two, or any combination of the four cards taken two at a time, but you must play two from your hand. And another thing there is usually no splitting of the pot unless someone has at least an Eight or lower for the low hand. That's correct, if no one has at least an Eight for low the entire pot goes to the high Poker hand. Yes, this makes for a very interesting game.

Number of Players

It is common for a table to seat eight to ten players. Yes, I know you can't play Seven Card Stud with eight players because 7 cards each x 8 players = 56 total cards. However, it's done in the casinos all the time. The reason? There is seldom a hand when all 52 cards are used. Invariably, at least two or three players drop after seeing their first few cards. In the case of Hold'em and Omaha, ten players is more the rule than exception. With Hold'em, the size creates the only reason to restrict the number of players. If larger tables were built, you could have thirteen players, or sixteen, or even twenty players. However, if tables were made large enough to accommodate that many people, the players at each end would need telescopes to read the cards at the other end of the felt.

8

ROTATE THOSE DEALERS

Why? If you caught 32 consecutive hands, all from the same dealer, which never exceeded a low pair, would you still think the dealer was a wonderful person? If a dealer was in collusion with another player, would you want that dealer at your table all night? Dealers rotate for the protection of the dealers, the game, and you.

The Dealer

When you're playing with your friends, relatives or whomever, you each take turns shuffling and dealing the cards. In the casino versions of Poker, the casino provides a person to do that for you. Yes, this prevents some card shark from stacking a deck, and is intended to keep the game honest and above board. Though I have seen shifts last for hours, dealers typically rotate every twenty or thirty minutes. In addition to dealing the cards, they provide chips when you need to purchase them, watch the pot to make sure all the players are contributing as they should, and announce the winning hands. The dealer is also there to answer any questions you may have, to explain all the basic rules, and settle any minor disputes. Do not hesitate to question the dealers, regardless of how busy they appear to be. For their services, dealers are compensated by the casino and the tips generously donated by the players. In games where the pot is small, the tip should be at least a half-dollar. When you win a good size pot, tip a dollar or more. Or, don't tip at all if you don't like the dealer. It's up to you. I think it is interesting to note that the dealers I've interviewed indicate they usually make better tips in the small and medium size games. One told me the story of the hand he dealt which ended with a pot of over $30,000. His tip: buy bonds.

Also, the "button" is used to identify each player, in turn, as the dealer so that the person first to the left of the button (pretend dealer) always receives the first card of a new hand. This simulates the act of changing dealers and assures a different rotation on every hand in terms of receiving cards.

Fixed Betting Procedures

At home, if you're playing a game in which the high hand wins, the first bettor will usually be the person with the highest card showing. In the casino, the first bettor will normally be the person with the lowest card showing. For games in which there is no card showing, like Hold'em, the first bettor is the person seated immediately left of the button.

The first bet is always a fixed wager, whether it be 50 cents, a dollar, or several dollars. Of course this depends on the level of the game you're playing. This first bet is known as the "blind" or "forced" bet, because the person on the hot seat (the first bettor) must make this wager. This person does not have the option of folding should he or she not appreciate the first cards dealt to them. The blind bet is always for a fixed amount, say $1 in a $1-$4 game. No more, no less. In some games,

9

A forced bet is used to get money from cheap players—the kind who always fold unless they have 3-of-a-Kind in their first three cards—and it's a neat way to play.

there are two blinds or forced bets. The first bettor must make, say, a $1 wager, the next person must make, say, a $2 wager; again, no more, no less. And, finally, there is another type of blind which is called a "live" blind. This describes a situation where everyone who stays in the game calls the bet of the blind, but no one raises. Should this happen, the blind then has the opportunity to raise herself.

> ## BLIND?
> **Surely you already figured this out. When it's your turn to make the "blind" bet you may as well be "blind" because looking at your cards is meaningless. You're in for the bet whether you like your cards or not.**

After the blind or forced betting has taken place, the rest of the betting must also follow a pattern. In a $1-$3 game of Stud, for example, you may not be able to bet $3 until the last round of cards has been dealt.

If you see a game advertised as $1-$3-$6, this would mean that a wager of $6 is allowed on the final betting round.

There is an ante in some games, none in others. When there is an ante, it is usually fairly small, like a quarter in a $1-$3 game.

Raise, raise, raise. That's correct, in most games the number of raises is limited to three. But, unlike most home games, when there are only two players remaining in the pot, there is no limit to the number of raises allowed. If two of you decide you have a hand that simply cannot lose, then you can raise each other until there is no money left.

Wanna get down and dirty in a completely legitimate manner? Then check and raise. Though this is very uncommon in most home games, it's allowed in virtually every casino Poker room I've ever seen Remember, you're playing with the "big" boys now.

House Take

Did you think the casino was providing this Poker room just so the dealers could make money? The casino needs to collect its share. In Poker rooms, their take is called the "rake" . . .as in the motion the dealer makes when they extend their arms over the pot and pull it over in front of them to take out the casino's share. Or, rake, as in the manner in which the dealers rake the chips into the secured money box attached to the edge of the table. Also, please recall that at the beginning of this chapter I mentioned that one advantage of playing real Poker is that there is no casino advantage . . .that you are not fighting a fixed percentage disadvantage. So, the question becomes, is the Rake the same as a casino advantage? Not exactly. Remember that you are not playing against the casino. The casino neither wins nor loses. The Rake is nothing more than an admission fee. You pay to play. And you only pay when you win. All those losing hands cost you nothing.

The size of the rake varies from game to game Here are some examples.

Betting Limit	% of Rake	With Maximum of
$1 - $3	10	$3.00
$3 - $6	5	$2.50
$1-$2-$4	10	$3.50
$1-$4-$8	5	$2.00

11

The rake will generally be more in Stud, less in Hold'em. This is because fewer hands are dealt per hour in Stud, and Hold'em typically has higher pots, so the casino collects the maximum more frequently. The amount of the rake, plus a list of the games and some of the basic rules is always listed near the entrance to any Poker room. Look until you find it. Ask if you don't find it. Ask before you take a seat.

What Are Table Stakes?

Example: At the beginning of a hand you are down to your last ten dollars, but you think that's enough to last. You're wrong. After the first two bets your $10 in chips is already in the pot. You don't want to fold. There's $70 in the pot at that point. You continue to play, but not bet. At the end, the pot is $200. You win. Guess what? You only get the $70 . . .the amount which was in the pot when you stopped contributing to the pot. The other $130 goes to the best hand of the remaining players . . .even if your hand is higher.

Minimum Buy-In

You can't sit down to play unless you have at least X number of dollars in chips. The amount of the buy-in is listed on the same board that tells you the rake, etc. In a typical $1-$3 game, the buy-in would be at least $20.

Once the game has begun, the table stakes rule applies . . .if you run out of chips you can only play for that portion of the pot to which you contributed. However, most places will allow you to purchase additional chips providing that your money is already on the table. In other words, you buy-in for $20. You set your $20 worth of chips on top of another $30 in cash. The cash counts as chips being on the table, so you can buy more chips at any time during a game.

If you don't already have cash on the table, you cannot go into your pocket, billfold or purse during a game. Of course, you can always purchase more chips between games.

Burn Cards

This is another way of keeping the game honest. It is possible for players to mark the cards as the game is being played. If a player does this, then they could identify the top card on the deck. To prevent this, the dealer shuffles, someone cuts, and then the dealer burns a card both prior to the beginning of the first round, and before beginning each subsequent round.

Placing of Chips in the Pot

At home, when you call a bet, or raise, you toss your chips into the middle of the pile which is accumulating in the middle of the table. In the Poker Room at the casino, you do it a little differently. Instead of tossing the chips, you slide the chips. Instead of sending the chips to the middle of the table, you slide them out slightly in front of your playing position. Instead of sliding your chips out in a stack, you slide them out so that they are slightly spread apart. When you raise, you slide out two rows of bets; one to call, the other to raise. Do it this way, and you'll make life much easier for the dealer and your fellow players. If the chips of each player are distributed as I indicate, a simply glance around the table will tell you who is staying, raising, re-raising, etc. After the betting is finished for each round, the dealers then scrape all the chips into one big pile in the middle of the table. If necessary, the dealers will even stack the chips in the various denominations, so they can tally the pot and determine the amount of the rake.

If you keep heaving your chips into the pile, the dealer and even regular old people like me might very well won-

> **ANOTHER NO-NO**
> If you fold, do not ever toss away your cards so that they land face up. Not kosher. Against the rules. Disturbing to other players. Will anger the dealer. Will convince every living soul in the entire casino that you are a worthless jerk. That, or even worse.

der if you really tossed six chips and not five. Get my drift? Should you desire to fold, toss your cards into the middle of the table. Yes, now it's okay to toss. You could also simply lay them all face down in front of or atop your player location.

Cards Play

There is no need for you to declare the value or rank-ing of your hand. Even if you have a Royal Flush and are so proud that you can't wait to announce it . . .don't. The dealer will read your cards and determine whether you have a winning hand. Allow the players to observe your cards and then calmly sit back while they gush things like "Wow, the SOB's got a

> **YET ANOTHER NO-NO**
> The game is over. Everybody turns over their cards except you. You wait until you see all the other hands. Then, if you know you lose, you toss away your cards, face down. Nobody knows what you had. You know what everybody else had. You keep doing this right up until the time the trap door opens and you are sucked through a tunnel of fire. Get the picture?

13

Royal." Or, "Man, oh man, I'm glad I dropped out."

You should know the ranking of your hand, so that you can recognize it immediately if the dealer makes an error, but the cards play themselves . . . turn them over and hope you have the best hand.

Conservative Play

If you're like me, and you're playing at home, and the game is of the nickel-dime-quarter variety, you never drop out of a hand which has even the most remote of possibilities. Consequently, it is not unusual to have seven players contending for a pot after the last round of betting. Obviously, this is something you will rarely, if ever, see in a casino Poker Room. In a Stud game consisting of eight players, the final round will normally see no more than two to four players.

You must decide for yourself how to play your cards. But if you play every hand which contains only marginal possibilities, you will be swallowed alive. If, on the other hand, you are accustomed to playing only those hands which offer sound possibilities your chances for survival are excellent.

Speed of Play

It won't take long for you to notice the difference. The game moves much faster than any you have previously experienced. There is not much idle chit-chat between players. The dealer makes every attempt to keep the game moving along. The more games played per hour, the better for both the casino and the dealers. The players, overall, are smarter, and take less time to make decisions. There's not much joke telling or friendly "kidding." However, there is conversation among the players and the dealers . . .usually during the shuffle or pot splitting. There is joking and wise comments . . .but seldom in the middle of the game.

Those are the basic differences between the game you play at home and the games you will play in a casino. The actual playing of the hands still depends on the style, intelligence and experience of the individual player. You can play Stud for hours and never see a winning hand better than 3 of a Kind, then lose with a Straight Flush. You can stay in a game of Hold'em hoping to fill a Flush and accidentally win with a Queen high because everyone else folds. You can stay in a game of Omaha simply because no one else is betting like they have anything, and either get massacred or win with a small pair. It's still Poker. You're playing in a different environment, but it's still Poker. And always remember this: Real men play Real Poker. Well, just kidding. Kinda. Real women play Real Poker, too.

14

2

Pai-Gow Poker

Firmly plant this image in your mind. You've just arrived at a casino. You've never been in this particular one. I don't care what the casino looks like. You can use your imagination. It can be old, run down and depressing. It can be bright, new and cheerful. None of that is important. Here's what is: You notice a small group of people clustered around a table in one of the Blackjack pits. You approach the group to see why everyone in the crowd seems to be studying the action taking place on the table. The players at the table consist of five Asians and one Caucasian. Instead of cards, you see these small plastic things on the table. On reflection, you decide these small plastic things resemble dominoes. No one in the crowd seems to have the slightest understanding of what is happening. The five Asians at the table seem to be having fun, but the lone Caucasian appears to be slightly perplexed. You look up and notice a sign which announces that the game you are watching is called "Pai Gow."

Okay, now that you have the picture, remember this: Do not attempt to play this game! Those plastic things that look like dominoes are actually the equivalent of Chinese playing cards. The figures which make them appear to

> ## SOUND ADVICE
> It is not a good idea to risk your money on gambling venues which are being played in a language you do not understand, by rules which you find incomprehensible. And, yes, this advice also applies to the newest of the slot machines found today in the casinos of America.

be dominoes are actually Chinese numbers. So, unless you can read Chinese numbers, it is virtually impossible for you to play this game. This is why the five Orientals at the table seem to be having fun, but the lone Caucasian is lost, and no one watching the game can figure out what is happening. Could you play Blackjack if the playing cards contained no numbers or figures? Of course not. So why try to play a game in which you are literally blind?

All of this is the bad news. Here is the good news. Same scenario: You are walking through a new casino and you see people clustered around a table in the Blackjack pit. At the table are seated two Asians and four players who are not Asian. There are playing cards distributed in front of each player, but it is obvious the game is not Blackjack. The dealer appears to be performing some sort of ceremony with a canister of dice. You say to yourself: "Oh, oh, this must be another one of those crazy games which can only be played by people with mysterious and special knowledge."

Special knowledge? Well, it would be nice if you knew the rules. Mysterious? Only at a glance. Crazy game? Not at all.

The game you are now observing is call Pai Gow Poker. Please note that the first game you discovered was call Pai Gow, and this game is called Pai Gow Poker. Again, unless you can read Chinese numbers, do not even think about playing Pai Gow. But please make every attempt during your next visit to play Pai Gow Poker, because it is an easy game to learn and a fun game to play, particularly if you find the pace of Blackjack and Craps to be too hectic.

Pai Gow Poker is a game which combines elements of the ancient Chinese game of Pai Gow, and the American game of Poker. So, if you have ever played Poker at any level, including Video Poker, you should be able to play Pai Gow Poker. So long as you have a basic understanding of the ranking of winning hands in Poker, you can play this game.

IT'S EASIER THAN IT LOOKS

Let's assume you decide to sit in for a few games. Here's what happens: First, you buy chips. Yep. Just like all the other games. Yep. If you're only going to be there for one hand, or if you absolutely need to do it, you could play for a cash wager but the casino will not encourage you. So, get chips and then make a wager. At most tables, the minimum is $10, though you may need to play for more expensive stakes if you're visiting over a weekend, or over a holiday period, or it's the Super Bowl, etc. You may think the $10 minimum seems a tad steep for your taste, but don't worry; in the time it takes to play one hand of Pai Gow Poker, you could have played 5-7 handsof Blackjack. As I stated earlier, this game has a nice pace to it, and is not played with the frenzy of some of the other games. As is the case with Blackjack, there will be a small circular or rectangular area on the felt in which you should place the chips for your wager. In fact, all you need to know regarding the table layout is shown in Figure 1.

17

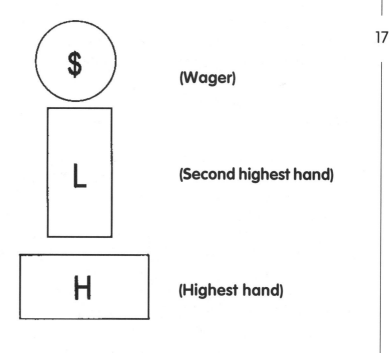

Figure 1

THE RITUAL

The dealer shuffles the cards and deals seven hands consisting of seven cards each in piles directly in front of her. The players don't get the cards yet. She starts dealing from her left, makes seven piles working to her right, then reverses her action, moving from right to left for the second card in the pile, then left to right again, etc. until each pile has exactly seven cards. She then counts the cards remaining in her hand to ensure that she has the correct number of cards remaining. She's been dealing for more years than you've owned an automobile, so she's in no rush. Maybe she notes how intently you are studying the action and gives you a wink from her twinkling blue left eye. You quickly multiply in your head that seven piles of seven cards each should be a total of 49 cards dealt, which means that she should have 3 cards left out of a single deck of 52 cards, but you are wrong. This playing deck consists of the 52 regular cards, plus one Joker, so when the dealer counts the cards remaining in her hand, she should find four.

Why the ritual? It gives the game more mystique and insures a clean game for both the public and the casino.

The next step is that the dealer picks up a small cup, usually metal, and shakes it to mix up the three dice contained inside. She then flips the cup over, reveals the dice, and counts the total of them. The dice, by the way, look like the same dice used at Craps, except that they are smaller and usually white with black dots. Each die exhibits the numbers 1 to 6, so that the total of the three dice could be any number from 3 to 18. The total of the dice is what determines which player is to receive the first hand. For, you see, if the piles of cards were distributed in the same order on every hand, the dealer may at times be accused of stacking the deck in her favor. Due to the fact that this particular dealer looks like your Grandmother we won't accuse her of being in cahoots with any of the players. But since the dice determine which hand she will be playing, ritual prevents her from predetermining which hand to stack.

The dealer's position is counted as number 1, number 8, or number 15, depending on the total of dice. That is, the Banker's position is counted as

18

number 1, 8, or 15, but since the dealer is almost always the Banker, just think of it that way and I'll explain the difference later.

Let's assume that the total of the dice was 4. The dealer counts herself as one, the first person to her right as two, the second person as three, and the third person as four. So the third person from her right is given the first hand, which is the first stack on her right, and then the rest of the piles are passed out to player number five, number six, number seven, the dealer, then players number two and three. If this sounds a little confusing, don't fret. You have no control over the distribution of the hands. The important issue at this point is that all that stuff, that ritual which looked so mysterious when you were watching other people play this game, is not so mysterious, after all. Also, here is diagram that may help you understand.

Player Positions

7	6	5	4	3	2
14	13	12	11	10	9
			18	17	16

Dealer Positions

1
8
15

Keeping this chart in mind, you can see that if the total number from the dice were 4, then the player at the number 4 position would receive the first hand, and the player at position number 3 would receive the last hand. If the total dice number came to 13, then the player at position number 13 (which is also position number 6) would receive the first hand, and the player at position number 12 would receive the last hand. The only time the dealer would receive the last hand would be if the dice total 2, 9, or 16. I hope this makes sense to you, but if it doesn't this will not effect your ability to play.

THE GAME

Now you have seven cards in front of you, placed there in a nice, neat stack by the dealer. Your next step is to pick them up, look at them, and hope you can make a couple of Poker hands out of them. Not one hand. Two hands. You are going to make up what you can think of as your highest Poker hand, and your second highest Poker hand. All of the other players at the table, plus the dealer, are going to do the same. The object of the game is for your highest Poker hand to be higher than the dealer's highest hand, and also for your second highest hand to be higher than the dealer's second highest hand. The ranking of hands is Five Aces, Royal Flush, Straight Flush, Four of a Kind, Full House, Flush, Straight, Three of a Kind, Two Pair, One Pair, and High Card. Those of you who have already seen the Rankings of Poker chapter may now be saying, wait a minute, you can't have a hand of Five Aces. The highest hand you listed before was a Royal Flush. What's with this Five Aces nonsense? Well, remember that we're now playing Pai Gow Poker. This is not a Real Poker game. It merely contains elements of Real Poker. Consequently, there is a ranking which is higher than the Royal Flush. And we can't achieve a hand containing Five Aces unless there is at least one card in the deck which can "pose" as an Ace. And while we are not playing with any truly "wild" cards, you may recall that we are playing with one Joker in the deck. The Joker is an Ace by itself, or it can be used like a "wild" card in Straights and Flushes. In other words, if you

> ### WARNING—WARNING—WARNING
> Don't touch your cards until the dealer is finished with the distribution process. Yes, this is another one of those "don't ever do it again unless you want us to rip off your toenails" issues.

> ### HIGH—HIGHER—HIGHEST
> Some people find it more convenient to think of the two hands as a high hand and a low hand. I prefer the highest and second highest terminology. But it's your choice. You can think of it any way you want, so long as you understand the basic concept.

20

have an Ace and a Joker, you really have two Aces. If you have three Aces and a Joker, you really have four Aces. Should you have an Eight, Nine, Ten, Jack, and Joker, you have a Straight. A hand consisting of Seven, Eight, Ten, Jack, and Joker, would also be a Straight. If you have four Spades and the Joker, you have a Flush. If you have a pair of Queens and a pair of Kings, plus a Joker, you really have a pair of Queens, a pair of Kings, and an Ace.

Again, you are going to make two hands out of the seven cards you are now holding. And please note that you must use all seven cards. Your best hand will consist of five cards and your second best hand will only consist of two cards. Since most Poker hands consist of five cards, developing a five-card hand for the highest possibility should not be difficult. You simply look at the seven cards, and separate the five which make the best poker hand. This then leaves you with

Remember that the Joker can serve as an Ace, and can also be used to fill in a Straight or Flush. And that's all the Joker can do. The Joker is not wild.

21

two cards which you can utilize as your second best hand. The ranking of the two-card hand is slightly different merely because it only contains two cards; subsequently the two-card hand cannot contain a Straight, a Flush, or any other ranking except for High Card or a Pair. Sounds easy enough, right? Well, it is a little more complicated than that because you must keep in mind that we want to beat both the dealer's best and second best hands. In fact, the only time we win is when we beat both of the dealer's hands. What? You mean I gotta beat both of them? Yes, that's what I'm saying, and I know that sounds pretty tough, but the news gets better. On those occasions when you only beat one of the dealer's hands, you lose nothing, you gain nothing; we have a draw and no money exchanges hands. And in order for the dealer to collect *your* money, the dealer must either beat or tie both of your hands. Yes, the dealer wins ties. But don't concern yourself too much with the news that the dealer wins ties, because ties seldom occur.

The bottom line here, as they say in the business world, is that you can play a lot of hands without either gaining or losing a lot of money and have a very good time while doing it. This is because if you play your cards properly you won't find many instances of the dealer beating you senseless unless your luck is simply very bad. And the reason is that unless we have cards which will make us two good hands, we always play for the tie. Yes, I know this sounds defensive, but it is also intelligent.

> **This is worth repeating. You can't win unless your highest hand beats the dealer's highest hand, and your second highest hand also beats the dealer's second highest hand. You must win both. One loss would create a push. A tie could create a push. You must win both hands.**

Now, one last piece of information you must have in order to play this game. Your best hand, the one which is made up of five cards, must be higher in rank than your second best hand. This makes sense, but this is also where a lot of people end up making mistakes. If you make the error of arranging your cards so that your second best hand is higher in ranking than your best hand, you lose automatically. You also lose automatically if you mistakenly place only three or four cards in your highest hand, or make any arrangement that does not consist of five cards and two cards. Sound harsh? Too bad. You gotta have rules, and this is one of them.

HOW'S ABOUT WE PLAY A FEW PRACTICE HANDS

Let's see if we can make sense out of all of this. You sit down, make a bet of ten dollars, the dealer shuffles, the dealer makes seven little piles in front of her consisting of seven cards each, the dealer shakes the dice, the total of the dice is 9, so the player all the way over at the end of the table (third base in Blackjack lingo) receives the first hand, and the player at position number 15, which is the dealer, gets the last pile of cards.

Your hand consists of the following: Ace S + Queen S + Joker + Nine D + 10 D + Queen C and the King S. Get out a deck of cards and deal yourself this exact hand and you'll find this example easier to follow. As you can quickly see, this hand definitely has possibilities. A person new to the game, upon receiving these cards, might immediately arrange their two hands like this:

Highest hand: Ace S + Joker + Queen S + Queen C + King S
Second highest: 9 D + 10 D

This means that their 5-card hand is a pair of Aces (remember the Joker is another Ace), a pair of Queens, and the leftover King. The second best hand is simply the 9 and 10 of diamonds, which were the leftovers. Two Pair is not a bad hand, and if you consider the ranking of hands, the dealer would have to have Three of a Kind or better to beat it. So let's assume for a moment that Two Pair could very well beat the dealer's best hand. That's one win. Now let's think about the chances you left for your 2-card second best hand. In that hand, your highest card is a 10.

> **A REMINDER**
> Just because it is the second best does not mean that you can merely throw all of your "junk" into the 2-card hand and hope for the best. You must think in terms of making the two best hands possible, even if it means reducing the value of the highest(5-card) hand.

Relative strength? Weak. Very weak. Probably a loser. In fact, as you will see when you start playing, a 10 high will seldom win. So, bearing that fact in mind, how else could you play this same hand and improve our chances of winning: A) at least one of the hands, or B) both hands?

How about this?

Highest hand: Ace S + Joker + Queen S + Queen C + 9 D
Second highest: King S + 10 D

Please note that you made only one small change, trading the King of Spades for the 9 of Diamonds. This swap does not effect the ranking of our highest hand, yet makes a definite improvement in our second highest. Or you could alter your thinking entirely, and play the hand this way:

Highest (5-card) hand: Ace S + Joker + 9 D + 10 D + King S
Second (2-card) highest: Queen S + Queen C

Here, you are playing a pair of Aces plus trash for the high hand, and a pair of Queens for the second highest. The thinking here is that while your pair of Aces may not win for high, your pair of Queens will almost assuredly win for the second highest and will come out of this with no worse than a tie.

And now for those of you who thought I had overlooked one of our best possibilities, what if you remembered that your Joker can be used as the fifth card if you have four towards a Straight or Flush, and thus arrange your cards like this:

Highest hand: 9 D + 10 D + Joker + Queen C + King S
Second highest: Ace S + Queen S

MACHO, MACHO MAN

Some gamblers insist on taking the "macho" approach and so they put all their high cards in the best hand. This means that every time they lose the best hand they also usually lose the second best because there's nothing good in it. Even when they win the best hand, they lose the second best. Bad strategy. Play more conservatively, keep more of your money, and play longer on less money even when you don't get decent cards.

A Straight for the best hand is quite powerful, almost a certainty to beat the dealer's high hand, and the Ace and Queen you have leftover for the second best hand is also very playable since it will probably lose to nothing less than a Pair. Arranging the cards in this manner provides you with nearly a "lock" for best, and a good shot at also winning second best.

Always remember that you need to arrange your cards so that you are making your very best effort of winning at least one of the hands.

Another example: You are dealt the 2 C + 4 H + 6 H + 7 D + 7 H + 8 D + 9 C. How do you arrange your hand? What about this?

24

Highest hand: 2 C + 4 H + 6 H + 8 D + 9 C
Second highest: 7 D + 7 H

Obviously, the person who would arrange their hand in this manner is thinking that the trash is worthless, so why not put it in the high hand? This way they can save the pair of Sevens for the second best hand. The logic sounds okay at first, but the result is that this person will lose their bet. Why? Because their second best hand carries a higher ranking than their best hand, which is definitely against the rules. This person has no choice but to arrange this hand thusly:

Highest hand: 7 D + 7 H + 2 C + 4 H + 6 H
Second highest: 8 D + 9 C

Yes, I know that this hand appears to have no chance of winning. A Pair of Sevens is fairly weak for the 5-card hand, and a 9 high is exceptionally weak for the 2-card hand. But, as in Real Poker, strange things happen. Every once in a while, the dealer is dealt a hand that contains Cow Pie. So even when you receive terrible cards, do not despair. There will always be times when you win with terrible cards. And, of course, even more times when you lose with fantastic cards.

Anyway, let's look at one more hand and contemplate your options. You receive the Ace S + 9 S + Jack S + 10 D + Joker (Yeaaaahhhhh) + 7 S + 3 S. You immediately recognize that you have a very nice Straight, and arrange your hands like this:

> ### COW PIE?
> Cow Pie sounds like the exact opposite of Pai Gow, and kind of rhymes, so some player some time in history decided the term Cow Pie was appropriate for describing a dealer hand which contains absolutely nothing . . .the type of hands you want to see associated with the dealer every time you play.

Highest hand: Jack S + 10 D + 9 S + Joker + 7 S
Second highest: Ace S + 3 S

25

What can I say? Nice try, but no cigar. There's a better way. You failed to note that you also have a very nice Spade Flush and could arrange your hands like this:

Highest hand: Jack S + 9 S + 7 S + 3 S + Joker
Second highest: Ace S + 10 D

This gives you a better hand for the highest, and even improves the 2-card hand from Ace + 3 to Ace + 10. The Flush will win for high the majority of the time, and your Ace is tough in the second highest hand.

Hopefully, these examples have shown some of the choices you'll need to make in order to play this game. You will not be rushed for time, so think twice about your selections. Actually, I should say that while you will not be rushed for time the dealer will expect you to make your decisions promptly. If you take too long, she will ask you to proceed. If you take real long, she'll tell you to either move quicker or risk getting hit in the face with a cream pie. If you take real, real long the dealer will magically produce a Samurai sword and quickly and deftly separate your head from the rest of your body.

26

Placement of cards is face down. When you place your two hands in the appropriate positions on the H and the L, they must always be placed face down.

WHAT'S NEXT?

We will assume your hand was the one we just finished talking about—with the Spade Flush for best and the Ace, 10 for second best. Here's what happens next: you place the best (five-card) hand in that rectangular box you saw in Figure 1, the one drawn horizontally on the table felt and labeled with an "H". The second best (two-card) hand goes into the other box outlined on the table, normally labeled "L" as in low and located immediately above the box for the highest hand. As stated earlier, the casino thinks of this as a high hand and a low hand, but I like to think of it as the highest hand and the second highest hand.

You weren't supposed to look at the cards of the other players when they picked them up, but I always try to get a glimpse. The casino doesn't want any players switching cards to improve their hands, or even discussing their individual cards, but don't worry too much about this aspect of the game unless someone infers that you should not try to stretch the rules.

Once all the players have their cards aligned in the boxes on the table, the dealer reveals all seven of the cards dealt to her. That's right, up to now she has been waiting for the players to do their thing, and now it's her turn. She turns over her cards, and spreads them out for all to see. You are hoping to see Cow Pie, but this time you are disappointed. The dealer's hand contains the 10 H + 10 C + 5 C + 5 D + Jack S + 7 D + 3 H. There is no doubt about what the dealer is going to do with this hand. It will be played like this:

Highest hand: 10 H + 10 C + Jack S + 7 D + 3 H
Second highest: 5 C + 5 D

The reason the dealer plays in this manner is logical. Just think about it. The dealer is playing for the tie, hoping that while she will probably lose with only One Pair in her high hand, she will win most of the second best hands with a Low Pair. The dealer is playing not to lose. In fact, the dealers make their decisions based on very tight rules established by the casino. The dealer will always play not to lose and wait for the good hands. The dealer, after all, will be there for thousands of hours. Also, remember that you are only playing against the dealer, but the dealer is playing against the entire table. She could arrange her hand so that it contained the Two Pair for the best hand and the Jack, 7 for second best, but then she would lose to everyone at the table who had Three of a Kind or better for best hand, and a Queen or better for second best.

DID YOU WIN OR LOSE?

The next step is that the dealer exposes the hands of the players, starting at third base and working backwards (counterclockwise) around to first base. All hands are compared to the dealer's hands, cards and bets for hands that are losers are collected as she works her way around the table, ties and winners are left out until she is done, then settled as required.

27

And then another hand begins. Difficult? Of course not. The game moves at a nice pace, you're not at all rushed, you do not win or lose on every hand because of the ties which occur, and there is probably not a pit boss standing over your shoulder. So, as I concluded after learning how to play this game, everyone should play. But, I need to mention a few important details before we finish with this chapter.

First, when you lose your bet, it is gone. However, when you win a bet, a 5% commission is collected, which is something similar to Baccarat. However, unlike Baccarat, this 5% charge on winning wagers is normally collected immediately at the end of each hand.

Even though you actually only win $9.50 for every $10.00 bet, I still think Pai Gow Poker is a worthy game. As you can figure for yourself, your disadvantage is less than the 5% commission you pay only on winning wagers. The reason it's less than 5% is this: you only pay the commission on winning wagers. The casino collects nothing, in terms of a advantage, when you win. Example. You play eight hands at $10 each. You win four and lose four. Your 5% charge amounts to $40 x 5% = $2. You wagered a total of $80. $2 is 2.5% of $80, so you can say that is your disadvantage. So, as you can see, any disadvantage you have will fluctuate depending on the number of wins and losses. The game is also flavored by the fact that the dealer wins all ties. This

increases the amount of your disadvantage, but the exact figure is difficult to determine. So, if you want to know what figure to calculate over the long haul, it's something less than 5%, but not much. And while even a 5%+ disadvantage means you have better odds at other games, Pai Gow Poker is every bit as fun as Roulette or Video Poker, and can provide a rest from the frenzy of Blackjack or Craps without creating exposure to truly ridiculous odds like those associated with Keno or Slot Machines.

Remember when I mentioned the Banker early in this chapter? I said that since the dealer is ordinarily the Banker, I would leave this for the end. Well, this is the end, so here's what you need to know about the Banker.

First, you, yes you, can be the Banker should you desire. Simply let the dealer know that you want to be the Banker and she will be sure to accommodate you. Being the Banker means that you are the person who either collects from or pays off all of the players at the table depending upon whether your two hands are better or worse thantheirs. In other words, you replace the dealer and everyone is playing against you. You won't be dealing any cards, but you will be paying off and/or profiting.

Moreover, being the Banker does not relieve you of the problem of beating the dealer. When a player is also the Banker, the first thing that happens is that the dealer compares her hand with the Banker's hand. She wins, loses, or ties, just like the players. The dealer then exposes all the rest of the hands, determines whether they win or lose when compared to the Banker's hand, then assists the Banker in either collecting or paying off bets. Yes, the house still collects the 5% commission on winning wagers.

Other than wanting to seem important, there is a legitimate reason for being the Banker. The Banker wins all ties. So if the player loses one hand(5-card) and ties the other(2-card), he or she lose their wager.

I have never been the Banker, even though winning all ties does improve the odds against me, for the simple reason that I play this game to relax between serious gambling sessions at Craps or Blackjack. Why would I want to make myself tense by worrying about whether I can beat everyone at the table? Should you choose to be the Banker, I suggest you study the betting habits of the other players at the table. If the other players are wagering more than you can collectively afford to pay off, don't become the Banker.

STRATEGY

As stated previously, the key to this game is deciding how to split your cards so that: A) you give yourself the best chance of winning both hands, or B) you come out of it by winning at least one of the hands and thereby gaining a tie. Of course, at times, it will be impossible to accomplish either. The manner in which you set your hands is entirely up to you, but here are a couple of suggestions.

For those times when you have nothing, nada, not even a lowly Pair, keep your highest value card in your 5-card hand along with the lowest four of the rest. Which automatically means that your 2-card hand will contain the second and third highest cards from your hand. Like this:

Your hand is Jack S + 10 S + 9 H + 8 D + 6 C + 5 D + 4 H
So your 5-card hand would be: Jack S + 8 D + 6 C + 5 D + 4 H
And your 2-card hand would be: 10 S + 9 H

Also, here is a rule of thumb which will serve you well. Regardless of the ranking of your 5-card hand, try to set your cards so that your 2-card hand contains at least a King.

For example, if you have Two Pair plus an additional King, you can consider keeping the Two Pair in your 5-card hand. Should you have Two Pair and no King, then you must place the highest pair in your 5-card hand, and the smaller pair in your 2-card hand. In other words, if you can't keep at least a King in your 2-card hand, play for the tie.

MONEY MANAGEMENT

Don't expect anything new here. This is nearly the same advice I dispensed for several of the other gambling venues. If you already know it and understand it you may want to skip to the questions. However, it does bear repeating, so here it is:

1) **Have a plan. In Pai Gow there are not a lot of betting options, so this part is easy. The plan is to win.**

2) **Practice, practice, practice. The options in this game involve making good decisions regarding the forming of the hands. The only way to become a whiz is to practice.**

3) **Loss limits. One of the most important elements of a good plan. You must set a "drop dead" number for yourself. When and if you reach that number, you quit. It's as simple as that.**

4) **Winning Goal.** You should set one. And please note that I said "should". If you are going to take this seriously, you **must** set a winning goal. If this is strictly recreational play time, you should or could set a goal, but that's not necessary.

5) Part of your plan should be to know when to begin **Dead Bolting.** I don't mean to turn you into a robot, but when you hit X number of dollars in profit a clear bell should sound in your head telling you it is time to start getting some of those chips off the table and into your pocket.

6) If you get ahead by as many as ten units, change your unit. If you unit was $10, for example, change it to $20. When you are winning, you must push for all you can. The player most feared by the casinos is the player who gradually increases his or her bets for maximum profits. If you increase your unit and start losing, go back to your original unit. If you win another ten units, increase your unit again.

7) Always quit when you arrive at your **MAXIMUM LOSS LIMIT FOR ANY 24 HOUR TIME PERIOD.** When you're beat, admit it. Give it up. There will be another day.

UNDERSTAND THE CONCEPT OF
DEAD BOLTING MONEY

Once chips are Dead Bolted, they cannot be put back into action. Period. If you change tables, take the Dead Bolted chips to the cashier and trade them for cash before beginning at the next table. If you keep them in your pocket, you will be tempted to use them before their time. Don't do it! Dead Bolted should mean Locked Away Forever. And Forever, as some of you may understand, is quite a long time. Even for gamblers.

3

Caribbean Stud

hat a perfect game for the casinos of the world. One of the best new games to hit the casinos in the last decade. One that had to work hard to earn its place in America. One that combines elements of 5-card Stud Poker with Slot Machines. For the person who is seeking the big hit, the huge jackpot, this game could be hypnotic. You can actually play a real game of Poker and at the same time try for a giant jackpot like those offered by various banks of progressive Slot Machines . . .jackpots which can easily climb to over $100,000! Nearly anyone can join the fun because the only tool needed by the player is a rudimentary knowledge of Poker. Yes, anyone who knows the ranking of Poker hands can attack this game. And those who have played 5-card Stud Poker will find this game to be a snap. However, as is the case with most casino games, the casino has a large, virtually unbeatable edge.

Like most of the newer table games which have been introduced in the 80s and 90s, this one is normally found in the Blackjack pit, and is played on a table which resembles a Blackjack table. As with all the other table games, the first step is to purchase chips. No difference here. If you already have chips

NEVER BUY IN FOR MORE THAN YOU WILL NEED

By now you understand that you should have a plan of attack and that the plan should define the size of the stake required. You should also know that the amount of money you put into play should never exceed the amount defined by the plan. Don't ever buy in for more than the minimum required for the plan.

from Craps or Blackjack, or Let It Ride you can use them here. But please recall that I suggest you always start with fresh chips. So if you've still got "used" chips, wander on over to the cashier and exchange them for cash. Then buy new chips when you get back to the Caribbean Stud game.

This is a *"you are playing against the dealer game."* Your cards must rank higher than the dealer's cards in order for you to win. This is not Real Poker. Five-Card Stud is a real game of Poker, but Caribbean Stud is not Real Poker. There is no bluffing, no checking and raising, no blind bet, etc. The rankings of hands is the same as for Real Poker, but you are not contesting against the other players at your table. They are the allies. The enemy is the dealer. Actually, the casino is the enemy. The poor dealer is just doing his job.

BETTING OPTIONS

The first thing you'll notice upon arriving at a Caribbean Stud table is that you will soon have the opportunity of making several different wagers. Figure 1 is pretty basic but shows everything you need to know in terms of where to place your wagers.

ANTE BET

This is the first and most elemental of the betting options. That's because you can't play unless you make this wager. There is no choice here. You gotta do it. Every hand. It is the price you pay for receiving cards It is the admission fee. The Ante Bet will range anywhere from a minimum of $2-3 dollars to a maximum of several hundred dollars. At most locations, the minimum will be

34

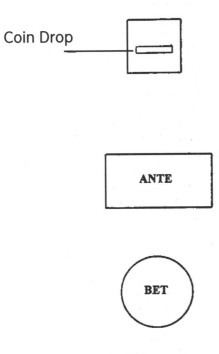

Figure 1

$5 and the maximum $500. You will find a square at your playing position clearly marked "Ante," so don't worry about where to place this wager.

PROGRESSIVE JACKPOT BET
Only $1. Never more, never less. Of course now that I've made that statement some casino will increase it to a $2 wager. Oh, well. Something changes every day. Anyway, this is the wager which is necessary if you want to participate in the pool for the Progressive Jackpot. Making this wager is like playing a Slot Machine. The only difference is that there is no handle to pull or button to push. And, believe it or not, it only takes a buck to win a jackpot which could be well over a hundred thousand dollars. There is even an electronic marque at the table. The purpose of the meter is to attract your attention and to continuously advance the meter which shows what the next lucky contestant could win. Every time some one at the table makes this wager the meter adds

about 50 cents to the pay-off. Which is pretty much what happens when you play the Progressive banks of Slot Machines. To make this wager, you need to set a $1 chip or token into a Drop Slot. After all the players have had a chance to exercise this option, the dealer will push a button and the coin or chip from each participating gambler will fall through the Coin Drop into . . .who knows? Maybe there's a little man under the table who collects all the bets. Maybe there is a funnel which directs all the coins and chips to the cashier's cage. Who knows? Anyway, when the dealer pushes that button two things happen. 1) The money disappears. 2) A light, usually red, ignites to prove you made the wager and are now officially qualified, money wise, to win the Progressive Jackpot should you come up with the right kind of winning hand.

BET TO CALL THE DEALER

Please note there is no way that I'm going to keep typing the name of this bet over and over. So, for the rest of this chapter, the Bet To Call The Dealer will hereafter be known as BTCTD. It is slightly different in that it is not made until after you receive your cards. Like the other two betting options, this one is also clearly marked on the table in a circle or square labeled "Bet." If you decide you have a hand which can beat the dealer, the requirement here is that your BTCTD must be exactly twice the amount of your Ante Bet. An Ante Bet of $10 would automatically require a BTCTD of $20. Bet $35 on the Ante Bet and your BTCTD must be exactly $70.

One game, three betting options. Sound easy enough? Of course. So let's see if I can make it a little more difficult.

> **A bet to call the dealer is a decision made after viewing your cards. Must be made if you want to continue. Must be twice the amount of the Ante Bet.**

ALL THE BASICS

Okay, you've got chips. As shown in Figure 1, you will note a spot in front of your playing position clearly labeled "Ante." You make your Ante Bet. I'm

36

going to assume your Ante Bet is $5. At the same time you make the Ante Bet, and prior to the dealing of the cards, you may also place a Progressive Jackpot Bet. Unlike the Ante Bet, this wager is not mandatory. Later on we will get into more detail about the Progressive Jackpot Bet.

Okay, you've anted $5. Each player and the dealer are then dealt five cards. At some casinos a very human dealer will shuffle the cards and then deal seven stacks of five cards in front of himself. At some casinos he will be dealing out of the hand. At others, the shuffling is done by a machine located to the dealers right. It is called a Shuffle Master because it shuffles the cards, and is manufactured by a company called Shuffle Master. The rea-son the Shuffle Masters have been introduced is so that the casino can create more "action." The Shuffle Master eliminates the time when the dealer would ordinarily be shuffling the cards. Less human shuffling means more actual playing time, which means more money in play. At some tables, the Shuffle Master actually deals out the hands, five cards at a time. At others, the dealer retrieves the shuffled cards from the machines and then he deals the hands. Regardless of how the cards are shuffled or dealt, you will end up with a hand of five cards placed face down in front of your position. The dealer's cards are dealt four face down, and the last face up.

MAN OR MACHINE?
No question here if you're the casino. More hands per hour = more action = more profit. And if you're the player? The game moves faster. So, if you want a slower game, avoid the tables which utilize automatic shufflers.

At this point you pick up your cards, and determine the value of your hand. Then you must decide whether you have cards which are worth playing. The question to be answered here is whether you think you can beat the dealer's hand. Yes, in this regard it is a little like Pai Gow Poker. I say this because a hand containing nothing higher than an Eight may win. Conversely, a Straight may lose. There is a basic strategy which can be used in this game, but we will get to that later.

I'm going to assume that you have picked up your cards and that you have a very playable hand; let's say 3 Kings. This is a terrific hand. So good you decide there is almost no chance of the dealer's cards beating you. So, now you exercise the BTCTD option by placing $10 worth of chips in the section of the layout labeled "Bet." This wager, as stated earlier, must be exactly and precisely twice our Ante Bet. Had your Ante Bet been $15, the Bet To Call The Dealer would have to be $30. Had the Ante Bet been $27, the BTCTD would have to be $54. In addition to matching the Ante Bet, you also lay down your cards, face down, alongside the Ante Bet section of your player area.

A quick glance around the table of players confirms that four of them are not pleased with their hands. All four of those players fold by placing their cards face down adjacent to the Coin Drop. There is no question about whether they are folding, because none of them placed additional chips in the Bet section.

Another player who has decided to play out the hand also places her cards face down near the Ante Bet location. This move, when combined with the action of adding chips to the Bet section, make it clear to the dealer that you are offering a challenge.

Now that everyone has made their intentions clear, the dealer starts picking up the cards of those players who are going no further in this game. He begins at what we know from Blackjack as third base and works back toward first. As he collects the cards, he places each hand in front of himself and spreads the cards to count them, to ensure each hand contains five cards. The reason he counts the discards? Some players may want to cheat by "saving" cards which they can slip back into the game when those cards can be more useful. Yes, again, the casino has to protect its backside. As he collects the folded hands, the dealer also retrieves the Ante Bets made by those players.

Once all the discards have been picked up, the dealer reveals his cards and you find out whether your hand won or lost. But, actually, simply beating the dealer's hand may not be enough. Sometimes it's not all that simple. Here's why: You've already made your intentions clear. But how about the dealer? What if the dealer doesn't want to play? Does he have a choice? Yes. For, you see, in order for the dealer to stay in the game at this point his cards must contain, at the very minimum, an Ace/King. Which means the two highest cards in the dealer's hand must be at least an Ace and a King. Note the "at least." Anything which ranks higher in value than an Ace/King would automatically qualify, also. If the dealer does not have at least an Ace/King, there is no contest. The dealer basically surrenders. The result is that you win the

Ante Bet . . .the Ante Bet and only the Ante Bet. Should the dealer's hand not reflect an Ace/King you have no chance of winning the BTCTD.

Now let's consider several possible outcomes for your hand of 3 Kings.

1) The dealer shows the following: Ace D + Queen S + 10 C + 8 H + 7 C. Does the dealer hand qualify? No way. The dealer has an Ace/Queen, which is definitely lower in value than a Ace/King. Consequently, even though you have a very nice Three of a Kind, you win only your Ante Bet. In this example, that amounts to $5. The other bet you made, the $10 BTCTD, you pull off the table. The dealer pays off your winning Ante Bet and collects your

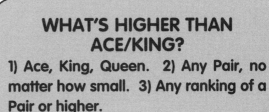

WHAT'S HIGHER THAN ACE/KING?

1) Ace, King, Queen. 2) Any Pair, no matter how small. 3) Any ranking of a Pair or higher.

cards. At this point, there is a difference in the standard operating procedure at various casinos. Once the dealer has surrendered, some do not bother to look at your cards. The fact of the matter is that you have won the Ante Bet regardless of what your hand contains, so why even bother showing the cards? The answer takes us back to that Progressive Jackpot Bet we might have made. Some casinos automatically reveal your cards to verify whether you have a hand that qualifies for a jackpot pay-off.

2) Different cards for the dealer: Ace S + King D + Queen C + 3 C + 2 H. Now what happens? Did the dealer qualify? Absolutely! Ace/King/Queen is definitely higher than Ace/King. And now it's time for you to rejoice. For, not only are you paid even money on your Ante Bet, you are paid at the rate of 3:1 on the three lovely Kings. Follow me on this. You had $5 on the Ante Bet, and $10 on the BTCTD. So how much do you win? $5 on the Ante Bet, and $30 on the BTCTD. A nifty net profit of $35. Hooray for our side.

3) Change the scenario again. This time let's give the dealer these cards: Jack D + 10 S + 9 C + 8 H + 7 C. Yes, that's a nice little Straight. Yes, a Straight beats the dickens out of your 3 Kings. So you lost not only the $5 Ante Bet, but also the $10 BTCTD. Like any other game, you pay your money and take your chances. There will be times when you will win with a Jack high and lose with a Full House.

These three examples provide nearly everything you need to know in order to play this game. In example #2, you won the hand and received a pay-off of 3:1. The casinos call this a Bonus Payout. Though there may be small differences from casino to casino, a typical Bonus Payout Schedule is shown below.

BONUS PAYOUT SCHEDULE

1 Pair	1:1
2 Pair	2:1
3 of a Kind	3:1
Straight	4:1
Flush	5:1
Full House	7:1
4 of a Kind	20:1
Straight Flush	50:1
Royal Flush	100:1

One additional comment regarding the pay-offs shown in Figure 2. All of the pay-offs should contain this addendum: up to table maximum. The reason? Let's assume for a moment you feel you have just received a sign from God. And He instructs you to bet $100 on the next hand of Caribbean Stud. You do so and are dealt a wonderful sight, a Royal Flush. Better yet, the dealer qualifies, so you are about to receive 100 times your $100 wager. Or are you? What is 100 X 100? That's right, it's 10,000.

It is worth remembering that If the dealer's hand does not qualify, you cannot win the BTCTD wager. However, the Progressive Jackpot has nothing whatsoever to do with dealer qualifications. If you have a coin or chip in the Coin Drop and a hand which is capable of earning a pay-off, you collect whether the dealer has zilch or a Royal Flush.

What is the table maximum? Probably no more than $3,000. So do you collect $10,000 for your Royal Flush? Absolutely not. Sorry, Charlie. However, your Royal Flush did win the Progressive Jackpot. Or did it? Did you put $1 into the Drop Slot before this hand? If you did, you win the Progressive Jackpot. Congratulations. Not only did you collect from the Bonus Payout, you also won the Jackpot.

Now, you ask, what would I have won had I drawn the Royal Flush at a time when the dealer could not produce a qualifying hand? I think you know this. As stated earlier, the dealer's hand must qualify in order for you to collect your BTCTD, which is paid off at the rates shown in Figure 2. If the dealer does not qualify you can't possible win anything except the Ante Bet. In this case your Royal Flush would have been a royal waste. This, however, is not the case when we are talking Progressive Jackpot. Each and every time you place that $1 in the Drop Slot, you qualify for the following pay-offs no matter how high or low the hand of the dealer. Which means that if you have a Full House and the dealer beats you with a Straight Flush you would still collect the Progressive Jackpot. So you could actually *lose* the BTCTD and still win a pay out from the Progressive. And as strange as that may sound, simply keep in mind that theProgressive Jackpot and the $1 you nudged into the Drop Slot have nothing whatsoever to do with whether you win or lose your Ante Bet or the BTCTD. Standard Progressive Jackpot Pay-offs are shown below.

HAND	PROGRESSIVE PAY-OFF
Flush	$50
Full House	$100
Four-of-a-Kind	$250
Straight Flush	10% of Jackpot
Royal Flush	100% of Jackpot

As was the case with Figure 2, there is a small addendum to these pay-offs. Should multiple hands qualify for the Progressive Jackpot during the same hand, the winners share the total Jackpot in ascending order. Here's what this means. We will assume that five of you are playing and that each of you has one of the hands listed in Figure 3. We will also assume that the Jackpot has grown to $100,000. Here is how the money is spread out. The plain old Flush receives $50. The Full House collects $100. The person with the 4-of-a-Kind is presented $250. Now add those up. $50 + $100 + $250 = $400. We subtract $400 from $100,000, which leaves us with $99,600. The stiff who was lucky enough to catch the Straight Flush receives 10% of that total, which is $9,960. And you, the lucky wretch who has the Royal Flush? You get everything that is left over. So $99,600 - $9,960 = $89,640. Granted, it's a shame you had to share the Progressive Jackpot, but $89,640 is still a nice pay-off.

Is this game easy enough? Of course. Should we play it? Well, let's take a look at the odds against us. This is basically a game of 5-card Stud and there are a total of 2,598,960 possible hands which could be dealt to us. The chart below shows both the type and number of hands which are possible.

ONE DECK
FIVE-CARD POKER HANDS

TYPE OF HAND	TOTAL POSSIBLE
Royal Flush	4
Straight Flush	36
Four of a Kind	624
Full House	3,744
Flush	5,108
Straight	10,200
Three of a Kind	54,912
Two Pair	123,552
One Pair	1,098,240
No Pair	1,302,540

You can see that the types of hands we are going to draw most frequently are in the no-pair and one-pair categories. The next chart now shows, based on the above mathematics, how often we can expect to draw any of the hands shown above.

TYPE OF HAND	CAN EXPECT 1 OUT OF EVERY:
Royal Flush	648,740 hands
Straight Flush	72,193 hands
Four of a Kind	4,165 hands
Full House	694 hands
Flush	508 hands
Straight	255 hands
Three of a Kind	47 hands
Two Pair	21 hands
One Pair	2.4 hands
No Pair	2.0 hands

Now go back and compare Figure 5 with the pay-offs shown in Figures 2 and 3. If we have a winning Full House, according to the Bonus Payout Schedule you will be paid at the rate of 7:1. However, Figure 4 shows that you will only draw a Full House once in every 694 hands. The true pay-off should be 693:1. Do you see a casino advantage here?

The odds of you hitting a Royal Flush are 648,740:1. So if you hit one with your $1 Progressive Jackpot Bet, and if it was going to be paid at true odds, you would receive $648,739. What can you expect here? The largest Jackpot paid to date was slightly over $300,000, and the average probably runs more in the range of $75,000. Do you see a casino advantage here? Of course you do. And it's huge.

Return again to that Progressive Jackpot. What happens when somebody hits it? Does it start all over again at a base of, say, $50,000? No. At most places it starts over again at a base of $10,000. In addition, about 46% of every dollar that is deposited into the Drop Slot goes to the casino, the rest stays in the pot. On the flip side, at least in terms of the Bonus Payout Schedule, the casino's advantage is not as severe as it first seems. Keep in mind that you hold the advantage of being able to look at your cards prior to deciding whether to double your basic Ante Bet. Also, the casino pays off every time the dealer does not qualify. But that's not the end of it. Consider what happens when you have a wonderful hand and the dealer does not qualify. A lot of Straights,

Flushes, etc. go unpaid. I have read articles by authors who claim to have figured out the casino advantage in Caribbean Stud. One claimed it was only 5%, the other wrote that it was less than 5%. Frankly, I don't have a clue as to how they came up with their figures. However, for my purposes, all I need to know is that the odds of catching a Straight in real life 5-Card Stud 254:1 but the the Bonus pay-off for a Straight in Caribbean Stud is only 4:1.

STRATEGY

The most sound advice I can provide is that you should not consider making a BTCTD unless you have at least a Pair. That should happen approximately every 2.4 hands. As I stated earlier, this is a game where a small Pair can win a hand, and then a Straight will get beat the next. I once sat at a table where two successive dealers went over forty-five minutes without producing a qualifying hand. Once we picked up on what was happening, all of the players started making the BTCTD on every hand, regardless of what we were holding. Needless to say, the entire table enjoyed healthy profits. Yet, I've have also sat at a table where over the course of five incredible hands the dealer never had anything less than a Flush.

Another issue to consider. You may recall that the dealer's hand is dealt with four of his cards face down and one face up. Does that help you in any way? Yes, but not much. If you're playing by a fixed set of rules in terms of when to make the BTCTD you wouldn't, or shouldn't, be dissuaded by any dealer up card. However, if you're playingon hunch and intuition the dealer's up card could prove very meaningful. If you have a playable hand, ignore the dealer's up card. If you have a marginal hand, meaning one that would not qualify for bonus money, the dealer's up card might very well convince you to fold.

44

4

Let It Ride

I hope you're not bored to tears by all of these games which have a connection to Real Poker, because here is yet another one. But unlike its predecessors, this one is a "WE WANT THE DEALER TO HAVE GREAT HANDS" kind of game. It's a dealer friendly kind of game. You can joke with and encourage the dealer. Which makes for a fun time.

In order to play, you need only to understand the rankings of Poker hands. Heard that before? Sound easy? It is. But what is truly refreshing is that you are not competing against the dealer. Yeaaaah! In fact, you actually want the dealer to have a good hand. I'll pause here for a moment while you pick yourself up off the floor. I realize this is a lot to digest in only a few seconds. But, as strange and foreign as it may sound, in this game it would be wonderful if the dealers could manage to deal themselves a high pair on every hand.

THE BASICS

Okay, we're going to move fast, here. After reading about all of the other Poker-based games you shouldn't need anything but the highlights for this one. Found in the Blackjack pit. You need chips to play, etc. The basic idea is that you will be dealt three cards, all face down. The dealer deals herself only two cards, which some people think of as a "flop" because they will be common to all hands. You end up with a total of five cards, only three of which are actually in your possession. You will win or lose depending on the strength of your 5-card hand. Standard Real Poker rankings apply. No wild cards, no Jokers. If your cards can produce at least a Pair of Tens, you will receive one of the pay-offs shown below, which is right behind the end of this sentence.

LET IT RIDE PAYOUT SCHEDULE

YOUR HAND	PAY-OFF
Royal Flush	1,000-1
Straight Flush	200-1
4 of a Kind	50-1
Full House	11-1
Flush	8-1
Straight	5-1
3 of a Kind	3-1
Two Pair	2-1
Pair of 10's or better	1-1

46

Figure 1, which appears on the following page, tells you everything you need to know regarding the table layout.

TIME TO PLAY

To begin this game, you must make three wagers. As shown in Figure 2, there are three betting circles: #1, #2, and $. Minimums required for this game range from $2 and up, so note the requirements when you join the game. For this discussion, I will assume a minimum wager of $5, so it will take $15 for you to play this first hand. Next comes the deal. The cards are usually dispensed from a Shuffle Master, which is probably appropriate since Shuffle

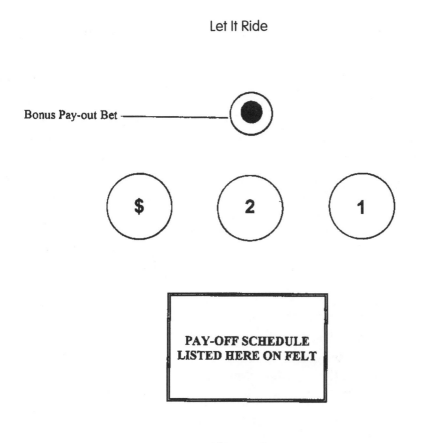

Figure 1

Master invented the game. Still, I have seen dealers actually shuffle and deal out of the hand. Either way, you are going to receive three cards, all dealt face down. So, pick up your cards. Yes, it's okay to use both hands. No, it is not okay to show your cards to the other players, though some casinos are more strict about this rule than others.

Three bets on the table, three cards in your hand. The dealer has two cards in front of her, both facing down so we can't see them. Time to make the first of two decisions. The question is this: Do your first three cards offer enough possibilities to warrant you remaining in the game? Remember that it takes at least a pair of Tens to collect a pay-off. If the answer is yes, you simply slide your three cards under the bet labeled as #1. This is done in the same manner as sliding your cards beneath your chips in Blackjack. This action denotes to

WORTH REPEATING
You must have at least the minimum wager in each betting circle. All three bets must be of the same value. It's required. It's the law.

the dealer that you want that #1 bet to stay right where it is . . . that you think you have winning possibilities . . .that you're not backing off. If, however, the answer is no, that you don't believe you have winning possibilities, then you want to have that #1 bet removed from the board. You want to reduce your exposure. You do this by scraping your cards against the felt just like you did in Blackjack when you wanted an additional card. You scratch the felt with the cards, the dealer shoves or nudges that bet off of #1 back to you. Easy enough? Once all the players have made this first decision, the dealer picks up one of the two cards in front of her position and turns it face up for all to see. Some people refer to this as the "flop." I don't. I mean, the cards are already laying out there and

HANDS OFF THE MONEY
Place the chips into the betting circles, then don't dare touch them again until the dealer is finished making the settlements. This is another "you could lose a finger if you touch those chips again" kind of rule.

all she does is turn one over. Far as I'm concerned, that action does not meet the definition of "flop". Yes, I know, I'm being picky. Anyway, you now have the opportunity of seeing the dealer's first card and making another decision. This will be the second, and last, decision. After this, the rest of the game is out of your control. The question now is whether the three cards in your hand, plus the fourth card out there in front of the dealer, when added together, warrant you staying in the game. Should you still not like your possibilities, you scrape your cards again and the dealer will nudge your chips off the bet marked #2. If your 4-card hand warrants playing, you slide your cards under the bet marked with the $ sign. But, you may wonder, why not slide them under the bet marked #2? Wouldn't that be the logically place to slide them? You might think so, but the answer is that once this second decision is made you are automatically in the rest of the way. You can toss your cards on top of your chips, adjacent to them, or you can slide them under the bet marked $.

Either way, there is no third decision. The money in the $ betting circle is going to stay there. Regardless of the action you took on the first two deci-

sion, regardless of whether you scraped the felt and got back both of those bets or left them out there, the $ bet stays right where it is until the game is finished. We have no choice concerning that wager.

> ## THE $ WAGER
> It's out there to stay, so what you really have here is two optional bets and one that is not. You put out a total of $15, but $10 of it is returnable.

Next, the dealer reveals the second and last card remaining in front of her playing position. It's your fifth card. It's also everybody else's fifth card. All of the gamblers can now utilize the three cards in their possession plus both the dealer's cards. Did you win? Depends on whether all five cards can generate, at the minimum, a pair of Tens. If they do, we are paid as shown in Figure 1. If they don't, the dealer takes your money.

49

SHOW ME SPECIFIC EXAMPLES

Okay. As before, deal these practice hands to yourself so you don't become confused. I insist on it. Go ahead, take out a deck a cards and get ready. Here we go.

1) You've got thirty dollars on the table . . .$10 on each spot. Your three cards are the 10C + 10S + 8S. What is your decision on the first bet? Are you kidding? This is a No-Brainer. Figure 1 clearly indicates that a pair of Tens pays at even money. You cannot possibly lose! You can only improve this hand.

Time to start wishing and dreaming that the dealer's hand contains some help. In this scenario you would slide all three cards, face down, beneath the bet marked with the $ sign. This way

> Any time you have at least a Pair of 10s on your first three cards, go directly to the $ bet and slide your cards under the chip or chips deposited there. You're a winner! Congrats!

the dealer knows that you are in the game all the way to the end. The dealer also knows that unless you have lost our mind, you probably already have a winning hand. The dealer then reveals the 4 of Hearts, which is of no help to you. But don't give up yet on improving the hand. Remember, this is one game where you fervently wish the dealer good luck. In this case, the dealer catches a 4 of Clubs on the last card, and all of a sudden you improve to Two Pair. Terrific! What great timing. The only thing that would have been better is if the dealer could have produced a couple of more Tens. But the good news is that all 3 of your bets are still on the felt. Two Pair pays 2:1. You're about to be paid $20 for every spot where you have a bet, which for you is three, which for you means a total pay-off of $60.

2) Your three cards are the 4 S + 5 D + 8 C. What is your decision on bet #1? What do you have? Think about it. No Flush. No Pairs. At best, you have three cards to a possible Straight with two holes. What are your chances of the dealer coming up with a 7 and a 6? Is this a joke? You have almost no chance. So scrape your cards on the table and let the dealer nudge your $10 off the first betting circle. Now, onward and upward. Your exposure has been reduced from $30 to $20. The dealer's first card just happens to be the 6 of

Hearts. And you are not sure whether to be excited or dejected. Your next decision just became more difficult. If you leave out bet #2 you know there's no way the dealer will produce a 7. If you scrape off bet #2 you know darn good and well that the dealer will produce a 7. What to do? What to do? You must think for all of three seconds. Why only three seconds? Well, what's the chance of filling the inside Straight? And if you don't fill the Straight, does your four-card hand offer any other winning possibilities? The second answer is that while you could pair up on the fifth card, you still wouldn't have the minimum of a pair of Tens. The answer to the first question is that there is only a distant possibility of filling the inside Straight. Yet, for those who enjoy a gamble, I'm going to assume that you have decided to "Let It Ride"! So you slide your cards under either bet #2 or the bet marked $. It makes no difference. Now your exposure is the $20 still remaining on bet #2 + $. Does the dealer reveal a 7 on her second card? Of course not. You're out

$20. And if you continue to draw on hands that offer such terrible possibilities, you deserve to lose.

3) With this hand we immediately see a lot of red. Namely, the King D + 10 D + Ace D. What's your first decision? Again, this is a No-Brainer! First of all, you have three cards to a Royal Flush. Second, you have three cards to a plain old Flush. Third of all, you have three cards to a Straight. Fourth of all, you have three cards to a Straight Flush. Fifth of all, you have three cards which could be matched to make a winner. Consequently, you slide your cards under bet #1, which tells the dealer your hand must contain good potential. The dealer then turns over the 6 D, and immediately destroys several of your possibilities. No longer a chance for a Royal Flush. The Straight Flush is no longer a threat. The Straight is dead. So, even though you still have the possibility of catching the Flush, you scrape and the dealer pushes bet #2 back to you. The fifth card? It's the King C and you're a winner. You col-

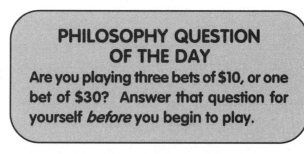

PHILOSOPHY QUESTION OF THE DAY
Are you playing three bets of $10, or one bet of $30? Answer that question for yourself *before* you begin to play.

51

lect $20 . . .$10 from bet #1, and $10 on the $ bet. Some people might suggest you should have stayed on all three bets, and I agree. With four cards to a Flush you should have taken your best shot, which was to go for it. You won't see four to a Flush all that often, plus you had high cards which could match and bail you out.

4) You receive the 5 S + 5 H + 10 C. First decision? Before you answer, ask yourself this question: Beginning with the three cards you are holding, what is the absolute best 5-card hand you can end with assuming the dealer reveals the exact cards you want? In this example, the answer is obvious: You could end up with four Fives, but only if the dealer manages to come up with another pair of them. Yet, it's possible. Right? So maybe you're thinking of "Letting It Ride" on bet #1. And then just before you make that decision, the person seated immediately to your left says, "A lousy pair of Fives. Why couldn't they be Tens?" You think she's talking about your hand, then realize she's talking about hers. So now what is your chance of ending with four Fives? Nonexistent. And, you see, this is why some casinos are quite strict about

players discussing their cards or showing their cards to each other. Anyway, you scrape off bet #1. The dealer's first card is the Jack of Spades. You scrape off bet #2. The dealer's last card is the 8 of Hearts. You lose the bet marked $. You began with $30 in exposure and actually lost only $10. Had the person seated at your left not allowed you to "see" her hand, you might have stayed in for at least bet #1.

Simple enough? Yes, and no. Most hands are very easy to play, but then when you are dealt those Straight and Flush possibilities and "Let It Ride" on all the bets, you can be burned severely. What is your disadvantage in this game? Think of this as being 5-Card Stud. Here's a reproduction of the chart from the chapter on Caribbean Stud.

TYPE OF HAND	CAN EXPECT 1 OUT OF EVERY:
Royal Flush	648,740 hands
Straight Flush	72,193 hands
Four of a Kind	4,165 hands
Full House	694 hands
Flush	508 hands
Straight	255 hands
Three of a Kind	47 hands
Two Pair	21 hands
One Pair	2.4 hands
No Pair	2.0 hands

Now compare these odds with the actual pay-offs as shown in the "Let It Ride Payout Schedule" at the beginning of this chapter. For example: The odds of drawing Three of a Kind are approximately 46 to 1. What's the actual pay-off from the Pay-off Schedule? 3 to 1. Anybody see a casino advantage here? Well, it's not as bad as it sounds. Think of it this way. You give me $30. I give you three cards. If you don't like the first three cards, I will refund $10 of your money. Then I'll give you another card, and if you don't like it, I'll refund another $10. Granted, the pay-offs aren't great, but the player definitely has the advantage when it comes to controlling the money.

STRATEGY

Keep it simple. Work out a strategy which makes sense for the way you play and stick to it. Here's my suggestions.

DECISION #1
Always scrape unless you have one of the following:
- A) A made hand. This means you have at least a Pair of 10s.
- B) Three cards to a Flush.
- C) Three consecutive cards to a Straight
- D) Three cards to a Straight with no more than one hole and at least two cards which are 10 or higher. This means you would stay on a Queen + Jack + 9, or on a 4 + 5 + 7, but not on a 9 + 8 + Queen, or on a 4 + 5 + 8.

DECISION #2
Always scrape unless you have one of the following:
- A) A made hand.
- B) Four cards to a Flush
- C) Four cards to a Straight with no holes. This means staying with 7 + 8 + 9 + 10, but not with 5 + 7 + 8 + 9.
- D) Four cards to a Straight with one hole and two cards equal to or higher than a 10. Which means you would scrape off Jack + 9 + 8 + 7, but would stay on Queen + Jack + 9 + 8.

BONUS PAY-OUTS

Somehow you knew there had to be more, right? Perhaps because Figure 1 shows a spot for a bet we've not yet discussed. Perhaps your intuition is working. Perhaps you decided that Let It Ride didn't sound thrilling enough . . .yet. We've been down this road before, so this will be short and sweet. Cost $1. Put a $1 token or chip atop the usually red spot which is located above the three betting circles. Pay tables vary, but this is pretty standard:

HAND	PAY-OUT
Royal Flush	$20,000
Straight Flush	$2,000
4 of a Kind	$100
Full House	$75
Flush	$50
Straight	$25
3 of a Kind	$9
Two Pair	$6

Of course the pay-outs aren't even close to what they should be. Gives the game that "Slot Machine" psychology. Bad bet because the pay-offs are terrible and over 50 cents of every dollar wagered is held by the Casino.

There are "experts" who have figured the casino advantage for Let It Ride to be only 3.5%, and, I don't have a clue as to how they came up with that percentage. But for my purposes, all I need to do is compare the true odds to actual pay-offs to see that the casino vigorish is deadly.

Okay, I'll confess. I'm a little down on Let It Ride because A) I know the odds are awful and B) I've tried this game many times and have yet to win at it. I have friends who have won. I have relatives who have won. Christ! Even my wife won one time. But not me. Not yet. And maybe not ever, because even though it can be fun to play there's no sense playing if you can't win. Which is advice dear to my heart . . .the kind I give to myself.

MONEY MANAGEMENT

As is the case with several of the other games we have discussed, how you manage your money in this game is pretty much dependent on whether you are running hot or cold. If you can't draw at least a pair of Tens over the first three or four hands of play, leave the table. If you can't draw any kind of decent hand, but the dealer keeps dealing himself a pair of Kings, stay right where you are. Other than that, apply the same Money Management suggestions I made for Pai Gow. It is also a Poker-related game, and the same basic plan could work.

54

5

Blackjack

There's a good reason for making Blackjack your game of choice: the odds can be more favorable for the player than in any other game. In fact, there are people, and most of the time you can include me on this list, who think that anyone who does not select Blackjack as his or her specialty is a masochist. The game is simple to play, the rules are clear and understandable. Properly played, the odds can actually be turned to the player's advantage.

A QUICK SYNOPSIS

I'll start with a basic description of the game. Some authors indicate that if you already know the basics, you should skip over this section and go on to the next, but I disagree. Even if you already know how the game is played, or *THINK* you know, read this. In fact, no matter how much you might think you know, take the time to read every section of this book. It can't hurt and it might help. And, besides, the really simple stuff will only take a few moments to read and I'll try to make it as fun as I can.

Blackjack is a card game played with a regular deck of cards. Which means a deck which contains four each of the following: Twos, Threes, Fours, Fives, Sixes, Sevens, Eights, Nines, Tens, Jacks, Queens, Kings and Aces. Of the four of each, one would be a Spade, one a Club, one a Diamond, and one a Heart. If you don't know what a Heart is, you're already in over your head. And I know this is so elemental it's actually aggravating to read for those of you who already know this, but the previous few sentences mean that each deck contains a Four of Hearts, a Four of Clubs, a Four of Diamonds, and a Four of Spades. Same is true for the other twelve types of cards. The total deck consists of 52 cards (13 different cards X four suits = 52). Some games are played with only one deck, others are played by combining two, four, six, or even eight decks, but more on this later.

The game is conducted and supervised by a DEALER. That's the person who provides you with chips, shuffles and distributes the cards for each round of play, and then either collects or pays off the wagers depending upon who won or lost. Dealers are easy to spot because they are always standing behind the blackjack tables with cards and chips spread out in front of them, and they are all wearing identical uniforms.

Dealers are mere mortals. They are not Gods. But when you are playing with cards there are times when dealers appear to have the powers of Gods. They know it, and now you know it.

Blackjack tables are found in what is commonly called the BLACKJACK PIT, which is an area most often located in the center of the casino. Yes, this means you'll need to navigate through hundreds or even thousands of slot machines and video poker machines before you can find this table-filled, sit-down oasis. A typical table layout is coming soon. Those people behind the dealer who are standing, loitering, and trying to look busy are the PIT CREW. Most of the time they are wearing suits or business attire. Their jobs vary, but for the most part they are there to monitor what is happening at the tables. This means they are making sure the dealer is conducting an honest game, which means they are making sure the casino is not being cheated. They don't want you to be cheated,

56

either, but since the casino provides their pay checks, well... everybody has their priorities. They are also there to assist you, the

When you exceed a total of 21, you "bust." When you "bust" you lose. Busting is bad. Busting is not good for the player. However, we want the dealer to bust on every hand.

player, whenever the need arises, whether it be for recommendations on restaurants and shows, proper gambling etiquette, freebies or the cost of milk in Poland.

The idea of the game is to beat the dealer. There are three ways to win. One, you win if your point total is higher than the dealer's when neither of you exceeds a total of 21. (Some people still refer to this game as Twenty-One.) Two, you win if your point total is less than 21 while the dealer's total exceeds 21. Three, you are dealt a Natural (described later) and the dealer isn't. Simple enough, right? You get two cards to begin the game, and then you can request additional cards until you either decide to stop or you exceed a total of 21. When you exceed a total of 21, something very bad happens . . .the dealer swiftly and adroitly retrieves your wager.

There is a ton of strategy to consider in this game. There are virtually thousands and thousands of options. You'll need to make decision after decision. And every one of them is at least semi-critical. But we'll get to all of that, later.

Figure 1 on the following page shows what you're looking for. Some may be of a slightly different shape, but this diagram tells you all you need to know. If you're at a large casino, there might be fifty to a hundred Blackjack tables spread around in four or five Blackjack pits. At smaller casinos there will generally be at least one or two of them. I've never seen a table with fewer than five player positions, or chairs, and I've never seen a table which contained more than seven. If there are numerous tables, they will be positioned so that they form an oval or a horseshoe; long sides back to back, with or without an entry at either end. Picture the wagon trains of the pioneers rounded up at night to ward off attack from any direction. No, I'm not saying Blackjack pits are like castles or fortresses, but the similarity is interesting.

57

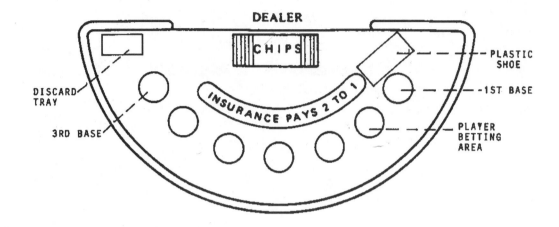

58

Figure 1

SELECTING A TABLE

This might not be as easy as you think. With today's preponderance of slot machines and video poker machines, the space for games like Blackjack is continually shrinking. Plus, you can't be satisfied with just any old table because you need to find a table where the game is being played for stakes you can tolerate. It is quite embarrassing to rush up to a table, ask for $20 in chips, and then discover the minimum bet at that table is $100.

You will usually find a small sign, atop the table, to the dealer's right or left, which will indicate the minimum and maximum allowable wagers at that table.

| Table Minimum $5 | Minimum Bet $25 |
| Table Maximum $500 | Maximum bet $2000 |

The sign you are looking for usually looks like one of the above. In addition to betting limits, these signs will often also contain specific rules used at that particular table. If the signs are obscured by ashtrays and empty drinks, don't hesitate to approach the dealer and inquire directly as to wagering limits and rules. At some Blackjack pits there is a large sign hanging above the tables which lists specific rules of play. For betting limits you can get a tip-off by simply observing the size of the wagers being made by the players. If all you see are green chips, it is probably a $25 table (the minimum bet is $25). If all you see are red chips, it is undoubtedly a $5 table. If you see dollar tokens, it could be a $1, $2, or $3 table. Assuming that you are a novice, you'll want to start with low stakes. If your hotel/casino does not offer a low-minimum table, go somewhere else, but not before complaining to any number of pit bosses, hosts, dealers, cashiers, and even security officers, that you are sadly disappointed because there are no, let's say, $5 minimum tables available at your casino. And, of course, you would love to gamble at your hotel as well as swim, sleep and eat there. If you tell that to enough people, somebody may eventually listen. A pit employee can change the table minimum in a matter of seconds. That same sign which indicates a $10 minimum bet can be turned over to reveal one which advertises a $5 minimum wager. And, believe it or not, the pit employees would love to accommodate you. However, if you are there are on a weekend and it's busy, save your breath. Or, if you are gambling in Atlantic City, and request they change the table minimum to $2,you will be made the laughing stock of the city. Fact is, in most places in this country you will have difficulty finding tables where the minimum is less than $5. Yes, I know that statement is not 100% correct, because there are places in states like Colorado and South Dakota where you can easily find a $2-3 minimum table. But do you live in Colorado or South Dakota? I didn't think so.

So, here's the point. Before you sit down at any table, before you even get to the tables, before you even get to the casino, determine what kind of player you are. And I'm not talking about good, bad, or indifferent. What will be your minimum wager? Until you know the answer to this question, you can't begin to select a table. If you decide the answer is $5, then you are what is commonly known as a $5 PLAYER. If your answer was $10, then you're a $10 PLAYER. If the answer is $25, then you're a $25 PLAYER. That's correct. You are what you bet.

 **If we ever meet, and we discuss Blackjack, and I ask what kind of player you are, the answer can only sound like this: "I'm a $5 player." Additionally, should you want to sound like a person who has spent a lot of time in the trenches, so to speak, you could also tell me that you are a "nickel" player. If you play $25 minimums, you could say you are a "quarter" player. Get it? The amount can change, but the answer should be in terms of your smallest wager.**

60

IN ORDER TO PLAY, YOU GOTTA HAVE CHIPS

Now it's time to dig into your wallet or purse and bring out the greenbacks. And let me emphasize that you will, indeed, be playing for money. In reality, you will be playing with the chips purchased with your money, but too many people forget that those red, green, and black chips represent authentic United States dollars, in most cases, hard-earned dollars. (Please note that I will continually refer to the colors of chips as red, green, and black. This is because virtually all of the casinos use these colors for $5, $25, and $100 chips. The logos or designs may be different, but the colors will always be the same.)

On my first trip to Las Vegas . . .yes, the streets were paved even then . . .I was playing Blackjack within 35 minutes of my arrival. I played from eight o'clock in the evening until two o'clock the next afternoon, and consumed great quantities of free drinks in the process. During that playing session, I forgot that I was playing for money. I was not making $5-$25 bets, I was playing with nifty-looking red and green chips. I was not losing money, I was losing chips. Mentally, I had made a fundamental blunder. The chips didn't mean anything to me. They were simply playthings; toys. That is, they were simply playthings until I finally quit and discovered that those playthings added upto $475 in losses! I have never made that mistake again. It was an expensive lesson. Absolutely true story. Except the part about it being $475. It was actually more than that.

For the most part, you do not have a choice of playing with either chips or cash. Most casinos will insist that you play with chips. Yes, you will see players making cash wagers. But at most casinos if you deposit cash onto your betting area the dealers are under instructions to replace the cash with chips. Yes, there are still places where you can do it, but why? Make it easy for both yourself and the dealer and use chips. However, never forget that you are playing for real money. You are *not* playing a friendly game of Monopoly. The casinos claim it is much easier and faster for the dealer to work with chips instead of cash, and that is true. The casinos claim it is easier for players to cheat when using cash instead of chips, and that may also be true. Yet it is also true that people tend to forget about money when playing with chips.

Another suggestion: Purchase only a few chips. If you are playing at a $2 table, don't start with more than $10. If at a $5 table, don't start with more than $20. Do not buy $100 worth of chips simply because you have a hundred dollar bill. You are not going to impress anyone, and you will not intimidate the dealer by dropping a hundred dollar bill on the table. Go to the cashier, break your hundred dollar bill into tens and twenties and *THEN* buy chips at the Blackjack table.

Another thing. There is an optional way to purchase

> ## FREE DRINKS
> Why do the casinos serve free drinks only to people who are gambling? Do they want you to become intoxicated? Of course not! Would they like to see you curb your inhibitions? Maybe. Do they simply want you to have a "good" time? That must be it.

chips. If you establish credit with the casino prior to your playing session, you can obtain chips by signing a MARKER. Which you can think of as being a credit receipt. Yes, in essence, the casino is making you a loan. Yes, they expect you to pay it back. Yes, if at all possible, they want it back before you leave. There are three reason to use markers. One, to some people they may help make you look like an important person. Two, using markers relieves you of the responsibility of carrying large sums of cash. Three, they make it easier for you to qualify for complimentary meals, shows, rooms, etc. Of the three reasons for using markers, at least two are legitimate. This, by the way, is all I'm telling you about markers. And that's because if you play the way I'm going to suggest, you won't be needing them.

NEVER START WITH MORE CHIPS THAN THE MINIMUM YOU WILL NEED TO PLAY

There are several reasons why I make this suggestion. First, having too many chips in front of you can create a false sense of security; as long as you can look down and see chips on the table, you will have a tendency to keep playing, even though you may be losing badly. Second, and conversely, if you only start with a small amount, and those chips suddenly vanish, you will have an automatic alarm clock to help make you aware that you are, indeed, losing money. There will be times when you can sit at a table and do everything right, but still lose. The trick is to conserve your losses when you are losing. So, if that first $10 or $20 (or, for you heavy hitters $500 or $1,000) disappears, change tables! A new table can improve your morale and may help change your luck. In addition, your first time at the Blackjack tables will be an experiment of sorts. You're going to find out if you really understand the game, so don't make it an expensive training session.

HERE'S HOW TO PURCHASE CHIPS

A) Sit down.
B) Remove that $10, or $20, or $1,000 from your pocket, wallet, purse or back pack.
C) Place the money adjacent to and slightly above your wagering area (See Figure 1). Not IN your betting area. Never IN your betting area. And, there is no need to wait until the present hand is concluded. You can plop down that money any time you feel like it.

62

D) If you really wanna sound like a beginner, say something like "Change, please" or "Chips, please."

E) When the dealer asks whether you want silver or red, be prepared to answer.

Here's what I mean. Let's assume you're going to play at a $2 table, but your plan calls for bets of $5. You put $20 on the table adjacent to your betting area. The dealer finishes the hand which had already begun when you sat down, then snatches your $20 and lays it in front of himself right smack in the middle of the table. (He does that so the "eye in the sky" can see it clearly.) Then he

> **WHERE DOES THE MONEY GO?**
> That hole in the top of the table by the discard tray feeds a box which is attached to the underside of the table. At certain times of the day or night you will see burly security guards exchanging full boxes for empty ones. They take the boxes to the "money" room, where it is counted, wrapped, and then either sent to the bank or put back in action at the casino.

63

might say to you, "All silver?" Which means all $1 betting tokens. Or, he might say, "All red?" Which means all $5 betting tokens (chips). All you gotta do is answer him. There is also the possibility that he will automatically give you $10 worth of $1 tokens and $10 worth of $5 chips. There is also the distant possibility he might be a sly jokester who would say something like, "Did you want two chips, or three?"

Most times you will not need to say anything. The dealer will automatically retrieve your cash, give it a quick inspection, smooth it out if it's crumpled, lay it out in front of himself, trade you for chips, and then deposit your cash into a slot located over by the discard tray This is all pure routine. If you put thirty of those $20 bills out onto the table, he would give all thirty of them the same treatment.

The reason it is important to place your money adjacent to and not IN your wagering area is that you don't want to risk confusing the dealer. If your $20 is inside the betting area, the dealer may believe that you want to make a $20 cash bet. All dealers are supposed to ask whether that is your intent. They are supposed to ask prior to dealing any cards. But you know with grim certainty that the first time you make this elemental mistake your particular dealer will be staring off at some hot chick who is walking by and go ahead and deal your cards without thinking or asking, and then you've got a problem. Don't leave any room for misunderstanding. Also, if the dealer does not give you the chips you want, do not hesitate to tell him you want something different. If, for example, the dealer gives you four $5 chips and you only want to play for $2 a hand, push two of the chips back at him and request $1 chips. The dealer simply needs to understand what you want.

Another point: The dealer can give you chips for your money, but the same is not true in reverse. He cannot buy back your chips when you leave the table. Chips can only be exchanged for money at the cashier's cage. The only cash to which the dealer has access is in his pocket, and his hands are never supposed to see his pockets while he is working. In fact, his hands are supposed to be above the table and in sight at all times. Again, for the benefit of the eye in the sky.

> **What is the eye in the sky?** It's the God-like camera which SEES ALL twenty-four hours a day, seven days a week. It is watching for cheats, dealer/player collusion, and bald heads which may exhibit snappy slogans!

64

Anyway, you buy with cash, but you can only leave the table with chips. So if you have a lucky $20 bill, don't give it to a Blackjack dealer. You'll never see it again. You might win thousands of dollars, but that $20 bill is gone from your life.

I'M AT THE TABLE, I HAVE CHIPS . . .NOW WHAT?

To make your initial wager, place chips inside the betting area for your player position(see Figure 1). On some tables this area is rectangular, on others it is circular. And there is probably somewhere in the known universe where the betting area is a three dimensional cube. It doesn't matter . . .the point is that your chips must be placed within the confines of your betting area.   Even though there are no extra points given for neatness, your chips should be stacked in an orderly fashion, one on top of the other. Yes, it's okay if the chips are slightly askew. They need not be stacked in perfect symmetry. But when you see dealers reminding people to stack their bets, please know they are not doing so because they are tidy people. The dealers are responsible for making sure that everyone is playing correctly at their table. Which means playing in a manner which would make it difficult for them to cheat the casino. So, yes, this is another one of those DO IT RIGHT SO WE KNOW YOU'RE NOT TRYING TO CHEAT US things. It is more difficult for a cheater to swindle the casino if the chips are stacked properly.

If you are making a wager which requires more than one denomination of chip, it is vitally important that the chips be stacked in the following manner: The largest-value chips should be on the bottom of your pile, the smallest-value  on the top, and any others in the middle. Are you a step ahead of me? Yes, this is another one of those D.I.R.S.W.K.Y.N.T.T.C.U. things (see paragraph above). Let's say, for example, that your wager, for whatever reason, is going to be $132. Think about it. It's like making change at the store. There would be several ways of making this bet, all of which work so long as you place the largest value chip on the bottom of your stack, the smallest on the top, and the others in-between in descending order. To make the $132 wager I could place a black $100 chip on the bottom, top it with a green $25 **chip,** top the green with a red $5 chip, and then top the red with a couple of dollar tokens. Or, I could go four green $25 chips, plus six red $5 chips and then the dollar chips or tokens. It makes no difference how much you are betting, it makes no difference what denomination of chips you are utilizing . . .simple follow the rules. Everything in order, biggest on the bottom, smallest on the top. The casinos insist that wagers be made in this manner to help prevent cheating by the players. If this sounds a little strange, let me explain. Let's say you want to swindle the casino. You look at your first two cards, discover a total of twenty, and decide you have a very good chance of winning the hand. The dealer is having a verbal joust with another player. Your hand is literally inches away from your bet.   So, with lightning-fast fingers, you quickly drop a few more chips on to your stack. Yes, I know that sounds silly. Who could possibly move that fast?

65

DOLLAR CHIPS or DOLLAR TOKENS—WHAT'S THE DIFFERENCE?

Dollar chips are usually made from the same material as all the other chips, and are simply a different color. Dollar tokens are usually metal, and silver in appearance. But the really big difference is that dollar tokens can be utilized for both table games and machines. Dollar chips can only be used at table games. So, if you only had dollar chips and wanted to play video poker, you would need to exchange them for tokens. But if you wanted to play blackjack with your dollar tokens they would be warmly received.

No one could possibly get away with such a trick. Right? Wrong. Dealers and pit bosses tell me that people try to do it all the time. In our $132 example, with your chips stacked properly, you'd only be able to add a few dollar chips or tokens to the top of your bet, which would hardly be worth the effort. But, were the chips stacked so that the $25 chip was on top of the pile, you could easily add another $50 or $100, which to some people might be worth the risk of getting caught. And that's why you must stack your chips properly.

THE BLACKJACK RITUAL

What happens next depends on how many decks are in use at your table. There are single-deck tables, double-deck tables, four-deck tables, and even six or eight-deck tables. Who knows? One day we might even see ten or twelve-deck tables. If you are in doubt as to how many decks are being used, ask the dealer. If there is a "shoe" (see Figure 1) on the table, at least four decks are being used. A "shoe" is a small plastic box which holds all the cards. Instead of dealing out of the hand, the dealer slides the cards out of the shoe. The more decks, the more benefit to the casinos. I prefer single or double-deck tables. However, there are many, many gamblers who love playing against a shoe. I think those players are at least a little deranged, and, conversely, they may feel as though I should be living on Mars. Some people prefer blondes, others prefer brunettes. Some people wake up bright and early, others merely wake up early. The casinos prefer to use a shoe because the dealers can generate more hands before reshuffling. The casino has an edge on every hand. Therefore, the more hands played, the greater the benefit to the casino. When only single or double decks are utilized, the dealer must reshuffle after one to six or seven hands. When dealing from a shoe, the dealer can easily generate twenty or more hands. The casino cannot make money while the dealer is reshuffling. The math is pretty simple. A dealer who produces sixty hands per hour should be making more money for the casino than one who is only producing thirty hands per hour. If you continue to play, you will develop your own preference. It is possible to win while playing against a shoe containing four or more decks. It is also possible to win playing against single and double decks. But consider this: We don't want to do anything that benefits the casino. They want you to play as many hands per hour as possible. Can you reach a conclusion based on those two statements?

Now for the cards. We will assume it's a new shuffle. The dealer carefully mixes the cards, flips a red plastic card at your playing position, usually right about where you place your bets, then holds the shuffled deck or decks in front of your playing position. Already figured out why? That's right. The dealer wants you to cut the cards. That red card, sometimes yellow or green, is used to cut the deck. The dealer will extend all the decks so that you can insert the plastic card somewhere in the pile. The dealer then cuts the cards at that point. So, simple slide the card in there anywhere you like.

After you've cut the cards, the dealers will discard the first one, two, or more cards into another small plastic tray to their right. It is called the "discard tray." This action is called "burning" cards. Later in this chapter I will explain its purpose. For now, suffice to say that burning cards is something the casino does to make it more difficult for players to win.

You can't just start playing any time you feel like it. You must wait for the dealer to finish settling the accounts for any of the rounds which may have been under way when you arrived.

67

SOME PEOPLE NEVER LEARN

The Never Touch The Cards With More Than One Hand Rule is probably violated more often than any other. As far as the casino, and some of the rest of us, are concerned there are only two kinds of people who attempt to use two hands. One, those who are trying to cheat. Two, those who are either very (here's an attempt to be kind) forgetful, or simply very new to the game. Try not to be either one.

OKAY, OKAY, LET'S START PLAYING

The burning completed, the dealer begins distributing the cards from her left to her right, from first base to third base (again, see Figure 1). Please note my shift in tone. The dealer is now officially a woman. In one and two-deck games the player's cards are all normally dealt face down. In multiple-deck games the player's cards are often dealt face up. In either case, the dealer always has one card face up, one face down. The dealer's face-down card is called the "down" card or the "hole" card. The dealer card which is face up is called . . .the "up" card.

You watch your two cards slide toward you, pick them up, and make your first mistake. You forgot where you were. You're not at home now. You're in a casino. And what did you do? You grabbed the cards with both hands. This is a no-no. A serious error! Should you make this mistake, do not be surprised if the dealer barks at you. For, you see, you can only touch the cards with *ONE* hand. Like most other casino rules, this one is to prevent cheating by the players. Should you be playing at a table where all the cards are dealt face up, you don't touch the cards at all.

AM I HAPPY OR SAD THAT I GOT THESE TWO PARTICULAR CARDS?

Time to calculate the value of your hand. Don't be rushed. Take your time. Not all of us are mathematically inclined, so try not to let it bother you when Mister Smarty over at the end of the table gives you an annoyed look. Each card has a point value. Tens, Jacks, Queens and Kings are worth ten

68

points each. Aces can be either one or eleven. All other cards are face value; a Six is worth six points, a Two is worth two points, and so forth.

The object of the game is to obtain a total of 21, or as close to 21 as possible, without exceeding 21. If you exceed a total of 21, you "bust" (lose automatically). If you do not bust, and your total is higher than the dealer's total, you win even money. For example, a $5 bet would win $5. Should your total be the same as the dealer's total, you tie (or "push"), and neither win nor lose.

Assume your first hand is a Jack and an Ace. Rejoice! You have a NATURAL, a total of 21 on your first two cards, which is an automatic winner. Not only do you win, but the payoff is three to two. A $5 bet would win $7.50, a $10 bet would win $15, a $7 wager would pay off $10.50, etc

A natural Blackjack is any two-card hand consisting of an Ace and any Ten-Value card. When you receive a Natural, expose your cards immediately; turn them over and lay them down in front of your bet. If you're at a table where the cards are being dealt face up you needn't do anything but collect your winnings. And please note that I described a Natural as any *TWO-CARD* hand. That's because you can only have a Natural on your first two cards. There is no

WHY BLACKJACK?

Why call the game Blackjack if black Jacks have no special meaning? I mean, why not make a hand containing a black Jack an automatic winner? Why not make black Jacks wild? Darned if I know.

other way. And, by the way, you will rarely hear any one referring to a Natural as a Natural. Every body calls them a Blackjack. I'll be using both terms, because they are interchangeable. A natural Blackjack cannot lose, but it can be tied by a dealer natural. If the dealer's up card is an Ace, she must peek at her hold card to see if she has a natural. If she does, everyone loses except the players who also have naturals. Those players tie, or push.

Anyway, you won your first hand. Congratulations. You are smiling joyously, so the dealer grins at you and then turns to the player at first base. That player is the first to choose from several available options. Since you were dealt a natural you don't need to exercise any options, but you still need to understand your alternatives. Here they are:

OPTIONS, OPTIONS, OPTIONS

1) You can STAND (or *STICK*, or *STAND PAT*). This means that you are satisfied with your first two cards and don't want any more. To stand in a game where the cards are dealt face down, you simply slide your cards under the chips in your betting area. However, you *MUST NOT* actually touch the chips with your hands; the casino might think that you're cheating. Remember when we discussed how to properly stack the chips in your betting area? Well, here's one way people try to cheat. They pick up their cards and note a Blackjack. They can't lose. So, in the same motion that it takes to expose their cards and place them atop their betting area, they also "palm" a few chips and add them to the stack. Sound slick? Pretty tough to do with one hand, but still possible. Which is why the casinos have that "eye in the sky."

If the cards are all dealt face up, simply wave your hand over the cards with your palm parallel to the table. You may also say, "I'm good," or "No more for me," or words to that effect. However, virtually all casinos prefer that you use hand signals, and most demand that you do so. For, you see, all of your intentions are clearly recorded by the overhead cameras . . .the eye in the sky. So make it easy for all concerned and use plain hand signals at all times.

2) You may request additional cards (HIT, or *DRAW*). This means that you are not happy with your first two cards and want to improve your total. If the cards were dealt face down, hold the cards in your hand—one hand—and brush them lightly against the top of the table. The dealer will give you another card every time you make this motion. If the cards were all dealt face up, you can accomplish the same by brushing your index finger on the table as if your finger were a dog who is digging for a bone. If by taking additional cards you exceed a total of 21, you bust. In that case you must expose all your cards by laying them face up on the table. The dealer will then collect your cards and your losing wager. You can take as many additional cards as you want as long as you do not exceed 21. When you are through taking cards, you then stand as noted in #1 above.

3) You can *DOUBLE DOWN*. Explained later.

70

4) You can *SPLIT*. No, this doesn't mean you can grab your money and run for the exit, even though your initial two cards may inspire that reaction. I'll cover this one later, also.

5) You can *SURRENDER*. Later.

6) You can buy INSURANCE. Later.

As you watch the dealer move from player to player, you'll see your fellow gamblers exercising these options. When all the players have acted on their hands, it's the dealer's turn. And this is what makes this game both unique and beatable. While the players have several options, the dealer has only two:

1) If the dealer's total is 16 or less, she *MUST* take additional cards until she totals from 17 to 21 or busts.

2) If the dealer's total is 17 or more, she *MAY OR MAY NOT* take additional cards. The reason I say may or may not, is because at some casinos the dealer must hit a soft 17, while at others the dealer must Stand on any 17, regardless of whether it is soft or hard. Yes, I realize that we haven't yet discussed the difference between hard and soft hands, so just bear with me. It's coming soon.

After acting on her hand, the dealer then settles all wagers, usually working from third base back to first base. Then the next round begins. You place your bet, receive your cards, decide which option to exercise, and win or lose. See, I told you this was simple.

What makes Blackjack so interesting to play is that the gamblers have many options, the dealer only two. For the person who enjoys making quick decisions, no other casino game is as challenging or rewarding.

But how do you know when to exercise the various options? Are there bad times to stand, good times to hit? And if you exercise your options properly, can you actually win? Yes, yes, and yes.

The following sections set forth the strategy you should use to win at Blackjack. You *MUST* study the charts, memorize and practice them if you are serious about winning. You cannot win by exercising your options with decisions based only on intuition or lucky feelings. You *MUST* know the basic strategies in this book. They may seem difficult at first, so take your time. You can learn them!

HARD HOLDINGS

I don't know how the term originated, but it is quite descriptive. Often a HARD HOLDING of 12-16 puts you between a rock and a hard spot, creates a hard lump in your throat, or causes you to cast a very hard, disgusted look at the dealer.

A Hard Holding (also called *HARD HAND* or *STIFF*) is a holding which can only be counted in one manner. A holding of Queen + Six can only be counted as 16. A holding of Eight + Seven can only be counted as 15. All hands are hard hands unless one or both of your cards is an Ace. And that is because Aces can be counted as either one or eleven.

What do you do if you have a total of 15 and the dealer's up card is an Ace? What if the dealer is showing a Two or a Six? Sometimes the decisions are agonizing.

The chart which follows tells you what to do in every instance with hard holdings. Study it, memorize it, test yourself on it. Don't worry, you can learn it. I have tested this strategy in over a hundred thousand actual hands, plus used it in over a quarter million practice hands. It works.

If you have 12 and the dealer is showing a Seven, you hit. If you have 12 and the dealer's up card is a Six, you stand. If you have a total of 11 or less, hit. Stand on any total of 17 or more. For now, this is all the basic strategy you need to know. If you stop right now, make an attempt to play Blackjack at a casino, and adhere to the HARD HOLDING STRATEGY you will be playing better and smarter than most of your fellow gamblers. Later, I'm going to provide you with a few options on the HARD HOLDING Strategy for the simple reason that some of these decisions are never right, never wrong, and mostly in between right and wrong.

72

HARD HOLDING STRATEGY

S=STAND   H=HIT

DEALERS UP CARD IS =		2	3	4	5	6	7	8	9	10
YOU HAVE A TOTAL OF:										
4-11		H	H	H	H	H	H	H	H	H
12		H	H	S	S	S	H	H	H	H
13		S	S	S	S	S	H	H	H	H
14		S	S	S	S	S	H	H	H	H
15		S	S	S	S	S	H	H	H	H
16		S	S	S	S	S	H	H	H	H
17-21		S	S	S	S	S	S	S	S	S

73

Figure 2

But, you also ask, why do I hit when I'm holding 12 and the dealer is showing an Ace, stand when the dealer is showing a Six, hit when the dealer is showing a Two? Good questions, all. The answers lie in Figures 3 and 4 which follow.

The percentages in Figures 3 and 4 will vary as the game progresses, but not much. Consequently, they are the percentages we must use to determine whether to hit or stand. It is these percentages, combined with the rigid rules governing the dealer's options, which produce the basic HARD HOLDING STRATEGY set forth in Figure 2. This is known as playing the percentages, or playing the odds. When the dealer has a high chance of busting, you do not want to hit. In those cases, you play for the dealer to bust. You want to shift the risk from your hand to the dealer's hand.

74

THE DEALER IS SHOWING	% OF TIME DEALER WILL FINISH WITH 17-21	% OF TIME DEALER WILL BUST
ACE	83%	17%
10	77%	23%
9	77%	23%
8	76%	24%
7	74%	26%
6	58%	42%
5	57%	43%
4	60%	40%
3	62%	38%
2	70%	30%

Figure 3

YOUR TOTAL HAND IS:	% OF TIME YOU CAN EXPECT TO HIT WITHOUT BUSTING	% OF TIME YOU CAN EXPECT THAT A HIT WILL BUST YOU
11 or less	100%	0%
12	69.2%	30.8%
13	61.5%	38.5%
14	53.8%	46.2%
15	46.2%	53.8%
16	38.5%	61.5%
17	30.7%	69.3%
18	23.1%	76.9%
19	15.4%	84.6%
20	7.7%	92.3%

Figure 4

For Example. Assume that your hand is Queen + Five for a total of 15. The dealer is showing a Nine. Figure 4 indicates that you have a 53.8% chance of busting if you hit. More important, Figure 3 indicates that the dealer will finish with a good hand 77% of the time. If you stand on 15, you will probably lose. If you hit your 15 there is a little better than 50/50 chance that you will bust. Sorry, but get used to it because you'll be seeing a lot of these types of hands. You're between a rock and a hard spot, which is why we refer to these as HARD HOLDINGS. This is nearly a no win situation. So, the question is this: Do you stand on your 15 and silently pray that fate bails you out, or do you take the offensive and go for the win? Are you nuts? Think about this.

One out of every two times you take the offensive you will bust. Which also means that one out of every two times you will not bust. If you stand the dealer is going to make a pat hand 3 out of every 4 tries. So, the answer is that you need to take the offensive and attempt to improve your hand. In this example the odds are telling you that the dealer has a heck of a good chance of making a good hand. Your chances are dismal. But standing with that hard 15 will result in losses three out of every four times.

Now let's change the dealer's up card. Let's say she has a Five showing instead of a Nine. Figure 2 indicates that you should stand. The reasons are twofold: First, you still have a 53.8% chance of busting if you hit. Second, the dealer has only a 57% chance of making a pat hand. Close call, but why push your luck? Don't forget that you go first. You must play your hand before the dealer acts on hers. If you hit and bust, you lose no matter what happens with the dealer. If you don't hit, there is almost a one in two chance of you winning. Why take the chance? Transfer the risk to the dealer. Let her risk busting *HER* hand. You may lose, but you're playing the odds.

76

RISK

Don't forget we are gambling. Yet, in some ways gambling is just like business or life. Whenever possible we must attempt to reduce risk. You can also call this hedging your bets, or protecting against losses, or whatever nomenclature works for you. The point here is that we want to massage the odds because reducing risk should increase our chances for gain.

Okay, enough of the negatives. Let's look at a positive example. You have a Nine and a King for a total of 19. The dealer is showing a Seven. That's right. Nobody in their right mind would hit a 19, because nearly 85% of the time a hit will bust you. And, in case you need to be reminded, figures like 85% are not just large numbers. This is gambling and 85% is a HUGE number. Only a nitwit would buck odds of 85 to 15 against you. So, I don't care if you have a direct pipeline to Lady Luck and she's screaming for you to take a hit, don't do it. Play the odds. Moreover, if the dealer has an Ace or a Ten-Value for her down card you beat her. If she has anything less than a Ten-Value she's gotta hit.

Yes, there's only a 26% chance that she will bust. But that's 26 times greater than your chance of busting if you stand. Similar examples can be drawn for all the other Hard Holding totals, but I'll let you figure them out for yourself. But remember what I said earlier. In many, many cases we are simple trying to make the best of horrible situations.

WHAT IF I HAVE MORE THAN TWO CARDS??

The basic strategy in Figure 2 does not change if your hand consists of more than two cards, especially if you're playing against a shoe. If you have a three or four card total of 15, you should still hit against a dealer Nine. If you have a three or four card total of thirteen, you should still hit against a dealer Eight.

> Since all Tens, Jacks, Queens and Kings count 10 points, we will refer to that entire group of cards as Ten-Values. This is called Keeping It Simple.

77

Assume you're playing against a shoe and you're dealt a Two and a Five. The dealer is showing a Queen. The basic strategy says to take a hit, so you do. You draw another Five, so now you've got a total of 12. The basic strategy says to hit a 12 against a dealer Queen; you do, and receive a Two, for a total of 14. Yes, I know you already have four cards, but that doesn't make any difference. Your lousy 14 will probably lose, so you must take another hit. You do, and receive an Ace. Now you have a 15 or 25, and since 25 is no good, you really have a hard 15. The sweat begins to trickle off your brow. The basic strategy says to hit a hard 15 when the dealer is showing any Ten-Value card. But you already have five cards, and you're convinced that if you take another hit you'll bust your hand. Your mind screams for you to stand pat. The other players are staring at you, waiting to see if you are stupid enough to draw a sixth card. It's decision time. And, since the basic strategy says to take a hit, you do so. Unfortunately, you receive a Jack and bust the hand, thereby losing your bet. Well, what can I say? You're not going to win every hand. The basic strategy is a guide which will help, but it will not miraculously cause you to win all the time. You might have caught a

Six and won. That's why it's called "gambling." Nothing ventured, nothing gained.

However, and this is a large HOWEVER, I want to point out that in single and double deck games I prefer to stand on any three-card 15 or 16. No, there isn't a strategy table telling me that in a single or double deck game I must stand with a three-card 15 or 16. . .just experience. So, yes, I am hereby notifying you that if your experience proves to you, over years and years of playing Blackjack, that there are certain pieces of the basic HARD HOLDING STRATEGY that don't work for you, then don't use them. And please note I just said over YEARS AND YEARS of play. You cannot use the basic strategy once or twice and decide that certain elements of it will not work for you. I'm talking about using the basic strategy for hundreds of thousands of hands. You convince me that you've played that many hands, and I won't argue if you determine that you have better results if you stand on 16 against a dealer Nine. Until then, don't even think about altering the HARD HOLDING STRATEGY.

LEARN OR BECOME OBESE

Let's say your experience is that seven out of every ten times you place your hand on your forehead you gain twelve pounds. Let's say this has been true for the last twenty years. Knowing this, how often would you place your hand on your forehead? Well, it's no different from the life experiences that years of gambling should provide. If, after playing thousands of hands you determine that seven out of every ten times you hit 14 when the dealer is showing an Eight you lose, and yet continue to do it, then I hope you become obese. But until you make that determination, stick to the basic strategy.

Whenever you are dealt an initial holding of 12, 13, 14, 15, or 16, your odds of winning are very slim. Again, that's why those totals are called Hard Holdings or stiffs. They are bad for your morale and bad for your pocketbook. Consequently, the strategy in Figure 2 is designed to make the best out of terrible situations. As I stated earlier in this chapter, it is possible to do everything right and still lose. But if you use the basic strategy you will lose less than the other players at your table who are relying solely on luck or whimsy. And I'm not discarding luck as being a valuable asset. What I'm saying is this: If you are using the basic strategy and you are still losing, you don't have any luck. Your karma is bad. Fate has decided to rob you of your money. You can't buck bad odds and bad luck. The basic strategy can't turn the odds in your favor, but it can help protect you against the horrendous losses commonly associated with "bad luck." But if you sit down at a Blackjack table and continually receive 12's, 13's, 14's, 15's and 16's, you are playing the wrong game. Leave the table and visit the hotel's steam room. If you use the basic strategy and still lose, you'll know fate is being unkind. If you DO NOT use the basic strategy, there is no way to determine whether your losses are the result of bad luck or poor, foolish card play. On too many occasions to count, I have observed players making numerous ridiculous plays at the Blackjack tables, and then heard those same gamblers complain about not having any luck. Play wisely, and you can create your own luck.

Yes, you will win some of the time when you have Hard Holdings. Yes, it is even possible to win a majority of those hands. However, overall, the odds are against you. If, in fact, you are winning a majority of those hands, you may wish to increase your bets. You could be on a "hot streak," or the dealer could be on a "cold streak."

In the next sections you'll see that there are ways for you to make up for all those terrible Hard Holding hands, options which will mean money in your pocket if utilized properly. On the Hard Holding hands, you are really striving to break even. On the other hands you swing the odds in your favor.

ABOUT THESE PERCENTAGES

I'm including this section for those who are interested in whether the percentages shown in Figures 3 and 4 were derived from somebody's magical or mystical imagination. Were they plucked from the air by whimsy? Or are they grounded in mathematical fact? Here's something to think about. And let me point out that the only reason we're covering this is because percentages in Blackjack are ever changing. What was true a few cards ago is no longer true. Even though Figure 4 indicates that you will bust 30.8% of the time by hitting a total of 12, this percentage fluctuates with every card which is dealt.

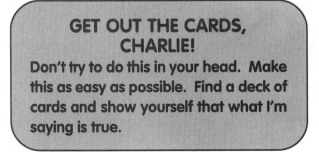

GET OUT THE CARDS, CHARLIE!
Don't try to do this in your head. Make this as easy as possible. Find a deck of cards and show yourself that what I'm saying is true.

Start with a deck containing the normal 52 cards. Deal yourself a King and a Two. You have a total of 12. What are the chances that the next card dealt will bust you? Mathematically speaking, that's pretty easy to determine. There are another 50 cards left in the deck. The only cards which can bust you are the Tens, Jacks, Queens, and three remaining Kings. That's a total of 15 cards which can hurt you. None of the other 35 remaining cards can hurt you. Some may not help much, but they will not bust your hand. So, 15 out of 50 can hurt. 15 divided by 50 = 30%. But Figure 4 says you will bust nearly 31% of the time. What's up here? Well, how many ways can you have a total of 12 with only two cards? What if your hand consisted of Nine + Three? In that case, all 16 of the Ten-Value cards could bust you, and they are all still in the remaining deck of 50 cards, so 16 divided by 50 = 32% chance of busting. Figure 4 shows 30.8%, which you can think of as being an average. If we take all the ways to make a 12 with a Ten-Value card, like King of Spades + Two or Hearts, Queen of Diamonds + Two of Hearts, etc., and combine those results with the results derived from all the times that 12 contains no Ten-Value cards, we end up with an average, and in this case it comes out to 30.8%. No magic here.

For Figure 3, the dealer busting percentages, we do it basically the same way. If the dealer is showing a Nine as her up card, there are 13 possibilities for a down card (2-Ace). Once we determine the dealer's hole card, the method for discovering bust percentages is the same as you saw in the last paragraph. So we gotta figure the chances of busting with each possible hole card, and then average them out, which is how we get the percentages for Figure 3.

Fine and dandy. But how often will there only be one hand dealt from the deck? If you're playing for real, the answer is never. It's always, at the very least, you against the dealer. And it could be you and six other players against the dealer. So what does this do to our percentages? Well, they keep changing . . .constantly . . .with the drop of every card. For example. You're sitting at third base. You catch a Nine and a Three for a total of 12. We just figured out a few minutes ago that you can expect to bust 32% of the time. But the dealer is showing a King. That's one less card that can bust you, so the figure becomes 30%. Then one of the other players draws two Queens, and your bust percentage drops to about 28%. The lower the bust percentage the better, so things are improving for you. But then the next player draws four Threes and a Four. Now your bust percentage climbs back up to 31%.

I could go on and on with this, but I'll stop now and hope that you understand the point I'm trying to make. Which is this: That 30.8% figure shown in Figure 4 might never be exactly accurate at any time during the game. But, neither will it ever be all that wrong. It will almost always be very close. Close enough that we can depend on the percentages in Figures 3 and 4 to help form our playing strategy.

That said, it is still important for you to understand that you will experience times when you swear that every time you hit a 12 you bust. Or that every time you hit a 14 consisting of Nine + Five, you catch an Ace. That's because aberrations happen.

One more tidbit pertaining to Figure 4. You've got a total of 14. I don't care what cards you wanna use to make up your 14. According to the percentages, you can hit without busting 53.8% of the time. Does that mean you will catch a card which will make a winning hand? Of course not. You might draw a Two for a total of 16 and be

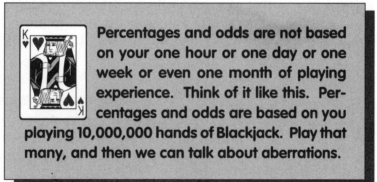

Percentages and odds are not based on your one hour or one day or one week or even one month of playing experience. Think of it like this. Percentages and odds are based on you playing 10,000,000 hands of Blackjack. Play that many, and then we can talk about aberrations.

forced to hit yet again. You might draw an Ace for a total of 15 and be forced to hit yet again. And you just might draw a Six for 21. Hurray!!! Yes, it does happen.

81

DOUBLE DOWN

Perk up, because your odds of winning are now improving. Pray that each new hand brings a double down opportunity. If you double down in the correct situations you can recapture the money you lost on all those miserable 15's and 16's. Here's your chance to get even with the dealer for giving you all those bad hands.

The term "doubling down" derives from two actions. First, you double your bet. Second, you receive one additional card which is dealt face down. Hence, you double down. At the overwhelming majority of casinos you can only exercise this option after seeing your first two cards. Yes, that means there are a handful of casinos which will allow a double down option after three or even four cards, but don't expect to find one in your lifetime.

The rules governing doubling down vary greatly across the United States. Most casinos allow you to double down on any two-card holding, whether it be 6 or 11, 4 or 10. At some casinos you can only double down on hands which total 9, 10, or 11. And at yet others, you may be restricted to doubling down on 10 or 11 only. It is to your advantage to play at casinos which allow you to double down on AND two-card holding. Why? For now, simply think of it this way. The more casinos restrict your options, the tougher it is to win. If there are only two casinos in your town and The Wild Rooster offers doubling down on any first two cards, and The Lame Lion does not, all other things being equal, you gotta fall in love with The Wild Rooster. Even if the drinks are cheaper at The Lame Lion. Even if the food is better at The Lame Lion. Even if parking is easier at The Lame Lion.

To double down, you must expose your cards to the dealer by placing them face up in front of your betting area. By "in front of" I mean slightly above your betting area. You can also place them adjacent to your betting area. Then you match your original bet

WHERE TO PLAY

I'll keep repeating this until you have it firmly implanted in your brain. You must play only at those establishments which give you the best chance to win. Which means you must play only at casinos which offer the best rules for the player. If you want to gamble, and none of your "home" casinos offer decent rules, you need to relocate.

with a like amount. If your original wager was $23, you gotta put up another $23. If your original bet was $2,345, you gotta put up another $2,345. At some casinos they prefer that you place your additional chips adjacent to your original chips. At others, they may prefer that you place them below your original stack of chips. You'll find out the first time you double down. If you place your chips adjacent to your original bet and the dealer moves them down below, she's just told you how this casino wants to play.

If you're playing against a shoe, where all the cards were dealt face up, simply extend the chips required to match your original wager . . .don't touch the cards . . .don't touch your original chips. When it's your turn, the dealer will then give you one card, face down. Some dealers will then say "good luck," others will say "hope you catch," some will even deal you the double-down card in a manner which will allow you to take a peek while it's airborne. Most will say or do nothing. You do not have the option of taking more cards. You receive one card, and one card only. This is the good news, bad news part of doubling down. The good news is that you have this option, the bad news is that you live or die with only one additional card. Yes, you may pick up that double-down card and look at it. However, most of us don't. Most of us wait until the round is ended and the dealer starts settling up working from third base back to first. We allow the dealer to reach out and flip over that card to reveal whether we're richer or poorer. Why? Because it builds the suspense.

Does doubling down sound risky? It's all in the timing. The chart depicted in Figure 5 will tell you when the time is right.

H = HIT   D = DOUBLE DOWN

THE DEALER SHOWS:	2	3	4	5	6	7	8	9	10	ACE
YOU HAVE										
9	H	H	D	D	D	H	H	H	H	H
10	D	D	D	D	D	D	D	D	H	H
11	D	D	D	D	D	D	D	D	D	D

Figure 5

We can condense this chart by saying you should double down on 11 against every dealer up card, on 10 against every dealer up card except a Ten-Value or an Ace, on 9 only when the dealer is showing a Four, Five, or Six. If you compare Figure 5 with Figures 3 and 4, you'll see how the doubling down strategy was developed.

> **WORTH REPEATING**
> The bet is doubled. You are dealt one card, face down. Double down. Some times the name does tell the whole story.

An example. Your cards are a Seven and a Four for a total of 11. The dealer is showing a Five. Lick your chops. It doesn't get much better than this. First, there is absolutely no chance of you busting when you take a hit. Second, the dealer is up against the worst busting percentage on the charts. Time to reap some profits. You have an excellent chance of winning, so take advantage of this double-down opportunity.

An example. Your cards are a Six and a King for a total of 16. The dealer is showing a Jack. Face the facts. You've got one foot in the grave. Why put both feet in a coffin by doubling down? Have you no brain? You have only a 38% chance of hitting without busting. The dealer is going to make a good hand 77% of the time. Who has the advantage here? This is not a double down opportunity. This is a joke.

An Example. Your cards are a Five and a Four for a total of 9. The dealer is showing an Ace. Time to double down? Forget it. This is not a true double down opportunity because you have no advantage. True, you can hit that 9 without risking abust, but even if you catch a Ten-Value you could still lose. With an Ace in her hand, the dealer is going to finish with 17-21 a high 83% of the time. You have no edge here. Therefore, you would not double down.

In essence, you want to double down 1) whenever the dealer has her highest probability of busting or 2) you have the best probability of winning. Doubling on 11 against a dealer Seven, Eight, Nine, Ten, or Ace is an offensive attempt. Remember that in a deck of 52 cards there are sixteen Ten-Value cards (four Tens, four Jacks, four Queens, and four Kings), so your chance of receiving a Ten- Value card on your double down is good. Also, you only want to double down on holdings which cannot be busted by the addition of one card; you would *NOT* double down on 12, 13, 14, or more.

I know one gambler who doubles down each time he has less than 12 and the dealer is showing a Five or a Six. Yes, I've seen him double down on a holding of 5. And, believe it or not, he wins more than he loses. However, when I tried the same strategy I was massacred. In any case, you don't want to be too greedy. Don't forget: When you double down you double your winnings, but you can also double your losses. Use doubling down wisely and you'll give yourself an edge over the casino.

At most casinos, you don't need to exactly double your wager. What if you don't have enough money to cover the bet? Simply say to the dealer as you make your move, "Double down for less," and extend whatever amount you have. For example, your bet is $10. You want to double down but only have $5. You say "Double for less," and extend the $5. The worst that can happen is that the dealer will tell you that option is not available. Which would be strange, because you are letting the casino off the hook when you double for less.

Watch the action at the tables. Sooner or later you will see somebody double down with a 12. Pity that person, for she or he thinks they are intelligent, and there are few things in life deadlier than thinking you are smart when you're not.

SOFT HOLDINGS

A soft holding is any hand which can be counted in *MORE THAN* one manner. Which can only happen when you have an Ace in your hand. Remember, an Ace can be counted as EITHER one or eleven. If you have a hand consisting of Ten + Five, you have a Hard Holding because this hand can only be tallied as 15. However, if you have a holding of Ace + Five you have either 6 or 16. Since a holding of 16 is tantamount to certain death, in this case it would be to your advantage to count the Ace as one, for a total of 6.

If you have a holding of Ace + Nine, you will want to count the Ace as 11, for a total of 20. You may also count it as one, for a total of 10, but why reduce a potential winning hand to an unknown?

Ace + Four could be 5 or 15. Ace + Seven could be 8 or 18. Obviously, having a Soft Holding gives you more flexibility. It is almost impossible to bust a Soft Holding. But, ordinarily, a Soft Holding does not stay soft very long.

Assume you're dealt Ace + Five. You treat the Ace as a value of one, so your total is 6. You take a hit (you can't possible bust) and catch a King. Your hand is no longer soft. Now you have a Hard Holding of 16 (1+5+10).

Another Example. You are dealt Ace + Three. You have either 4 or 14. You take a hit and get a Two. Now you have Ace + Three + Two, which is worth either 6 or 16. You take another hit, an Eight. Ace + Three + Two + Eight totals 14. It must total 14. You have no other choice. If you treat you Ace as eleven, you total would be 11 + 3 + 2 + 8 = 24!

Soft Holdings can make for very interesting hands. I am sure that this has happened to all seasoned Blackjack players, but I will relate this experience as an example. I was in a crowded casino on New Year's Eve, playing at a six-deck table. On one hand, my initial two cards were Ace + Two. The dealer was showing a Jack. I took a hit. I received another Ace, giving me either 4(1+1+2) or 14(1+11+2). My second hit was another Ace, as was my third. My hand was then Ace + Ace + Ace + Ace + Two for either 6(1+1+1+1+2) or 16(1+1+1+11+2). I then took another hit and received yet another Ace. Remember, I was at a six-deck table, so there were twenty-four Aces in the shoe. Anyway, my six-card total was still only 7 or 17. I could have stopped at that point, but since the dealer was showing a Jack, and since I could not possible bust my hand with another hit, I brushed my cards on the felt and received aFive, which gave me a total of 12 (1+1+1+1+1+2+5). At that point, my Soft Holding finally became a Hard Holding. The interesting point is that my hand stayed soft for six cards, which does not happen very often.

In case you're interested in whether I won or lost that hand, I suppose I should finish the story. I had to take two more hits to complete my hand. One was a Two, the other was a Five. My final hand was Ace + Ace + Ace + Ace + Ace + Two + Five + Two + Five for a total of 19. The dealer had 18.

Figure 6 shows you what to do with various Soft Holdings against all dealer up cards. With Soft Holdings you really have three options: stand, hit, or double down. When you read Figure 6 you'll see many doubling down opportunities. The reasons for doubling down a Soft Holding are threefold: First, you cannot possible bust your hand. Second, in each of the situations depicted in Figure 6 there is an excellent probability of the dealer busting. Third, there is a chance you will receive a card which will improve your hand. Explore this chart, study it, memorize it. And if you're interested in seeing how the Soft Holding strategy was developed, refer back to Figures 3 and 4. You'll find that some of the situations call for defensive action, others for offensive action by the player.

Note that you always stand on Ace + Eight and Ace + Nine, because those hands are worth 19 and 20, respectively. A case could be made for doubling down on either of those hands against a dealer Five or Six, and I wouldn't argue against doing so. In fact, there are certain times when doing so would be a very wise play. But, for now, let's stay slightly conservative.

As with the chart for doubling down, astute use of Soft Holdings will increase your winnings.

SOFT HOLDINGS
S = STAND   H = HIT   D = DOUBLE DOWN

THE DEALER IS SHOWING =	2	3	4	5	6	7	8	9	10	ACE
YOU ARE HAPPY TO HAVE:										
ACE + NINE	S	S	S	S	S	S	S	S	S	S
ACE + EIGHT	S	S	S	S	S	S	S	S	S	S
ACE + SEVEN	S	D	D	D	D	S	S	H	H	H
ACE + SIX	H	H	D	D	D	S	H	H	H	H
ACE + FIVE	H	H	D	D	D	H	H	H	H	H
ACE + FOUR	H	H	D	D	D	H	H	H	H	H
ACE + THREE	H	H	D	D	D	H	H	H	H	H
ACE + TWO	H	H	D	D	D	H	H	H	H	H

Figure 6

Okay, now give a few moments thought to how this strategy was devised. I'll provide an example, but if you're even semi-serious about making Blackjack your game of choice you really need to take the time to figure some of this out for yourself. Why? Because that's the only way you'll ever truly understand it.

Get out a deck of cards. Deal one hand to yourself and another for the dealer. One of dealer's cards should be down, the other up. Your cards can be either up or down . . .makes not difference. Rig the cards so that you start with Ace + Seven for yourself. This is either 8 or 18. And 18 is a decent hand. Make the dealer's up card a Four. Check the chart in Figure 5 and ask yourself why you would want to count your Ace + Seven as 8 and double down against a dealer Three, Four, Five, or Six? This is easy, folks. Go back and take a look at Figure 4. Here's the question. With what up cards showing does the dealer have the greatest chance of busting? Right. Three, Four, Five, and Six. So, number one, we are playing for a dealer bust. And, by the way, the act of doubling down has not changed because you have a Soft Holding. If you have possession of the cards, flip them over above your wager and match your wager with a like amount. You can do this as soon as you see your cards, or you can wait until it's your turn. You needn't wait until the other players sitting to your right have exercised their options. However, as you will see later, it may be to your benefit to wait for your turn. If the cards were all dealt face up, simply match your wager. But, you say, with a Four showing the dealer only has a 40% chance of busting. Does that percentage provide enough of a player edge to warrant doubling your bet? Of course not. Now we gotta move on to reason number two. Again, you're sitting there with Ace + Seven. On a one-card draw, how many cards can help you and how many can hurt you? Figure it out. An Ace would give you 19, a Ten-Value would keep you at 18, a Nine would drop you to 17. You already have one Ace, so that means a total of 23 cards will leave you with a playable hand. The other 26 cards remaining in the deck (don't forget to include the dealer's Four) will hurt. This means that 47% of the time you can expect a card which will give you a playable hand (23 decent cards divided by 49 possibilities). Conversely, the other 26 cards provide a 53% chance of you ending up with a terrible hand.

There's two factors to consider here. The dealer bust percentage, and your chance of improving your hand. Neither one, taken by themselves, would be reason enough to double your wager. However, when both of them are combined we have just enough edge to make doubling down the correct play.

So, why not double down an Ace + Two against a dealer Two? Let's do another analysis. What's the chance of the dealer busting? Only 30%. What's the chance of improving your hand to a playable total? I'll tell you it's roughly 41%, but you need to verify it for yourself. Now look at it another way. There's a 70% chance of the dealer ending with a playable hand. You have only a 41% chance of ending with a playable hand. Double down? No way. You have less than a 50/50 chance of improving your hand. The dealer has a greater than 50/50 chance of improving her hand. The edge here is non-existent for the player. No edge, no double down.

SPLITTING PAIRS

When you split your initial two cards you actually turn one hand into two. Each hand is then treated as it's own entity. This magic can only happen when your first two cards are a pair. If your first two cards are Two of Hearts + Two of Spades, you can split them. You can split Three + Three or Four + Four, or any pair including any two Ten-Value cards (Ten, Jack, or Queen, King). So a pair consisting of Ten + Jack could be split, as could a pair consisting of King + Queen. Suits don't matter. Obviously, if you're playing with only one deck, there is only one card of each suit; one Jack of Spades, one Three of Diamonds, etc. If you're playing with six decks, there would be a total of twenty-four Jacks, and six of them would be the Jack of Spades, so you could, literally, split a pair consisting of the Jack of Spades + Jack of Spades.

Since you will now be playing two separate hands after splitting your cards, you must double your bet. The procedure is the same as that for doubling down; expose your cards to the dealer and match your bet with a like amount. If the cards were dealt face up, simply match your bet. But unlike doubling down, take care to create a space between your cards when you expose them.

If you are splitting a pair and you lay them down so that one card is on top of the other, the dealer may think you want to double down. In any case, make sure the dealer understands that you want to split. It is quite common for mishaps to take place when the pair you are splitting consists of Fours and Fives. A pair of Fours is a total of 8, and some people, depending on the

89

> ### HERE WE GO AGAIN
> How many times must I tell you? You just made a move to split a pair, and in your haste to follow my instructions pertaining to creating a space between the two cards you used two hands. Bad, bad, bad. Two hands of cards does not equal two hands ON the cards. One hand only!!!!

dealer's up card, would rather double down on 8 then start two hands with only a value of 4 each. If you expose a pair of Fives, most dealers will inquire as to whether you are doubling or splitting, but don't leave room for a misunderstanding. When you intend to split a pair, create several inches between the two cards when you turn them over. If the cards are dealt face up, the casino doesn't want you to touch the cards, so give the dealer a clue by creating several inches of space between your original bet and your matching bet.

The dealer will issue a hit to the first card of your pair (the first of your two separate hands) and wait to see if you want additional cards on that hand. Let's say you split a hand of Eight of Hearts + Eight of Diamonds. Let's further assume that the Eight of Hearts is the card the furthest to the right at your playing position. It will be the first to be acted upon. Once you are finished acting on that hand, the dealer will deal a card to your Eight of Diamonds.

Both hands are played like any individual hand, using the strategies we discussed earlier. You can hit or stand, and the casinos which offer the best rules will also allow you to double down or re-split. The manner in which you play each of the hands should not be affected by the fact that you are now playing two hands instead of one. If your Eight of Hearts catches a Three, you've got 11 and should double down. If your Eight of Hearts catches a Six, you've got 14, and should execute the basic HARD HOLDING STRATEGY.

If your Eight of Hearts catches another Eight, say the Eight of Clubs, most casinos will allow you to re-split, which simply means that you'll split this new pair, match your bet again, and play three hands (one of which is started with the Eight of Hearts, one with the Eight of Clubs, and one with the Eight of Diamonds).

SPLITTING PAIRS
S = Stand $ = SPLIT   H = Hit   D = DOUBLE DOWN

DEALER HAS ON DISPLAY =	2	3	4	5	6	7	8	9	10	ACE
YOUR HAND CONSISTS OF										
2 + 2	H	$	$	$	$	$	H	H	H	H
3 + 3	H	$	$	$	$	$	H	H	H	H
4 + 4	H	H	H	H	H	H	H	H	H	H
5 + 5	D	D	D	D	D	D	D	D	H	H
6 + 6	$	$	$	$	$	H	H	H	H	H
7 + 7	$	$	$	$	$	$	H	H	H	H
8 + 8	H	H	H	H	H	H	H	H	H	H
9 + 9	$	$	$	$	$	S	S	S	S	S
10 + 10	S	S	S	S	S	S	S	S	S	S
ACE + ACE	$	$	$	$	$	$	$	$	$	$

Figure 7

There are rule variations for splitting, but one rule is the same at every casino. If you split a pair of Aces, you will receive only *ONE* card, usually dealt face down, on each of your Aces. You have no options. You live or die with the single card that you are dealt on each Ace. In addition, should one or both of your Aces be dealt a Ten-Value card, you do not have a Natural. You simply have a total of 21 and are paid even money if you win. Remember, the only time you can have a Blackjack is on your initial two cards. As to why you should always split Aces, consider that when you do so you have a 64% chance of catching a card which will make a playable hand. That alone makes it worthwhile. Then add in the possibilities of the dealer busting, and you can see why splitting Aces is always a good idea.

You never split Fours. Why? Well, if I told you that every hand of Blackjack you will ever play will begin with a Four, how long would you play? Right. That's why we neversplit Fours. More importantly, your total of 8 can survive a hit, even if it's a bad one. And, yes, for those of you who are wondering, there can be times when it is prudent to even double down with that pair of Fours. But even in the best of circumstances you would only double down a pair of Fours against a dealer 4, 5, or 6.

> ## THE STRATEGIES DON'T CHANGE
>
> **I don't care if you split fourteen times, the strategy for playing each hand remains the same. Don't get all nervous and frozen brained just because you're playing more than one hand and have lots of bets spread all over the table. The Hard Holding Strategy does not change, the Soft Holding Strategy does not change, the Double Down strategy does not change, the Splitting Pairs strategy does not change. Can I possibly make this any more clear? Simple play them one hand at a time.**

You should *ALWAYS* split Eight + Eight. You should *NEVER* split Ten + Ten or Five + Five. Figure out the whys for yourself.

You will note that at times you are taking the offensive, at other times the defensive. Holding Seven + Seven is no great joy. By splitting Sevens you may draw cards which will improve your chance of winning (nearly anything is better than 14). Splitting Nines is an offensive attempt when the dealer is showing a card worth Six or less. Yet we do not split Nines against a dealer Seven for the simple reason that if the dealer has 17, you will beat her with your 18. Against a dealer Eight you should Stand on Nine + Nine, hoping for a tie. Against a dealer Ten or Ace there are a lot of people who say the correct play is to split a pair of Nines. I don't advocate it for the very simple reason that my experience is that with a pair of Nines I have 18, and when I split them I'm lucky to end with 19 or 20 on even one of them. Consequently, I love Nines if the dealer has a bust card showing. Otherwise, I stand on my 18 and hope for the best.

There are pros and cons pertaining to several of the decisions I have listed in Figure 7. As with all the various strategies, we are often attempting to make the best of dreadful situations. Splitting opportunities do not present themselves very often, but you should know how to handle them when they occur.

INSURANCE

This is one of the least understood of all the player options. Yet it can be quite beneficial once you know what buying it really means.

The only time you can buy Insurance is when the dealer's up card is an Ace. In that case the dealer will ask all the players whether they want to buy Insurance. If you want to buy Insurance, place an amount equal to half your original wager into the area marked Insurance (see Figure 1). The dealer then peeks at her hold card to see if she has a Ten-Value card for a Blackjack. If she does, you lose your original wager(unless you also have a Blackjack), but you win a payoff of two to one on your Insurance bet. If your original bet was $10, the Insurance wager would cost you $5. So, if the dealer does in fact have a Natural, you would lose your original wager of $10, but win a payoff of 2:1, or $10, on your $5 Insurance bet. The end result? You break even for the hand. If the dealer does not have a Blackjack, you lose your Insurance bet and the game continues in the normal manner, with each player then acting on their hands. Which means that you are already down $5 before you even take a hit, which means, unless you double down or split, the most you can hope to win is half of your original wager.

The truth of the matter is that you are not really buying Insurance. In essence, you are simply making an additional wager. You are betting on whether or not the dealer has Blackjack. Clearly, this is a case of the casino misleading all those who don't know any better. Technically, this should be called "OPPORTUNITY TO MAKE A HIGH RISK WAGER." And unless you are a card counter (explained later) this is a bad bet to make!

What's my move if I'm holding Ace + King, and the dealer asks for Insurance? The majority of people you will meet at Blackjack tables, the overwhelming majority of dealers and pit employees, and even a few noted authors will tell you that if you have a Natural as your holding you should always buy Insurance. So, let's say your wager is $10. You draw a Blackjack. But the dealer is showing an Ace, so you have the option of the Insurance bet. Insurance would cost you $5. Now think about this. Follow the mathematics.

WARNING! WARNING!
Unless you are a card counter, never buy Insurance. No matter how many dealers or fellow players tell you otherwise. No matter how many dealers or fellow players look at you like they consider you an imbecile. Don't do it. Get it through your head right now.
Do . . .not . . .do . . .it!

First, we will assume that the dealer does have a Natural. What happens? Did you lose your original wager? No. You tied the dealer, so you have a push. Your original $10 wager stays right where it is. And, on your extra Insurance wager of $5, you win at the rate of 2:1, which is $10. So, just to confirm, the net result here of purchasing insurance when you had a Blackjack is that you actually ended up with a payoff for the hand of 1:1. Your original bet was $10, and you ended up winning $10. But don't forget that it really cost you $15 to win $10. And you had a Natural!

Now, regarding the above. In most casinos instead of purchasing the insurance you can simply toss your cards on the table, face up, and say "Even money." I've never been in a casino which denied the player this option. What it means is that instead of receiving a payoff of 3:2 for your Blackjack, you receive a payoff of 1:1, and you collect before the dealer looks at her hole card. Correct. You get paid whether the dealer actually has a Blackjack, or not. You eliminate the risk of tying the dealer's hand. But you give up a third of your potential profit to do so. However, should the dealer also have a natural Blackjack, you then have profit instead of a tie. Is this a good deal? Read the next couple of paragraphs before you decide.

Example. You have a Blackjack. The dealer is showing an Ace. You decide not to purchase the Insurance option. What's the worst thing that can happen? Well, if the dealer also has a Natural, you tie. You push. No money exchanges hands. Is that so terrible? Yes! Darn it, those Blackjacks don't come along all that often, so we would like to be collecting money when we are fortunate enough to receive them. I mean, it's not like tying the dealer with a 17, or 18. A Blackjack pays off at the rate of 3:2. And it is frustrating to be denied that payoff.

Last example. Same deal. You've got Blackjack. Dealer has the Ace up. You decide not to purchase the Insurance option. Best case, the dealer does not have Blackjack and your Natural collects at the rate of 3:2. Is this what we want? Absolutely!

So, there you have it. You have a Natural, the dealer is showing an Ace. You can purchase Insurance. You can pass on the Insurance. You can request even money. What's your choice? Lemme give you a hint.

Play for the highest possible return on your investment! You only need one reason to understand this decision. Why do you think the casinos allow players to call out "Even money!"? Is it because they want to see you rewarded for that Blackjack? Is it because they are not interested in profits? No, no, no. It's because it is to their advantage to provide you with even money.

Always remember that anything which benefits the casino is automatically bad for the player. Good For Them = Bad For You. G.F.T. = B.F.Y.

My advice is to never take even money on a Natural Blackjack unless you are a card counter. Yes, there will be times when you're gonna get beat by doing this. But every time the dealer does not have a Blackjack you're giving up 50% of your potential payoff.

Also, check your karma. You get a Blackjack. The dealer has one, too. If that happens more than once at a table, you may want to seriously consider moving on.

SURRENDER

Yes, this player option is exactly what the word implies. You surrender your hand to the dealer. You give up. You wave a white flag over your head. And the result is that the dealer takes only *HALF* your wager. If you are a card counter this option can be very beneficial. If you are not a card counter this option may not be as great as it sounds.

To Surrender your cards, simply turn them over and expose them to the dealer. If the cards were all dealt face up, simply say "Surrender" or "I Surren-

95

der." In either case, *DO NOT* touch your bet. The dealer will take half of your wager. The casino does not want you fooling around with your chips because, as I've already stated several times, they are always on guard for cheaters.

Technically, there are two forms of Surrender; late and early. Here's the difference. With Early Surrender, if the dealer has a Ten-Value or Ace showing, you have a chance to surrender BEFORE the dealer checks her hole card to see whether she has a Natural. With Late Surrender, if the dealer has a Ten-Value or Ace for an up card, you cannot surrender until AFTER she checks her hole card to see whether she has a Natural. If she has the Blackjack Natural, you lose . . .unless you can tie her with a Natural of your own. Now go back to the first sentence in this paragraph. I said TECHNICALLY. And the reason I said technically is that I've never seen Early Surrender offered . . .no where, no place, at no time. Consequently, and for all practical purposes, there is really only one type of Surrender, and that is Late Surrender.

You may only exercise the Surrender option *BEFORE* acting on your hand. You cannot take a hit, bust, and then surrender. You must surrender your original two cards.

Example. Your first two cards are the Queen of Hearts + the Five of Diamonds. Lovely. Even worse, the dealer is showing an Ace. Think about Figure 4. You're gonna bust this hand the majority of times you hit it. Think about Figure 3. The dealer is going to make a hand 83% of the time. It appears you are dead meat. So, you toss your cards out on the table and say "I Surrender," or "I give up," or any words to that effect. Actually, you could also say something like this. "After carefully analyzing my player options, the contents of my hand, the powerful dealer card currently on exhibit, and the sad state of affairs concerning my present gambling stake, I have decided to run for my life. Please, please allow me to escape with a few meager chips." If the Surrender option is

> **EARLY AND LATE SURRENDER**
> Do the casinos advertise "Late" Surrender or "Early" Surrender? No. And that's because there is really only one kind. Go ahead and ask, though, just in case. Early Surrender is definitely a benefit to the player. If you can find it.

96

offered at this table, the dealer will remove half of your wager and collect your cards. You don't even need to leave. You can play again the very next hand.

Is this good? Well, if you are a card counter, this can be a life-saving option. If you're not a card counter, there are only a few situations in which you would definitely want to surrender. Like this example. You are sitting at third base. There are six other people at your table. You are playing a single deck game. The dealer is showing a Ten. The guy over at first base takes three hits. Two of them are Sixes and one of them is a Five. The next player takes three Hits. Two of them are Fives and one of them is a Six. The next player takes three hits. Two of them are Fours and one of them is a Five. The next player takes three hits. Two of them are Fours and one of them is a Six. The next player takes four hits. All Threes. Now it's your turn. Is this a no-brainer example? Yes. You've just seen 15 of the 19 cards which could benefit your hand. All the Sixes are gone. All the Fives are gone. All the Fours and Threes are gone. Yes, there could still be four Twos still left in the deck, but a Deuce would only give you 17. Plus, there were no Ten-Values in the last 15 cards. Any chance the next one might be a Ten-Value? Are you kidding? It is nearly guaranteed. Get out of Dodge! Run for cover! Surrender, surrender, surrender.

This is a good option, but don't overuse it. If you are not a card counter, there are only a few times when you should exercise this option. Such as, if your hand is 15 or 16 and the dealer is showing an Ace or Ten-Value card; or if your hand is a 14 made up of Seven + Seven and the dealer is showing an Ace or Ten-Value card. Otherwise, play on. Remember that it's called GAMBLING. Take the hits and hope for the best. And if you continue to receive lousy hands like the ones just mentioned, it's time to change tables. Not all casinos offer this option, so always ask the dealer whether it is available.

This can be a terrific option to have at your disposal, so it is to your benefit to play at casinos which offer it. All things, that is, being equal. In other words, if you can choose from three different casinos and all of them have the same rules, but casino number three also offers the Surrender option, that's where you ought to be taking your money.

CARD COUNTING

Okay, we've already mentioned it several times in this chapter, so now it's time to explain why I have stated over and over again, "unless you are a card counter," or "if you are a card counter". Here's what this is all about. Card counters are gamblers who have the ability to count certain cards in order to ascertain whether the deck is in favor of the players or the dealer. Yes, a deck of cards can fluctuate quite a bit in favor of one or the other. It has been conclusively proven by numerous mathematical studies that the deck is favorable to the players when the ratio of high cards remaining in the deck is greater than the ratio of low cards. When the deck contains a high ratio of low cards, Twos through Sixes, the dealer gets very tough. When the deck contains a high ratio of high cards, Ten-Values and Aces, it's the player's turn to multiply his or her winnings.

> ### GOT IT?
> **Low cards are the dealer's friend. High cards are the player's friend. Lots of high cards remaining in the deck usually means good times for the players.**

If you are not a card counter, you may have even confused a favorable deck with "luck." Assume that you play at a six-deck table and that, by the time you begin to play, the majority of the low cards have already been played. You then win five hands in a row and decide that your luck is good. But, in fact, you won because the deck was favorable for the players. Of course, the reverse could also happen. You could sit down at a time when the deck is favorable for the dealer, lose five hands in a row, and decide that you have bad luck.

Card counting is not difficult. It can be if you use a complicated counting system, but exotic counting systems are best left to the experts. What you need is a system which is easy to use and easy to remember, a simple system which will help you win more and avoid losses. I will cover what I feel are the two easiest ways to count cards, and also a third, slightly more difficult option.

COUNTING TEN-VALUES

If you watch closely, whether the cards are dealt face up or face down, you will see every card that is played when players bust or when the dealer makes the settlements. Obviously, when the cards are all dealt face up you see every card. And even when they are dealt face down, the dealer will expose all the cards before making payoffs. She does this so the "eye in the sky" can photograph every card in every hand. And if the "eye in the sky" can see them, so can you. All you must do is count the number of Ten-Value cards that you see. Will it help? Immensely! Is it worth the effort? Absolutely!

There are 52 cards in each deck, sixteen of which are Ten-Values. This means that approximately one of every three cards is a Ten-Value. If the deck is "even" (the Ten-Values are spread equally through the deck), one Ten-Value should be played for about every three cards. When only a few Ten-Values are dealt on a hand, the next round will be "rich" in Ten-Values. When a lot of Ten-Values are dealt on a hand, the next round should be "poor" in Ten-Values. Again, if the deck is rich, the benefit is to the players. If the deck is poor, the benefit is to the dealer.

Common sense would tell us that if the deck is rich in Ten-Values, the dealer has the same opportunity of being dealt a good hand as the players, and common sense would be correct. The fact that a deck is rich in Ten-Values, does not mean that you will be dealt a pair of Ten-Values on the next hand. It might be the dealer who catches that pair of Ten-Values. So how does counting Ten-Values, knowing whether the deck is rich or poor, improve our chances for earning a profit? The answer is that knowing the composition of the remaining cards in the deck allows us to modify all of the basic strategies and therefore optimize our chance of success.

Example. The dealer is showing a Ten-Value. You have 11. The basic strategy says you should double down. However, from counting the Ten-Values, you know that the deck is very poor in Ten-Values. Should you still double down? Absolutely not! You already know that the deck has a less than normal ratio of exactly the cards you are hoping to catch. Play the odds. You've got no edge here.

Example. The dealer is showing a Ten-Value. You have a Hard Holding of 15. The basic strategy says to hit. But you know that the deck is very rich in Ten-Values. Should you still take a hit? No! You are almost certain to bust. Go back to Figure 4. With an even distribution of cards you are going to bust that 15 nearly 54% of the time. For every extra Ten-Value still in the deck, that percentage escalates. So, cross your fingers and pray the dealer doesn't have a

99

playable hand. Yes, you will probably lose. But if you bust before the dealer plays, you have no chance. None.

Example. The dealer shows an Ace, and asks if you want to buy Insurance. You know that the deck was very rich in Ten-Values at the start of that round. Should you buy Insurance? Of course. This is why I told you earlier that you should almost never buy Insurance unless you are a card counter. Make sense now?

I can't tell you how many times this has happened to me. I'm playing Blackjack. The dealer is showing an Ace. I have terrible cards. My hand is maybe 14, maybe 15,maybe 16. I have been counting cards. I know the deck is very rich in Ten-Values. I glance around the table. I don't see any Tens, Jacks, Queens or Kings in anybody's hand. I buy Insurance. I win the Insurance bet because the dealer has the Natural. When the dealer see my cards, she says "You were insuring a stiff?" Or another player says, "Why would anybody insure such a bad hand?" Well, guess what? First of all, as you should know by now, I didn't purchase Insurance. I merely made a wager on whether the dealer's hand contained a Blackjack. And, considering what I knew at the time I made the extra wager, I had an edge. I already knew the dealer had an Ace, and I already knew there was a very good chance the dealer would also have a Ten-Value for the Natural. I had an edge. I took advantage of it. You can do the same.

Another Example. The dealer is showing a Ten-Value, a Nine, an Eight, or a Seven. Your have a miserable 15. You know that the deck is rich in Ten-Values. Should you hit? Stand? No, you should do neither. This is a perfect example of when you should surrender, if you have that option.

Example. The dealer is showing a Five. You have a total holding of 8. You know that the deck is rich in Ten-Values. Should you hit? No! Instead, you could double down. The dealer's chance of busting is even greater than normal, so take your best shot.

By counting Ten-Values, you can modify the basic strategies to greatly narrow the odds against you. What's the difference? One percentage point, maybe two. Which, over the course of a long weekend of play is definitely meaningful. My best estimate is that by utilizing a good basic strategy you can cut the casino's advantage down from 6 or 7% to between 1 and 2%. By counting cards you can further reduce the disadvantage. And there are times when the count is so good that the percentage actually swings in the favor of the player. Not a lot. Perhaps a half of a per cent, maybe a full per cent. But Blackjack is still the only game in which the players can find themselves in a position where the odds are actually in their favor.

> ## WORTH REPEATING
> Counting cards provides you with information which you can utilize to modify the basic strategies to either a) take advantage of favorable situations or (b) protect yourself against losses.

Another outstanding benefit to knowing if the deck is rich or poor is that you can bet accordingly. If the deck is rich, to your advantage, you should increase your bet. If the deck is poor, make a minimum wager. Of course if there is a huge swing in the size of your wagers, the casino will take measures to negate your play. But if you keep your wagers in the 1 to 4 unit range you shouldn't encounter any difficulty. We'll discuss money management a little later, so for now suffice to say that it would be wise to bet one unit when the deck is average or poor, 3 to 4 units when the deck is rich.

101

Technically, in order to count Ten-Values you must have two counts going. One for the total cards played and another for the Ten-Values.

Example: Six players + the dealer at the table. You count a total of 22 cards in the first round. Two are Queens, two are Kings, one is a Jack, and one is a Ten. Is the deck now rich or poor? Well, figure it out for yourself. Remember that one out of roughly every three cards should be a Ten-Value. What's 22 divided by 3? The answer is 7.3333, and everything to the right of the decimal needs to be rounded off, so the answer we are really looking for is 7. Seven Ten-Values should have been played in that round of cards. How many did you count? Six. Consequently, the deck is slightly, by +1, rich in Ten-Values.

Example: Six players + the dealer at the table. You count a total of 37 cards in the first two rounds. Four are Queens, one is a King, one is a Jack, and three are Tens. Is the deck now rich or poor? Here's the formula. Total cards (37) divided by 3 should = the number of Ten-Values you should have counted. Any deviation from this result will tell you whether the remaining deck is rich or poor. In this example 37 divided by 3 = 12.333, which we will call 12. You actually counted 9 Ten-Values. So, the deck is rich, by +3, in Ten-Values. And that is meaningful.

Too hard, you say? Isn't there any easier way?

Yes. You don't really need to do all that mathematics. You will find that, on the average, 3.2 cards are used by each player during each round. Some will play with their initial two cards, others will take multiple hits, but the average is usually 3.2 per player. One out of every 3.25 cards in the deck is a Ten-Value. This means that you should see, or count, one Ten-Value for each player, including the dealer, at your table on each round.

Example. Six players plus the dealer. On the first hand of a new shuffle you count twelve Ten-Values. Is the deck rich or poor for the next round? Figure it out. Six players + the dealer = seven people. Seven Ten-Values should have been played; one for each player and one for the dealer. Since twelve were actually played, the remaining deck is very poor in Ten-Values.

> ## SURE YOU CAN COUNT, BUT CAN YOU PLAY?
>
> **Don't be stupid. Don't ruin a good thing. You're counting cards. You're doing well. You're winning money. The count is so good for the next hand that you jump your bet from $10 to $200. Well, guess what? You just ensured that the dealer is going to stop and shuffle up. Way to go. You just killed it for all of us who are playing at your table. We had a favorable deck, we were all looking forward to the next hand, and you just couldn't control yourself. Fine. You can count, but will the casino allow you to play? Not likely. Next time, don't ruin a good thing. Don't be stupid. Play it smart.**

Example. You are playing at a table with four other gamblers. For some undetermined reason, you are playing against a shoe of six decks. On the first round of cards you count three Ten-Values, on the second round you count only two Ten-Values, and on the third round you count six Ten-Values. Is the deck rich or poor in Ten-Values for the next round? Here's how to figure it out. You + four other gamblers + the dealer = a total of six people. So, approximately six Ten-Values should be played on each round. Three rounds of play should have seen eighteen Ten-Values. But how many did you count? Three + two + six = eleven. Consequently, the deck at that point is very rich in Ten-Values. This is exactly the kind of situation which calls for a maximum bet of five units.

If there is too much fluctuation in your bets, particularly if you are winning, the fact that you are a card counter will be obvious to casino personnel. And, the casinos don't care whether you are counting cards so long as you are losing, or not winning much, or at least keeping your bets in the 1 to 3 or 4 unit range. They do, however, care if you're winning. Moreover, when players make great jumps in their bets, they become alarmed. So, to destroy your count, the casino will then either have the dealer reshuffle after every hand, or even ask you to leave. However, unless you are changing your bets from, say, $10 to $500, you need not worry about being tossed out of any casinos.

A good rule of thumb is that your maximum wager should not be more than three to four times your normal minimum bet. Some people recommend that your maximum bet should not exceed five times your normal wager, but I've found that if you suddenly increase your bet from, say, $10 to $50, you become a closely-watched gambler. Which makes some people quite uncomfortable. And for most of us it is difficult to execute perfect strategy when two pit employees are standing at the edge of our table. So, keep it simple. If you normally bet $5 on each hand, your largest bet should be $20. If you normally bet $10 on each hand, your largest bet should be $40. Of course there are exceptions to this rule, such as when you are using a progressive betting system. But dealers and pit bosses know the difference between professional counters and people who are simply using good money management.

If you are counting Ten-Values and you begin to gain confidence, here's a suggestion. I'll assume you are varying your bets from $5 to $20. Instead of wagering $5 when the deck is even (neither rich nor poor), bet $10. Then, when the deck is poor you can drop down to a $5 wager, when rich go up to $20. The reasons are twofold. First, varying your bets by one or two units will not cause anyone to become alarmed, even if they know you are a counter. Second, knowing the richness or poorness of the deck gives you enough additional knowledge to increase to $10, even if the deck is only even. Counting Ten-Values makes you a smarter player so you can afford to wager more.

Counting Ten-Values is an easy way to help turn the odds in your favor, but it is not an exact science. However, knowing whether the deck is rich or poor gives you that extra bit of information which will add winnings to your gambling stake, or . . . and this is just as important . . . help protect you from unnecessary losses.

Please remember this: The deck can only be "rich," "poor," or "even." If it's even, you would continue to use the basic strategy outlined earlier in this chapter. If it is rich or poor, use your common sense. There are only a few minor adjustments that need to be made if the deck is rich or poor, and these have already been covered in the examples.

COUNTING ACES

This will not help as much as counting Ten-Values, but when the deck is rich in Aces you have an increased opportunity of being dealt a Natural Blackjack. Also, when the deck is rich in Aces you have more opportunity of being dealt a Soft Holding, which gives you much more flexibility. And when the deck is rich in Aces, doubling down on a holding of 9 or 10 makes for an even greater chance for success.

In addition, if you can manage to count both Aces and Ten-Values, you could be one of the best informed players in the casino. Try it; it's not all that difficult. Or play with a friend. You can count the Ten-Values, your friend can count the Aces.

One in every thirteen cards should be an Ace. So how many players are in the game? How many cards have been dealt? How many were Aces? Is the deck rich or poor in Aces? Use your head and figure it out for yourself.

Every time the deck is rich in Ten-Values and Aces, people are invariably dealt Natural Blackjacks. It never fails. And what's the common complaint you will hear from players who have been dealt a Blackjack? Yes, even though they've just won a 3:2 payoff they still have a complaint. Usually they will make some sort of comment about never having a large bet on the table when they catch that Ace and Ten-Value. You'll hear comments like, "Darn it, I started to double my bet that time, then changed my mind." Or how about "I knew it! I knew as soon as I backed off on my bet I'd catch a Blackjack!" Well, you'll never hear me making any comments like that, because whenever I note

104

that the deck is rich in Aces and Ten-Values, I make my largest bet. You might be amazed at how many times I've been dealt a Blackjack with a maximum bet on the table. And don't forget that a Natural Blackjack is paid off at three to two instead of even money. This is one way to start beating down the odds against the player which are so inherent in this game. The idea is to make your largest bets whenever there is a situation which can be honestly exploited. Counting Aces will help by providing the kind of information which can inform you when there's a situation to be exploited.

Even though few in number, Aces are powerful cards. Aces create Blackjacks and Soft Holdings. You should like both. Consequently, try to be aware of those times when it becomes likely that you will have an elevated chance of receiving an Ace.

POSITIVES AND NEGATIVES

For those of you who are willing to devote time to serious card counting, here's your system. If you can master it, you'll be one of the toughest, hardest-to-beat Blackjack players in any casino. But let me warn you: It takes a *LOT* of practice.

This system can be worked with infinite variations, so I'll explain the most popular version. And, by the way, I only use this system when I'm playing against a shoe. If I'm playing against one or two decks, I simply count Ten-Values and Aces. Not that counting Ten-Values and Aces is better . . .it's simply less mentally demanding and fatiguing.

Here's what you do: Assign a value of minus one (-1) to all Ten-Value cards. Count all Aces as minus two (-2). Assign all Threes, Fours, Fives and Sixes a value of positive one (+1). Do not bother to count Twos, Sevens, Eights or Nines. Suits are meaningless. The object is to keep a running total as all the cards are played. If the running total is negative, the deck is in favor of the dealer. If the running total is positive, the deck is in favor of the players.

Think about it for a moment, and it will start to make sense. If the count is a positive number, a lot of low-value cards have been played, which then means the rest of the deck has a high ratio of high-value cards remaining in it. And you, as a player, want to be aware of situations when the deck is made up of a high ratio of high-value cards.

Try a few examples. The following cards are played: Ace, Three, Two, King. What's the count? The Ace is worth minus two(-2). The Three is worth positive one (+1). The Two has no value assigned, so don't count it. The King is worth minus one (-1). So what you have is, (-2) + (+1) + (-1). Added together, the count becomes a total of minus two (-2), which tells us that of the cards played thus far, more high-value cards have been played than low-value cards.

Another example. These cards are played: Jack, Four, Five, Seven, Eight, Three, King. What's the running count? This time add the totals just as you would in a real game. The Jack is a minus one (-1). The Four is a positive one (+1), so now the total is zero (0). The Five is a positive one (+1), so your total becomes positive one (+1). The Seven and the Eight do not count. The Three is a positive one (+1), so your total adds to positive two (+2). The King is a negative one (-1), which brings the running total back down to positive one (+1). In this example, your running total of positive one (+1) tells you that of all the cards played thus far, more low-value cards have been played than high-value cards.

The easiest way to learn this counting system is to take out a deck of cards and expose them to your eyes one at a time. When you get to the end of the deck, shuffle and start over. Then, when you get to the point where you can go through a complete deck and finish with an accurate count, start dealing practice hands. At first, deal all the cards up. If you are still proficient, start dealing the cards face down and expose them in the same manner as the dealer; when a player busts, or at the end of the round when money is collected and paid off, etc.

Again, a positive running total tells you that the deck is composed of a favorable ratio of high-value cards. Positive means good, negative means bad for the players. The more often you have a positive running total, the more often you will win.

Now the question is, how do you adjust your play to reflect this new information? Again, keep it simple. Use your brain. Use some common sense. Personally, I've found that the total must reach at least a count of four, whether positive or negative, before I make any changes in my bets or in the basic strategy. Consequently, I have set a few parameters for my play, adjustments I make automatically whenever the count reaches four. You can make whatever changes make sense to you. But here are a few to help you along.

1) **With a running count of plus four (+4), double your wager. If you've been betting $5, bet $10.**

2) **With a running count of plus six (+6) or more, triple your bet. If you've been wagering $5, wager $15.**

3) **With a running count of plus six (+6) or more:**
   a) **Double your bet after every winning hand. If you had bet $30, make your next bet $60.**
   b) **Always buy Insurance.**
   c) **Double down on all totals of 8 against all dealer Fours, Fives, and Sixes.**
   d) **Do not Hit any Hard Holding of 15 or 16.**
   e) **Surrender any Hard Holding of 14, 15 or 16 against a dealer Ten-Value.**

4) **With a running count of minus four (-4):**
   a) **Do not double down on a holding of 11 unless the dealer is showing less than a Ten-Value.**
   b) **Do not double down on a holding of 10 unless the dealer is showing a Four, Five, Six or Seven.**
   c) **Do not split Aces unless the dealer is showing a Five or a Six.**
   d) **Never Surrender any hand, regardless of how bad it seems.**

The list could go on and on, but common sense should prevail. All these rules mean additional winnings or reduced losses, so try to remember them when you are using the Negative-Positive counting system. It is the most troublesome system to learn, but it is also the most accurate.

107

I should now explain two statements which I made earlier in this chapter. First, I indicated that, if at all possible, you should sit at third base. The reason for choosing that position is that by sitting at third base you are able to see, and therefore count, more cards before you need to exercise any options on your hand. This is beneficial even if you're not a card counter, but it is especially beneficial if you are utilizing a card-counting system. The more cards you can count, and the more accurate your count, the more you turn the odds in your favor.

> ## THE REALLY, REALLY GOOD NEWS
> Counting cards will make you a tough player to beat. You will be more informed than other players. You will amend the basic strategies where warranted. You will fluctuate your wagers to compensate for favorable situations. This is good. Do it.

Example. At the start of a round of play, you note that the deck is "rich" in high-value cards. Consequently, you know that the remaining portion of the deck should be favorable for the players. You are dealt a Seven and a Four. The dealer is showing a Queen. Since the remaining deck is composed of a high ratio of high-value cards, you are foaming at the mouth with anticipation. You can't wait to double down. But you are seated at third base, and the five or six players who act on their hands in front of you all take hits. They all receive Ten-Values. Would you still double down? Perhaps not. By the time it is your turn to exercise your options, the deck may no longer be "rich" in high-value cards.

Your second choice of places to sit should be at first base. The reason? At first base, you are able to exercise your options before all the other players. In the example stated above, had you been seated at first base, you would definitely have doubled down. Had you been at first base, the other players would not have depleted the high ratio of high-value cards remaining in the deck.

And now, allow me to thoroughly confuse you by offering a third choice. Many people, particularly those who can't see very well, think that the best place to sit when you're a counter is right smack in the middle of the table, because from there it is easier to see all the cards which are dealt. The larger the tables and the poorer your eyesight, the more important this becomes.

108

Don't get miffed at me. I know, I mentioned sitting at everywhere except on the floor or the dealer's knee. So this is another one of those times when you gotta figure out what works for you. Which means that our bottom line is that you should sit wherever you feel most comfortable and confident.

I also mentioned earlier that dealers will "burn" one or more cards from the top of the deck or decks before beginning each new deal. Now that we're talking about card counting, I can tell you that the reason the top card (or cards) is "burned" is to make life more troublesome for card counters. When counting cards, it is imperative to see as many cards as possible. If the dealer burns the top four cards, and all four cards are Ten-Values, your count will never be entirely accurate. The more cards the casino burns, the more difficult it is to count cards.

While I'm thinking of it, here's another point I'd like to make. To my way of thinking, the players are all in a war against the dealer. No, that doesn't mean we should hate all dealers. To the extent that we players are all trying to win, it makes sense that we should help one another as much as possible. Therefore, if the cards are dealt facedown, don't be afraid to let the players on either side of you see your cards. I am a card counter. So when the people around me try to conceal their cards so I can't see them, I sometimes become perturbed. The more cards I can see, the better my count, and the greater my chance of winning. Conversely, I always let the people around

THE REALLY, REALLY BAD NEWS

Casinos know that counting cards benefits the players. Consequently, more and more of them are shuffling up quicker and quicker in order to negate the benefits of counting cards. As recently as three or four years ago it was possible to find double deck games which would provide 4 or 5 hands to a full compliment of players. Now the casinos shuffle after 2 hands. As recently as three or four years ago it was possible to find six-deck shoes where all but the last deck of cards was dealt out. Now the casinos shuffle up after dealing three decks. So, if you're going to be a card counter, look for casinos which deal deep into the deck or decks.

109

me see my cards, in the hope that a small amount of additional knowledge may help them. If I have a holding of 11 and everybody around me has two Ten-Value cards in their hand, I will certainly think twice before doubling down. Don't hide your cards from the other players!

Should you attempt to play the game of Blackjack without A) learning basic playing strategy, and/or B) without learning a counting system, the casinos will hold an edge of approximately 4-7%. Should you, however, learn a good basic playing system, like the one outlined earlier in this chapter, you can reduce the casino's advantage so it falls into the 1-3% range. And here's the best news of all:

People who play with confidence never attempt to hide their cards. People without confidence, and those with poor playing habits, nearly always attempt to conceal their cards. I know this. Now you know this. So quit worrying about making mistakes. Quit worrying that I'll try to tell you how to play your cards. Relax. I'm simply trying to win. You're simply trying to win. So, let's try to help each other.

Should you learn both the basic playing system and a counting system, you can actually turn the odds in your favor. Not a lot, but at least in the 1-2% range. So, the question is this: Would you rather give up a 4% edge to the casino, or have 2% on your side? Isn't it worth the effort? Or do you wanna continue donating to the casinos for the rest of your life?

RULE VARIATIONS

Not all casinos use the same rules governing player and dealer options. What follows is a list of the differences which you may find. Remember to ask about the rules *before* you start playing. Many casinos have this information posted on small signs standing on the Blackjack tables. Others exhibit the rules on large signs hanging above the pit. Regardless where they are on display, find and read them. Know your options *before* you place any bets.

110

1) **DOUBLING DOWN:** In most casinos the player can double down on any initial two-card holding. However, there are also casinos which will allow you to double only on holdings of 10 or 11, which limits double down opportunities and is subsequently a disadvantage for the player. Actively seek out those casinos which allow doubling on any first two cards.

2) **SPLITTING:** Some casinos allow pairs to be split and re-split; others allow splitting but no re-splitting. Seek those casinos which will allow you to re-split.

3) **SURRENDER:** This is an optional rule in Nevada and most other States, so ask everywhere you play. This is a good option, so seek it out.

4) **DOUBLING DOWN AFTER SPLITTING:** Assume that you split a pair of Sixes and then receive a Five on the first Six. At most casinos, you may then double down on your 11. This is very beneficial to the player, so seek out casinos which offer this option.

5) **DEALER OPTIONS:** In some casinos the dealer *MUST* stand on any 17. In others the dealer *MAY* stand on a soft 17 (Ace , Six). In still others, the dealer *MUST* hit a soft 17. It is to your advantage to play *ONLY* where the dealer *MUST* stand on all 17's, whether soft or hard.

6) **DEALER BLACKJACKS:** At some casinos, if the dealer is showing a Ten-Value or Ace the dealer must look at their hole card before the players can exercise their options, so that they can determine whether they have a Natural Blackjack. If they do, the game stops at that point. Consequently, should you double down or split, only to find out later the dealer does have a Natural Blackjack, you lose only your original wager. At some casinos the dealers are not allowed to peek at their hole card.

7) **DOUBLE EXPOSURE: In some casinos both the dealer's cards are dealt face up. This, of course, gives the player a tremendous advantage as it eliminates any speculation about the dealer's hole card. If the dealer is showing a total of 20, for example, you would hit your total of 19. But what the casinos give you with the right hand, they take back with the left. Here's what I mean. Though you have the advantage of seeing the dealer's hole card in this game, you are only paid even money if you receive a Natural Blackjack. Also, most casinos count all ties or pushes in this game as losses for the player. Only a fool would play against such heavy odds. If you haven't tried double-exposure Blackjack yet, you might want to try it at a one-dollar or two-dollar table, using your "fun" money. And make sure you know ALL the rules before you start making bets.**

6

Red Dog

lthough the casinos call this game Red Dog, most people have heard of it under names such as Acey-Deucey, In-Between, Between the Sheets, or Split the Sheets. This is a game which may have been played by your great grandfather if he was a cowboy or miner, or a man who frequented the bars of the wild west back in the 1800s. The rules are extremely simple and the game can be fun to play . . .even though this is another game where the odds are stacked heavily against you.

This is also a game which will simply not go away. By that I mean you may find it at your favorite casino today, come back in a month and discover it's gone, then come back two months later and find it there yet again. It may be at Sam's Town today, the Four Queens next month, and at neither by the end of the year. Consequently, don't be surprised if you can't find a table.

WHERE'S IT AT?

Red Dog tables are generally found adjacent to, in the middle of, or somewhere close to the Blackjack tables. It is played on a Blackjack table, but the felt reflects a different layout.

GIMME THE BASICS

There is a dealer. There is a shoe containing at least six decks. You begin by placing a wager. Typical minimum is $5, but it's possible to find games for less. The dealer exposes two cards by placing them face up in front of his position, right out in the middle of the table for all to see. The question is: Will the value of the next card off the top of the deck fall between the value of the two exposed cards? Aces are always high. Suits are meaningless, so it makes no difference if the cards are Hearts, Diamonds, Spades or Clubs. If there is no spread between the first two cards, like a Nine and a Ten, there is an automatic tie; you neither win nor lose, and a new round begins. If the spread is at least

 This is worth repeating. You're not seeking to win with a higher card than anybody else, you're not looking for a better hand, or the best hand. You merely want a card which fits in between the two which are exposed.

one card, you have a decision to make prior to the dealer exposing the third card. You can leave your wager as it is, or you can double it. That's right, you really only have two decisions in this game. First, you must decide on the size of your initial wager. Second, after seeing the nature of the spread, you must decide whether to double your wager.

When the first two cards exposed by the dealer are the same (a Pair), you cannot double your bet. But don't worry, if this happens you cannot lose.If, for example, the first two cards are a Pair of Queens, the dealer will dispense a third card to see if Three of a Kind can be made. If Three of a Kind is not made, you have a tie, or push, and a new round begins. Should the third card make Three of a Kind, the players are all paid off at the rate of 11:1. This sounds very nice, except that the true pay-off for this wager should be 24:1.

HOW MUCH DO I COLLECT?

The pay-offs for all bets are dependent upon the spread between the first two cards. A one-card spread (Jack-King) pays off at 5:1. It's called a one-card

114

spread because only one card will fit between a Jack and a King . . .a Queen. A two-card spread (Jack-Ace) pays off at 4:1 if the third card is a Queen or King.

A three-card spread (10-Ace) pays off at the rate of 2:1 if the next card is a Jack, Queen or King, and any spread higher than three pays off at even money. To clarify, a one-card spread is any two cards with one rank missing in between. 2-4 is missing the 3, so it would be a one-card spread. 7-9 is missing the 8, so it's a one-card spread. 7-10 is missing the 8

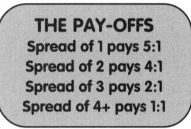

THE PAY-OFFS
Spread of 1 pays 5:1
Spread of 2 pays 4:1
Spread of 3 pays 2:1
Spread of 4+ pays 1:1

and 9, so it's a two-card spread. 9-King is a three-card spread because the 10, Jack, and Queen will all fit between those two cards. But don't be concerned about trying to count the spread on every hand because the dealer always announces the size of the spread, gives you a moment to decide whether to double your wager, and then deals the third card.

To keep yourself out of trouble in this game, study the chart in Figure 1 while keeping in mind the pay-offs listed above. Those of you who are interested can determine the house edge on your own. I'll merely state that it is very high. Yes, you do benefit by being able to double your wager in favorable situations, but even if you cut the house edge in half, you're still better off playing Roulette. However, this is another one of those games which can be fun to play, so at least give yourself a chance by studying this chart.

Spread	Win %	Lose %	True Odds
0	4%	96%	24-1
1	8%	92%	11.5-1
2	16%	84%	5.25-1
3	24%	76%	3-1
4	32%	68%	2-1
5	40%	60%	1.5-1
6	48%	52%	1-1
7	52%	48%	1-1
8	60%	40%	1-1.5

Figure 1

HOW DO YOU READ FIGURE 1?

Look at the first column. It shows the spread. The 5 listed in that column means a spread of 5. The next column, the Win %, is the percentage of time you can expect to fill a spread of five cards. The Lose % is the percentage of times you will not be able to fill a spread of five. And the last column shows the true odds of filling a spread of five.

SO, LIKE, WHAT DOES FIGURE 1 REALLY TELL ME?

Probably the most important fact is that in order to have a 50/50 chance of winning a bet you will need a spread of six cards. Any less, and the odds are against you. Any more, and the odds are in your favor. But take a moment to consider what a spread of six really means. In order to have a spread of six you need cards like 4-Jack, or 7-Ace, or 2-9. When you see cards like 5-Queen hit the table the spread appears to be huge . . .big enough to drive a tank through. And yet spreads like 5-Queen provide you with only a 50/50 chance.

116

WHAT'S THE MATHEMATICS ON THIS?

Here is how I came up with the figures you see in Figure 1. Consider a spread of 4. The first two cards are a 7 and a Queen. You determine the odds by thinking of this as a one-deck game in which only two cards have been dealt. Starting with 52 cards in the deck, you now have only 50 left because one of the 7s and one of the Queens have already been played. You must draw either an 8, a 9, a 10 or a Jack to be a winner. There are four of each of these cards in the deck, so there are 16 total chances of you winning. All of the rest of the cards in the deck will cause you to lose, so you have 34 chances of losing.

The number of winning chances (16) divided by the total number of chances (50), tells you that you can expect to win 32% of the time when the spread is five. The ratio of winning chances (16) to losing chances (34) can be determined by dividing 34 by 16, for a result of 2.13, which is listed in Figure 1 as 2, or odds of 2:1.

HOW DOES THE CASINO PROFIT?

How do I love thee? Let me count the ways. First, they make money due to the disparity between pay-offs and true odds. The pay-off for a one-card spread is 5:1. A true odds pay-off for a one-card spread would 24:1. Second, go back and look at Figure 1. With a spread of one you're only going to win 8 out of every 100 hands. Which means the casino is going to win 92 out of every 100. Even when you get up to spreads like seven or eight, the odds don't exactly turn overwhelmingly in favor of the player. Third, players assume that filling the spread is easier than it really is. The dealer may announce "Spread of four", but so long as it "looks" like there might be a chance a lot of players will double.

WHAT'S THE BEST STRATEGY

It does not take a superior intellect to determine that your best chances of winning and collecting on proper odds is when the spread is at least 6. Whenever you have a spread of 6 or more, you should definitely double your bet. Go beyond that fairly dry piece of advice and you're on your own.

DOES COUNTING CARDS HELP?

Even though a split second of shallow thinking might lead you to believe otherwise, the answer is: only a little. Granted, if you know that a high number of ten-value cards have been played, and you have a spread that needs a ten-value card, you should not double your wager. Conversely, when you have a spread of only 3 or 4 which requires a ten-value, you may want to double if the shoe is abundant with ten-values, even though the chart indicates the odds are against you.

Unfortunately, since the spread changes on every hand, and since the exact cards required also changes, counting cards does not help as much as you would hope.

For example, a spread of 4 on this hand could be 6-Jack, then on the next hand it might be 2-7, and then again it might be 9-Ace.

MONEY MANAGEMENT

This is another of those "fun" games. So play it only with "fun" money. The only way to win here is through good fortune. If you're having some, increase your basic unit. If you're not, leave.

In other chapters I talk about having a Plan, setting Loss Limits, establishing Winning Goals, etc. Forget all of that . . .except for the Loss Limits. Sit down, test the waters with a small amount of money, and stay only if you're winning. Buy in for no more than $20. If you lose it, vacate the game.

118

7

Craps

Craps tables remind me of carnival side shows. There ought to be carnival barkers reaching out to every person who walks by. Come one, come all! Step right up! Hurrrr-ray, hurrrr-ray, hurrrr-ray! Watch as two small cubes of ivory mesmerize and tantalize. Observe and be dazzled by the whims of fate. Don't pass us by! Step right up! Hurrrr-ray, hurrrr-ray, hurrrr-ray.

If you are old enough to remember the days of carnivals and side shows you were probably like a lot of us. Did we dare go in? Were we about to be fleeced, or was the show actually worthwhile? You may have felt slightly intimidated, yet thrilled at the prospect of seeing something new and exciting. Well, what can I say? Step right up.

Yes, this game provides all the carnival atmosphere . . .and all the intimidation. In fact, the game of Craps intimidates far too many people. You see enthusiastic gamblers clustered around a large table with chips of all colors being thrown, shifted, placed and removed with alarming speed. If there is human-generated noise in the casino, go ahead and assume that it is coming from the Craps tables. The money changes hands so fast it is puzzling for the novice, and there are so many betting options that most people don't have the foggiest notion what is happening. Pass, Don't Pass, Come, Don't Come, Hard Eight, Wrong Bettors, Right Bettors, Buying numbers, placing numbers, laying the odds, taking the odds, Any Craps, Hard Way bets. Is it any wonder why so many know so little about this game?

If the dice are "hot," and depending on how you are betting, you can virtually win or lose a fortune in a matter of minutes. If the dice are "cold," you can still virtually win or lose a fortune in a matter of minutes. Sound strange? You'll see rabid-looking rollers covering nearly every bet on the layout. You'll see serious players who never make more than one bet at any time. An inexperienced eye is amazed and awed, but to an experienced eye this game is as easy to play as Monopoly. Yet, before you rush to the first Craps table you see, a firm understanding of the game is necessary. For, unlike in Blackjack, when we play Craps it is impossible to obtain an edge over the casino. No matter what bet you make, the casino will have the advantage. However, that advantage is very small on some of the wagers. So small, in fact, that Craps is one of the few games I actually recommend that you play.

The game is played on a large table normally covered with green felt, with each betting option clearly marked by yellow or white lettering and boundaries (see Figure 1). The layout may vary moderately from casino to casino, but once you familiarize yourself with one layout, all are quite easy to understand. Craps tables are normally located in the same area as the rest of the table games, but there are no chairs. You gotta stand up to play this game. Most tables will "stand" up to twelve gamblers . . .officially. Actually, when the dice are hot you might find fifteen or more people squeezed up to the table. One person at a time rolls the dice, twelve or more may be making wagers.

Two DEALERS, a STICKMAN, and a BOXMAN supervise the action. The dealers settle the bets, assist the players in making proper wagers and, in general, do an incredible job of keeping track of the action. The stickman assists the dealers, controls both the dice and the center

120

> ## GENDER ISSUES
> Technically speaking, I should be calling the stickman the stick person. The boxman is the really the box person, etc. But for this chapter I have decided that all of the dealers, stick people and box people are male.

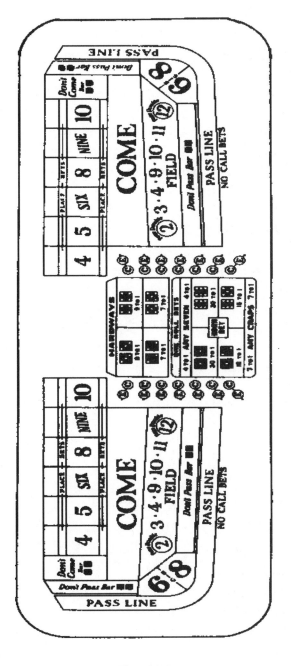

Figure 1

table bets, and keeps up a constant chatter to enliven the game. The two dealers and the stickman rotate their positions, each working the stick and both ends of the table on a fixed timetable. The boxman is the person sitting behind the table who looks like he is guarding the casino's chips; in fact, one of his responsibilities is to safeguard the casino's money. In addition, the boxman watches the game to ensure proper pay-offs, keeps a sharp eye on the dice, and is constantly on guard for cheaters and/or collusion between dealers and players. As I've mentioned before, the greatest danger, in terms of cheating, to the casino is an employee gone bad.

UNDERSTANDING THE POSSIBLE COMBINATIONS

Two dice are used. They are shaped just like the cubes of sugar you used to get at restaurants. Each has six sides, and each side exhibits a small dot or dots. Dice are usually red, the dots are usually white. Each side has a different number of dots, from one to six of them. When the two dice are rolled, there are 36 possible outcomes (totals of two dice). Before you can understand the various bets and your chances for success, you *must* understand how each number can be rolled. Study Figure 2 until you *fully* understand it.

122

OUTCOME	CAN BE ROLLED IN THESE COMBINATIONS OF TWO DICE
2	(1,1)
3	(1,2) (2,1)
4	(1,3) (2,2) (3,1)
5	(1,4) (2,3) (3,2) (4,1)
6	(1,5) (2,4) (3,3) (4,2) (5,1)
7	(1,6) (2,5) (3,4) (4,3) (5,2) (6,1)
8	(2,6) (3,5) (4,4) (5,3) (6,2)
9	(3,6) (4,5) (5,4) (6,3)
10	(4,6) (5,5) (6,4)
11	(5,6) (6,5)
12	(6,6)

Figure 2

What's the easiest number to roll? Seven. There are six different ways in which 7 can be rolled. 6 and 8 can each be rolled in five ways. 5 and 9 can be rolled in four ways. 4 and 10 can each be rolled in only three ways, 3 and 11 in only two ways. 2 and 12 can only be rolled in one way each. The chance of any of those numbers being rolled on any given throw of the dice is depicted in Figure 3.

NUMBER	CHANCE OF BEING ROLLED
2 or 12	1 out of 36, or 2.8%
3 or 11	2 out of 36, or 5.6%
4 or 10	3 out of 36, or 8.3%
5 or 9	4 out of 36, or 11.1%
6 or 8	5 out of 36, or 13.9%
7	6 out of 36, or 16.7%

Figure 3

123

In order for you to comprehend the various bets and why they work the way they do, it is essential that you understand Figures 2 and 3. As in all games, at least if you want to avoid financial perils, you must have knowledge of how the odds are stacked against you. In Craps, while it is impossible to gain an edge over the casino, some bets are better than others. So keep it simple. Give yourself a chance. Make only those

THE PERCENTAGES NEVER CHANGE

The odds of rolling any particular number do not vary. Not ever. It doesn't make any difference whether this is your first roll or your millionth roll. Even if you roll a 12 sixteen times in succession, the chance of rolling another one is still only one out of 36. The odds are still 35 to 1 against you. You still only have a 2.8% chance of rolling a twelve. The odds and the percentages never change. Never.

bets which provide you with the greatest opportunity for profits. Which means you absolutely MUST study and understand Figures 1 and 2.

LET'S GET STARTED

Strolling through the casino early one morning, you see a Craps table being opened. No one is playing there yet, so you decide this is an opportune time to finally master this game. You station yourself next to the stickman and purchase chips from the dealer on your end of the table. You do this by simply dropping your money on the felt, preferably on a spot which is not designated as a bet. You cannot hand your money to the dealer; you must lay it down. Remember that the casino is terrified that you may be operating in collusion with the dealer, so they don't want to leave any room for error or misunderstanding. When you lay your money out on the table it is there for everyone, including the ever-present "eye in the sky" to see.

124

BE SPECIFIC REGARDING THE CHIPS YOU NEED

If you are going to be making $2 wagers, it doesn't do you any good to get all $5 chips. If you're going to be making $25 wagers, it's easier to work with $25 chips than with five of the $5 chips. Keep it simple. When the dealer reaches out and snatches your cash, speak up! Tell him exactly what kind of chips you want. It's just like when you get change at the cashier. Be specific. If you want $10 in $5 chips + ten $1 chips for your $20 in cash, simple say so.

All right. The money is on the table. The dealer will provide you with chips. They are the same chips you saw when you tried Blackjack. Basic casino chips. Usually in denominations of $1, $5, $25, and $100. If there is a high roller at your Craps table you could even see chips worth $500 and $1,000. As with all games, there is a minimum wager required. However, unlike other table games, you will seldom see a Craps table which requires minimum wagers in excess of $10. Which doesn't mean much. Even $5 bettors could have $30-$40 spread over the layout for the next roll. However, and this goes for all games, you should always know the minimum required wager, and any pertinent rules prior to the time you make your first wager. So if the minimums and rules are not posted, simply ask the dealer who is on your end of the table.

Okay, you've checked and found out the minimum here is $5. The rules are posted on a sign hanging down above the table, and you don't see anything out of the ordinary. You've got your chips. Actually, you're hoping that no one else tries to play at this particular table so you can learn the game at your own pace, but before you can ask the dealers what you're supposed to do, thirteen other gamblers swoop around the table like locusts in a corn field. Suddenly, you're in the middle of a hot bed of activity. Players start throwing chips all over the layout, issuing instructions to the dealers like, "Eight the hard way!", "C and E!", "Place the numbers!", "Gimme the Yo!", etc. The stickman suggests, "Cover the field!", or "Bet the line!" Then he announces, "New shooter comin' out!", pushes five or more dice in front of you, and then looks at you as if you're supposed to do something.

Know the minimum required wager. Know the rules before you begin play. If you don't like the minimum or the rules, don't play. Go somewhere else. Go home. Or go to a movie. But don't play.

125

TIME TO ROLL THOSE BONES

You sense a slight tingling in your stomach, feel foolish for an instant, and almost decide to leave the table for the simple reason that this is your first time and you don't want to screw up and embarrass yourself. Fortunately, because you've already read this book, you merely take a deep breath while you compose yourself.

First, you must place a bet if you want to throw the dice. Only the roller is required to make a wager. If all the rest of the people at the table simply want to watch, they can do so without making a bet so long as nobody else wants the space they are inhabiting. But since there are so many different types of wagers to be made, it is quite common for a person to play and not have a bet on the table for each and every roll of the dice.

If you're going to roll, you gotta have a bet on the table. More specifically, you must make a bet on either the Pass Line or the Don't Pass Line.

Of course we're assuming you want to roll the dice, so your next step is to select two of the dice which the stickman has pushed in front of you. Remember that there are at least five of them, but you can only roll two at a time, so you need to select the two which are going to make you rich. No pressure here. It's just that if you don't pick the right dice most of the people at the table may want to strangle you within the next few minutes. Just kidding. Actually, the casino allows you to choose from five or more dice so that they can avoid being accused of any wrongdoing. Actually, it doesn't make any difference which two you select. The percentages which control this game will be in force no matter which dice you use. However, if you want to look like an experienced shooter try to look as if you have a specific plan. You know what I mean. Touch two of three of the dice. Maybe turn one or two of them over. Push two of them to the side as though you are narrowing the field. And then close your eyes and pick up whichever two happen to meet your fingers. And don't ever touch the dice with both of your hands. Yep. Just like in most of the card games. Yep. Same reason. Less chance of the casino being cheated.

Now throw them. And not just anywhere. And not just any way. The first rule for the shooter is the "one hand only" thing. The second rule is that

> **If you don't care to roll the little cubes, just tell the stickman, or wave him off, and he'll pass the dice to the first person on your left.**

126

> ## SHOOTER
> **The person rolling the dice. Or the person next in line to roll the dice, as in "next shooter." Or the person who just finished rolling--the "last shooter," etc. If you've ever rolled the dice, you were a "shooter."**

you must keep the dice over the table and in full view at all times. Failure to do so will draw an immediate reprimand from one of the crew; a reprimand which could be severe and harsh. If you ever want to get a rise out of the boxman, just grab the dice and make a move for your pocket. Just kidding. There are still places where a move like that could mean you would soon be eating those dice.

> ## AVOID PROBLEMS—
> ## KEEP IT SIMPLE
> **The game moves right along, and people are able to develop a rhythm, when everybody follows the rules. When people screw up and there are stoppages in play, rhythms are broken and your fellow gamblers become angry. Don't be the person who breaks the rhythm. Play by the rules.**

The third rule is that when you heave those cubes you must hit the far end of the table. If you're standing at the left end of the table, the dice must strike the right wall. If you're at the right end of the table, they gotta strike the left wall. If you're in the middle, you must go to the wall which is FURTHEST away from you. The casino wants a "true" roll. They take several steps to ensure a true roll. One, they insist you throw the dice the furthest distance possible. Second, you must hit a wall. Third, the walls are padded with special cushioning which is shaped to provide a true bounce. If you fail to do one of more of these three items, the stickman or boxman could call "No roll!" Of course there are reasons why the casinos want a "true" roll, but they all come down to one issue; the casinos don't want to be cheated.

Yes, I know this all sounds pretty darn restrictive. Just relax. We're already over the hump. For now, as to the exact manner in which you accomplish all of the items listed above, you have nearly limitless options. You could make every attempt to make it appear as if you've done this hundreds of times before, but in reality there is no such thing as a "correct," "cool," or "slick" way to toss the dice. Everyone has their own special and unique way of tossing the bones. You can hold the dice in your hands for a moment, shake them, blow on them, and give them directions as to what outcome you'd like, such as "Come on, seven!" You can hold them between your thumb and your pinkie and scream at the top of your lungs as you release them. You can remain completely silent and stoic. You can fling the dice with all your strength, or you can loft them softly. You can pray or you can swear. You can chant or sing. Whatever. Anything goes. Whatever works for you.

CRANK 'EM UP AND LET 'EM FLY

And now, knowing all that you need to know regarding the requirements for rolling the dice, you pick those cubes up and let'em rip. In fact, you heave the dice so hard that one of them flies over the end of the table, ricochets off the back of a pit boss, and skitters across the floor. The other completely destroys a pile of chips accumulated by a gentleman at the other end of the table, then impacts the padding and rebounds all the back to your end of the layout. If this happens, don't fret. The stickman will simply pass you more dice and let you start over again.

You're the shooter. You've made several numbers. You're feeling like these are pretty lucky dice. Then one of the die flies off the table. To ensure you get that same die back, you simply call, "Same dice." Then, instead of passing you more dice to choose from, the stickman will wait until your errant die is recovered and inspected by the boxman. Then you'll get it back.

DOES MY ROLL HAVE MEANING?

Absolutely! Your roll means everything. The outcome for every bet on the table will be determined by your rolls. Which is why some of the gamblers at your table will be, depending on how long you roll and what numbers you roll, either elated or dejected, happy or even irate. But don't worry about the other players. Just concentrate on what your rolls are doing for YOU.

If your very first roll produces a 4, 5, 6, 8, 9 or 10, you have established what is called the POINT. If your very first roll produces any other number several bets may be decided, but you will need to keep rolling until you gener-

128

ate a 4, 5, 6, 8, 9 or 10. During all of your rolls chips will be flying, people will be screaming their ecstasy or muttering their dread, and it may seem as though mass confusion reigns. Don't worry about anything. The actual length of time you will continue to be the shooter will depend on:

> ## WORTH REPEATING
> You don't have a POINT until you roll either a 4, 5, 6, 8, 9, or 10. People may win or lose money for all the other outcomes you can roll, but a POINT is not established until you roll one of the numbers listed above.

A) how long it takes to establish a Point

B) whether you throw your Point number again, or

C) whether you throw a 7 before repeating your Point number.

129

If your first roll is an 8, and your second a 7, you're done. If you keep matching the Point numbers, you could roll the bones a hundred or more times. But we're not concerned about any of that yet. More on this is coming. Right now, simply keep rolling the dice until the stickman pushes them in front of someone else. When you give up the dice, they are then rotated clockwise around the table to the next shooter. You may then either leave the table or make additional bets. What you do, is up to you.

In the following sections a short description is given for each bet available in Craps. If you don't understand the bet after your first reading, don't feel stupid. *KEEP READING UNTIL YOU UNDERSTAND*!! After several readings, you will find that there is no great mystique to this game, and, once you understand the bets, this is an easy game to play. We'll start with those bets which normally require several rolls of the dice before your stash of chips either grows or shrinks. Yes, it is possible to make a wager in Craps, then watch the shooter throw the dice time after time after time after time before you either win or lose.

PASS LINE

Please note in Figure 1 that this bet covers a large portion of the Craps layout. This is both one of the most popular bets and one of the easiest to understand. Yet here is a statement which may, at first, sound troublesome. A Pass Line bet should be made only BEFORE a Come-Out roll. That's important to remember. So, what the dickens is a Come-Out roll? It is the first roll which a shooter makes which establishes a Point. And having given you that definition, I need to get technical for a few seconds. Here's the deal. Picture yourself as the shooter. You're about to toss the dice for the first time. The stickman yells, "New shooter coming out!" You then roll an 11. Well, guess what? You did not establish a Point, so you need to roll again. And, once again, the dealer announces, "Coming out!" And, you ask, how can I be "coming out" again? I just did that." Well, the answer is that until you establish a Point, every time you roll it is a Come-Out roll. Think of it this way. If your Come-Out roll does not produce a Point, it really wasn't a Come-out roll, after all. Consequently, as many of you have already determined, it may take several rolls of the dice before you actually experience the true Come-Out roll. And why is it important to know whether the next roll is the Come-Out roll? Because of the types of betting options. More on that, later. For now, it is only important that you understand that there is such a thing as the Come-Out roll.

There are only two types of rolls. Come-Out and Point. You already know what a Come-Out roll is, so all you need now is to understand that a Point roll is every roll made after a Point has been established. Which means there can only be one true Come-Out roll, but there may be many Point rolls.

IMPORTANT TO KNOW
Once a COME-OUT roll has been made, meaning a Point has been established, all the rest of your rolls are called POINT ROLLS because you are chasing the Point, which means you are attempting to roll that same number again.

Fine. But what if you're not the shooter? How then would you know whether the shooter is about to make a Come-Out roll or a Point roll? Good news. We finally have an easy answer. If you approach a table and do not know whether the shooter is making Come-Out or Point rolls, look for a large white disc (or "puck") which will be placed on one of the numbers 4, 5, 6, 8, 9, or 10 on the layout. If the disc is on any of those numbers, the next roll *CANNOT* be a Come-Out roll. The disc (puck) indicates a Point has already been established and any subsequent rolls will be

> ### BLACK AND WHITE
> The "point" disc actually has two sides. When the white side is exposed and placed on the layout, you know a Point has been established. If you see it laying near the dealers with the black side exposed, you know there is no Point.

Point rolls. So, if the white disc is on one of the numbers, you SHOULD NOT make a Pass Line bet until the shooter either makes the point or passes the dice to the next shooter.

HOW DO I MAKE THIS BET?

To make this wager, simply place your chips within the Pass Line boundaries. More important, place them directly in front of your playing position. If you place them too far to the left or right or your position, there is no guarantee that you will be identified as having made the bet. Which can only be bad news for you.

131

Your wager will be won or lost depending on the following events:

1) **If the shooter throws a 7 or 11 on the Come-Out roll, you win. The pay-off is even money. A $5 bet wins $5.**

2) **If the shooter throws a 2, a 3, or a 12 on the Come-Out roll, you lose. A $5 bet means a loss of $5.**

3) **If the shooter throws a 4, a 5, a 6, an 8, a 9, or a 10 on the Come-Out roll, you have a Point. Then, on the subsequent rolls, if the shooter can produce that Point number again *BEFORE* rolling a 7, you win even money. If the shooter rolls a 7 before rolling your Point, you lose.**

Example: The Come-Out roll is 8. Your bet remains on the Pass Line. The shooter then rolls a 4, a 3, an 11, a 9, a 6 and another 6. What effect do those numbers have on your bet? None! Only 7 or 8 (the Point) can make you a winner or loser. So, let's say the shooter then throws a 3, a 2, an 11, and an 8. Congratulations. You just won because the shooter rolled your Point (8) before rolling a 7.

When betting the Pass Line you are essentially wagering on the shooter, betting that the shooter will either throw a 7 or an 11 on the Come-Out or make the Point. To analyze this wager, or any others, refer to Figures 2 and 3.

RIGHT AND WRONG

People who bet that the shooter will produce winning Pass Line wagers are called "Right" bettors. Right, as in truth, justice, and the American way. Right, as in "let's all support the shooter". People who bet that the shooter will not produce winning Pass Line wagers are called "Wrong" bettors. Wrong, as in villainous and dastardly. Wrong as in "I don't think this shooter can make a point."

Seven can be rolled in six ways, 11 can be rolled in two ways; 2, 3, and 12 can be rolled in a total of four ways. On the Come-Out roll, eight combinations (outcomes) can win for you, and four will cause a loss; consequently, the odds are in your favor on the Come-Out.

However, if a Point is established, you lose the advantage. Remember when I said that if a Point has already been established you should not bet on the Pass Line? This is why. While you would be permitted to make the Pass Line wager after a Point has been established, you would be welcoming trouble. Regardless of what Point is established, there is a greater chance of 7 being rolled than any other number.

To summarize, on the Come-Out roll you have a 22.2% chance of winning, an 11.1% chance of losing. After a Point is established you have an 8-14% chance of winning, a 16.6% chance of losing. Where did those % figures come from? Follow along. On the Come-Out roll you can win with a 7 or an 11. Look again at Figures 2 and 3. There are six ways to roll a 7 and two ways to roll an 11. That's eight ways out of a total of thirty-six possibilities. 8 divided by 36 = .2222222 which is the same as 22.22%. Figure the losing percentage

132

for yourself. After a Point is established, the % depends on the Point number. Let's say the Point is 4. There's only three ways to make a 4. Same math. 3 divided by 36 = .83333 which is the same as 8.3%, which I have stated as a flat 8%. If the Point was 6, the math looks like this: 5 divided by 36 = .1388888 which is the same as 13.8%, which I have stated as a flat 14%. And the 7? 6 ways to make it divided by 36 possible outcomes = .166666 which is the same as 16.6%, and that's what I'm calling it.

"Making the Point" is a common expression meaning that the shooter has established a Point, and needs to roll that same number again in order to "Make the Point."

133

DON'T PASS

Does the word "don't" mean anything to you? I hope so. With one slight exception, this bet is the exact opposite of a Pass Line bet. The rules governing winning or losing are reversed, for now you are betting that the shooter cannot make the Point.

As with the Pass Line wager, the Don't Pass wager can be made only *BEFORE* a Come-out roll. Place your chips in the Don't Pass section of the layout, directly in line with your player position, and wait for the dice to determine your fate.

1) **If the shooter throws a 7 or an 11 on the Come-Out, you lose.**

2) **If the shooter throws a 2 or a 3 on the Come-Out, you win even money; $5 wagered wins $5.**

3) **Here's the small twist. Figure 1 makes it look like the layout says Don't Pass Bar 6 + 6. Actually, those are two separate statements. The first is Don't Pass, which identifies that section of the layout as the Don't Pass betting area, and the second is Bar 6 + 6, which means that if the shooter throws a 12 on the Come-Out, you tie. On some tables, a roll of either 2 or 3 may tie instead of**

12, but on most tables it is the 12 which produces a tie. In any case, the symbols in the Don't Pass section of the layout will tell you which number ties.

4) If the shooter throws a 4, a 5, a 6, an 8, a 9, or a 10, you have a Point. If the shooter rolls the Point before a 7, you lose. Should the shooter roll a 7 before the Point, you win even money.

In terms of odds and percentages, the situation is pretty much reversed. On the Come-Out roll your chance for success is only 8.3%, your chance of losing 22.2%. But if a Point is established your chance of winning improves to 16.7%, and your chance of losing drops to 8-14%, which puts you in a very nice place.

COME BET

This wager, with one exception, is *IDENTICAL* to a Pass Line bet. The lone difference is that a Pass Line bet is made *BEFORE* a Come-Out roll, while a Come bet is made only *AFTER* a Come-Out roll. Yes, I realize this sounds slightly twisted. But stay focused. You know what a Come-Out roll is. You also know that you can only bet the Pass Line BEFORE the Come-Out roll. So what happens if you want to be a RIGHT bettor . . . that is, you want to support the shooter . . . but when you walk up to the table a Point has already been established? Well, darn it, you want to bet the Pass Line but it's too late. So whataya do? YOU MAKE A COME WAGER! Again, you are betting on the shooter. Place your chips in the Come area of the layout, directly in front of your position at the table, and wait for the next throw of the dice.

1) If the shooter's very next roll is 7 or 11, you win even money.

2) If the shooter's very next roll is 2, 3 or 12, you lose.

3) If the shooter's very next roll is 4, 5, 6, 8, 9, or 10, that is the Point for your Come bet. Then, on the subsequent rolls, if the

shooter can produce that Point number again *BEFORE* rolling a 7, you win even money. If the shooter rolls a 7 before rolling your Point, you lose.

Note: The Point for your Come bet will probably be different from the Point established on the original Come-Out. In fact, it will seldom be the same.

Example: I'll start at the beginning. On the Come-Out roll the shooter throws a 6, so 6 is the Point for the Pass Line bettors. Now you approach the table and bet Come. The shooter's very next roll is an 8, so 8 is the Point for your Come bet. Had the shooter rolled a 5, then 5 would have been the Point for your Come bet. But don't letall these numbers confuse you. Here's the most important thing for you to remember. Your Point is determined by the very first roll of the dice after you make your Come bet. That's all you must remember. In fact, you don't even have to remember it. As soon as the Point is established for your Come bet the dealer will remove your chips from the Come section and drop them in above area you see on the layout which is under "Place Bets" on whichever number represents your Point. Simply follow your money. If your Point is 6, your money will travel from the Come section to that box which has "PLACE" written both above and below it. (See Figure 1)

The percentages for winning or losing a Come bet are exactly the same as for a Pass Line bet.

135

DON'T COME

That's right, a Don't Come bet is nearly the exact opposite of a Come bet. A Don't Come bet is also exactly the same as a Don't Pass bet, with one exception: a Don't Pass bet can be made only *BEFORE* a Come-Out roll, while a Don't Come bet can be made only *AFTER* a Come-Out roll. You are betting against the shooter. Wrong. You, that is. You are now a WRONG BETTOR. You could be right, but you're definitely Wrong.

Place your chips in the Don't Come section, as directly as possible in front of you, then win or lose in the following manner:

1) **If the shooter throws a 7 or an 11 on the very next roll, you lose.**

2) **If the shooter throws a 2 or a 3 on the very next roll, you win even money.**

3) **Here's the same twist as with the Don't Pass wager. If the shooter rolls a 12 on the very next roll, you tie.**

4) **Any other outcome is your Don't Come Point. If a 7 is then rolled before your Don't Come Point, you win even money. If the Don't Come Point is rolled first, you lose.**

As soon as the Point for your Don't Come bet is established, the dealer will move your chips from the Don't Come section to the box just above your Don't Come Point. Again, watch your money. There may be several bets in that little box, and you want to make sure you know which is yours.

136

Making a pass has nothing to do with sex or gender issues. Making a pass means that the shooter has made money for the Right bettors by either rolling a 7 or 11 on the Come-Out or by making the point. The more passes the shooter makes, the more the Right bettors will rejoice.

The percentages for this wager are identical to those for a Don't Pass bet. Now, just in case you're confused, let's recap these first four bets. Pass Line and Come bets are won and lost in exactly the same manner. The only difference between the two is that Pass Line bet can be made only *BEFORE* a Come-Out roll, while a Come bet can be made only *AFTER* a Come-Out roll. Don't Pass and Don't Come bets are won and lost in exactly the same manner. The only difference between the two is that a Don't Pass bet can be made only *BEFORE* a Come-Out roll, while a Don't Come wager can be made only *AFTER* a Come-Out roll.

And guess what? With only these four options, you can play Craps all day. All four of these wagers are even money pay-offs, all have the same overall advantage for the casino, which is approximately 1.4%. Yes the game is stacked against you. But with a disadvantage which is this small you have a legitimate chance of winning.

ODDS BETS (ALSO CALLED "FREE ODDS")

When you bet Pass Line, Don't Pass, Come or Don't Come, you are allowed to make a corresponding Odds bet after the shooter establishes a Point. With Pass Line and Come, you are *TAKING* the odds on the shooter making the Point. This means you believe the roller will make the point before tossing a 7. With Don't Pass and Don't Come you are *LAYING* (or *GIVING*) the

When the shooter Craps Out, it means the shooter is throwing 2s, 3s, or 12s on the Come-Out . . .all numbers which create losses for Right Bettors.

137

odds against the shooter making the Point. This means you believe the roller will toss a 7 before making the Point. Another way to think of it is that Taking the odds means you will win more than your bet if you are correct. Laying the odds means you will win less than your bet if you are correct. Why is that? Because when you Take the odds, the odds are against you. When you Lay the odds, the odds are on your side. These odds are also called Free Odds because the pay-offs are exactly correct—the casino holds no advantage over the player. Since it is easier to picture these Odds wagers if I call them Free Odds, I'll try to remember to refer to them as Free Odds from here on out, but if I slip up please know that Odds and Free Odds are the same wager.

If you go back to the table layout shown in Figure 1 you will not find an area in which to make Free Odds bets for the very simple reason that there is none. Because of this fact, many players are not aware that these bets are available. By Taking or Laying odds the player actually reduces the casino's advantage on Pass Line, Don't Pass, Come, and Don't Come from 1.4% to .8%.

Free Odds bets are excellent wagers for the player. You run the risk of losing faster because of the additional wager, but you can also increase your winnings. I'll explain them one at a time.

PASS LINE ODDS BET

First, you MUST make a wager on the Pass Line. No option here. You cannot make a Free Odds wager on the Pass Line without first making a Pass Line bet. Then, as soon as a Point is rolled, you can back up your Pass Line bet by Taking the Free Odds on the Point. The exact amount of this wager depends on the casino's guidelines, but you can normally bet at least as much as your original wager on the Pass Line, and in some casinos you can wager as much as one hundred times that amount. Yes, this means that you could put $5 on the Pass Line and then back it up with $500 in odds once a Point is established.

To make this bet, place your additional chips an inch or two behind your original Pass Line bet . . .just behind the line . . .making certain the additional chips are outsideof the Pass Line betting area outlined in Figure 1. Both your Pass Line bet and the Odds bet will then either disappear or grow depending on whether the shooter can make the Point. Same rules for the Odds bet as for the Pass Line bet. If a 7 is rolled before the Point your money will be swept away by one of the dealers. If the Point is rolled before a 7, the dealer will be paying you off and your chips will grow. The Pass Line bet still pays even money, but the associated Free Odds bet pays in the following manner:

1) **If the Point is 4 or 10, you are paid two to one (2:1). A bet of $5 would pay you $10.**

2) **If the Point is 5 or 9, you are paid three to two (3:2). A wager of $6 would pay you $9.**

3) **If the Point is 6 or 8, you are paid six to five (6:5). A wager of $5 would pay you $6.**

138

Please note that these pay-offs reflect the exact true odds of any of these numbers being rolled. There are six ways to roll a 7, there are five ways to roll either a 6 or 8. Therefore, the odds against a 6 or 8 showing up before a 7 are 6:5. Figure the rest for yourself.

Now, remember when I said something about the other bets requiring a thinking, alert brain? Here's the first evidence. Because of these pay-offs, you must take care to always wager the correct amount to receive the correct pay-offs. I'll provide examples, but if you're ever in doubt, simply ask the dealer. Most of them will be able to take a quick glance at your Pass Line bet and tell you exactly what to wager for your Free Odds.

GO NOT FURTHER
If you can't figure out why the Odds pay-offs are what they are, you have no business making Odds wagers. Go back to the basics. Do not attempt to make Odds wagers until you better understand what you are doing.

Note that a Free Odds bet of $5 when the Point is 4, 10, 6 or 8 could be paid correctly, but a $5 bet on 5 or 9 would produce an uneven pay-off of $7.50. On uneven pay-offs the casino will round down to the next lowest even pay-off. So a winning $5 Free Odds bet on 5 or 9 would only pay $7. This is because the lowest value chip used by most casinos is $1. They will not give change of fifty cents or twenty-five cents. Therefore, Free Odds bets with a Point of 5 or 9 should be made in multiples of $2; bets on 6 or 8 should be made in multiples of $5. And Free Odds bets on 4 or 10 should be made in. . .you guessed it . . .it doesn't make any difference because a 2:1 pay-off can be made accurately no matter what you wagered.

Example: You bet $10 on the Pass Line. The shooter rolls an 8, which becomes your Point. You then place an additional $10 behind your Pass Line wager. The shooter then throws a 4, a 5, a 6, a 9, an 11, another 11, a 2, and a 3. None of those numbers mean anything to you. The only outcomes which affect your bets are 7 and 8. If 7 is rolled before 8, you lose both the Pass Line bet and the Odds bet. If 8 is rolled before 7, you win both the Pass Line bet and the Odds bet. In this example, you could lose $20 or win $22. The Pass Line bet would pay even money of $10, and the Odds bet would pay off at the rate of $6 for every $5 wagered, which would be $12 and a total pay-off of $22. If the

139

Point had been 4 or 10 you could have lost $20 or won $30. Had the Point been 5 or 9, you could have lost $20 or won $25. No, I'm not divulging how I came up with those pay-offs. Figure them out for yourself. If you can't, you're already over your head.

COME BET—ODDS BET

If you understood Come wagers, this ought to be easy. Come bets-Free Odds bets are identical to Pass Line Free Odds bets. They are made in the same manner, they win or lose in the same manner, they have the same pay-offs. Here are the only differences:

1) **As stated earlier, your Come bet can be made only after a Come-out roll.**

2) **Instead of placing your Free Odds bet on the table, you drop your chips nearly anywhere within the reach of the dealer and say, "Odds on my Come Point." Or, if your Come Point (for example) was 8, you could say, "Come Odds on my Eight." The dealer will then place your Odds bet on top of and slightly out of line with your Come bet.**

DON'T PASS—ODDS BETS

First you MUST make a wager on Don't Pass. No option here. You cannot make a Free Odds wager on the Don't Pass without first making a Don't Pass bet. Then, as soon as a Point is rolled, you can back up your Don't Pass bet by laying the odds on the Point. The exact amount of this wager depends on the casino's guidelines, but you can normally bet at least as much as your original wager on the Pass Line, and in some casinos you can wager as much as one hundred times that amount. Yes, this means that you could put $5 on the Don't Pass Line and then back it up with $500 in Free Odds once a Point is established. Since you are laying, rather than taking the odds, the pay-offs are reversed.

1) **If the Point is 4 or 10, the pay-off is one to two (1:2). A $6 wager would pay $3.**

2) **If the Point is 5 or 9, the pay-off is two to three (2:3). A $6 wager would pay $4.**

3) **If the Point is 6 or 8, the pay-off is five to six (5:6). A $6 wager would pay $5.**

All the examples are in units of $6. To ensure proper pay-offs, always make this wager in multiples of $6. But, you ask, what if my Don't Pass wager was only $5? Will the casino insist that I make it $6? No. Enough said for now.

To make this bet, place your chips for the Free Odds bet immediately adjacent to your Don't Pass bet, or on top of your Don't Pass bet at a slight offset. If you do it wrong, the dealer will show you how. If the Point is rolled before a 7, you lose both your Don't Pass and Free Odds bets. If a 7 is rolled before the Point, you win both your Don't Pass and Free Odds bets.

Need an example? The new shooter is skinny. You don't like skinny, so you decide to be a Wrong bettor and bet $12 on Don't Pass. The shooters first roll is a 10. You know in your gut, that there's no way a skinny shooter can make a 10, so you want to load up on the odds. But you're not a big spender, or a high roller, so you merely match your Don't Pass wager with another $12. The ugly and skinny one then rolls a 7. Congrats. You were right to bet Wrong. Your Don't Pass bet pays off even money of $12. Your Odds bet pays off at the rate of 1:2, so that $12 worth of Odds earns $6. Total pay-off of $18. Now stop and take the time to calculate what the pay-offs would be if the Point were a different number. And don't go any further until it all makes sense.

141

DON'T COME—ODDS BETS

Right again. Don't Come-Free Odds bets are identical to Don't Pass-Free Odds bets. They are made in the same manner, they win or lose in the same manner, they have the same pay-offs. Here are the only differences:

1) **As stated earlier, your Don't Come bet can be made only *AFTER* a Come-out roll.**

2) **Instead of placing your Odds bet on the table, you drop your chips in front of the dealer and say, "Odds on my don't come", or "Odds on my don't four," or words to that effect. The dealer will then place your Odds bet in the Don't Come section of the box just above your Don't Come Point.**

Again, the overall casino advantage on Pass Line, Don't Pass, Come, or Don't Come is about 1.4%. If you Take or Lay the corresponding Free Odds bets, the casino advantage is reduced to about .8%.

If you never learn any more about craps, it is okay, because knowing only what we have covered thus far you can play Craps right alongside all the heavy hitters. You can stay at the table for hours and hours. In terms of the casino's advantage, you will be making the very best bets which are offered. Simply understanding Pass, Come, Don't Pass, etc. and how to take advantage of the Free Odds will make you one of the more knowledgeable gamblers at the next Craps table you approach. Just remember to keep it simple. Walk up to a table, buy chips, and put $2 (or the table minimum) on the Pass Line before the next Come-Out roll. You will win or lose as described earlier. Should you win, bet another $2.

142

$2--$5--$10--$20

Please note that although I am suggesting $2 bets for your "testing" period, the wager you make is totally dependent on you and your bankroll. If you want to "test" the waters with $10 wagers, then do it. In other words, there is no "magic" in $2 bets. I suggest staying with low bets early in your development in order to reduce the risk while you are learning.

If you lose, bet another $2. But stay with that simple Pass Line wager the entire time you are at the table. All hell may be breaking loose, with players shouting all kinds of directions to the dealers, tossing chips everywhere, and pleading for their numbers to be rolled. Some of the players may be wagering thousands of dollars. But none of that should mean anything to you. Simply keep at least one eye on your Pass Line wager and let the dice decide your fate.

Once you are more comfortable with the game, make the Pass Line wager and then take the Free Odds. Don't Pass and Don't Come can be worked in the same manner. You could actually stop reading this chapter right now and play Craps as well as anyone. The odds against you on these first four betting options are about as low as you're going to find anywhere in the casino, so don't hesitate to try them. However, there are many other wagers waiting for your chips, so let's investigate them.

PLACE BETS

These bets can only be made on the numbers 4, 5, 6, 8, 9 and 10. Do not attempt to make this bet by yourself! Making a Place Bet requires the assistance of the dealer who is positioned at your end of the table. Yes, to the casino this is one of those IF YOU TRY TO DO THIS WE WILL BREAK YOUR FINGERS kind of things. But that's okay, because making these wagers is simple. All you gotta do is drop your

KNOW THE BET--KNOW THE PAY-OFFS

Due to the nature of the pay-offs, it is vitally important that you know how much $ you want or need to wager, and also how much your wager will pay when you win. As with other Craps wagers, you need to make wagers in multiples that guarantee correct pay-offs. This is elemental. This is critical. Simply ensure that you understand what lies at the bottom of the canyon before you leap from the rim.

143

chips in front of the dealer and tell him what numbers you want to place. You can be as creative as you like, but make certain that your directions contain words like "Place the eight," or "I want to place the nine," or "Place the six and the ten, please," etc. It's hard to do it wrong so long as you mention the words "Place" and the "number" or "numbers" you want to cover. If you give the dealer either too much money or too little, he will ask you to be more specific.

You may Place any or all of the numbers. There are six Place numbers. You can have bets on as few as one number or as many as six . . .all at the same time. You may make or remove this bet at any time. Correct. This bet has nothing to do with the Come Out Roll or whether a Point has been established. Which, again, means that you can make it or remove it at any time. When you want to remove your bet, keep it simple. Tell the dealer "Off my Place bets," or "My Place bets are off."

To clarify matters, it is to your advantage for Place bets to be on at all times. Whether you win or lose a Place bet is determined in the following matter:

1) **If a 7 is rolled before your Place number, you lose.**

2) **If your Place number is rolled before a 7, you win. Here are the pay-offs:**

   4 and 10 pay nine to five (9:5), a bet of $5 pays $9
   5 and 9 pay seven to five (7:5), a bet of $5 pays $7
   6 and 8 pay seven to six (7:6), a bet of $6 pays $7

144

Please note that these pay-offs are less than those for the Free Odds bets which are associated with Pass, Don't Pass, Come and Don't Come. Not a lot less, but enough to increase the casino's advantage. On 4 and 10 the casino's advantage is about 6.7%. For 5 and 9 it is 4%. For 6 and 8 it is only about 1.5%, which makes 6 and 8 the best numbers to Place.

Now, why? Why would you want to make this wager? The answer? Consider the following. If you make a bet on Pass or Come and the very next roll is a 2, 3, or 12, you lose. But if you Place a number and the very next roll is a 2, 3, or 12, those numbers do not effect your wager. With Pass and

> ### THE WONDER OF IT ALL
> **See if you can follow the intent of this rule: Unless the player makes a request for the Place bets to be off, they are always on for all rolls except the Come-Out roll, when they are always off unless requested to be on. Actually, it's not that difficult to understand. Read it again three or four times.**

Don't Pass, you need to live with whatever number the shooter throws. With Place bets you get to choose your number. In addition, and this is big, for most gamblers Place bets provide an opportunity to get more action by covering more numbers quickly. Why wait for the shooter to establish your favorite Point numbers when you can Place any or all of them immediately? Yes, there are many other wagers these folks could be making if they want more action, but the casino advantage, particularly on 6 and 8, is still within the "reasonable" range.

Placing numbers is another simple and effective way to play Craps. Walk up to the table. Drop your chips in front of the dealer and say "Place the six, please." You don't care what the point is. All you need concern yourself with is whether that 6 shows up before a 7. Think about it. Go back and study the charts. If we eliminate the 7, which numbers can we expect to see the most often? Right. 6 & 8. So play the odds. The only number which can beat you is that 7.

Want more excitement? Place both the 6 and the 8. Got a hot shooter? Place the 6, the 8, the 5 and the 9.

I can't emphasize this enough: Pass, Don't Pass, Come, Don't Come, taking or laying the Free Odds and Placing numbers. These are by far the best bets at the Craps table. And if you are serious about winning money you must play only those games and make only those bets which have the smallest edge against you. A long-winded sentence, but worth remembering. This is part of becoming "Gambling Smart," or "Gambler Smart." Yes, there are still more betting options, but, quite frankly, unless you are going to become *very* serious about Craps don't even attempt to learn all of them at this time. I will explain 'em, but that doesn't mean you gotta try 'em.

BUY BETS

Buy bets are very similar to Place bets. As with Place bets, you are essentially wagering that the shooter will roll your number before a 7. Buy bets can be made or removed at any time, they are made on the same numbers as Place bets, and you make the bet by dropping your chips in front of the dealer. But now you say, "Buy the eight," or "Buy the four." The similarities end with the above. Here are the differences:

1) A small marker, which looks as if it came from a tiddlywinks game, is set on top of your chips to distinguish your Buy bet from a Place bet. The marker has "Buy" stamped on it.

2) The pay-offs are different:
   4 and 10 pay two to one (2:1)
   5 and 9 pay three to two (3:2)
   6 and 8 pay six to five (6:5)

3) On Buy bets the casino charges a five percent service charge in multiples of $1. If you want to bet $10, it will cost you $11. A bet of $20 would cost $21. A $40 bet would cost $42 ($40 x 5% = $2). The charge is always in multiples of $1 because the casino does not give change of fifty cents or twenty-five cents. Obviously, only a fool would make a $10 Buy bet at a charge of $1, because then the fool would be giving up a 10% advantage to the casino, and that's much too heavy duty.

146

The casino advantage on Buy bets is approximately 5%, which is not great for the player, but still not as bad as some of the other wagers.

So why a Buy bet? I'll give you one reason, figure any others by yourself. If you Place the 4 or 10, your disadvantage is approximately 7%. If you Buy the 4 or 10, your disadvantage is only 5%. So if you are lured by that very nice pay-off of 2:1 for the 4 or 10, and can afford to wager at least $21, it is smarter to Buy than to Place.

LAY BETS

You ought to be catching on by now. The opposite of Pass is Don't Pass. The opposite of Come is Don't Come. The opposite of Buy is? Right. Lay bets are nearly the exact opposite of Buy bets. Here, you are betting that the shooter will roll a 7 before your lay number. You can make a lay bet on the 4, 5, 6, 8, 9 or 10. Toss the dealer your chips and say, "Lay the odds on the six" or "Lay the eight." The dealer will place your chips in the Don't Come section of the number you request, then put a small Buy marker on top of them. Lay bets are always on, even on the Come-Out roll. If a 7 is rolled before the number you lay, the pay-offs are:

4 and 10 pay one to two (1:2)
5 and 9 pay two to three (2:3)
6 and 8 pay five to six (5:6)

As with Buy bets, there is a five percent service charge involved, but the 5% is based on your potential winnings instead of on your bet.

Example: You want to make a $40 Lay bet on the 4. If you were to win, the pay-off would be $20. Five percent of $20 is $1, which is added to the cost of your bet. So, in order to be paid correctly on a bet of $40, you need to bet $41. Sound dumb? The casino advantage on Lay bets is 2.5% on the 4 and 10, 3.2% on the 5 and 9, 4% on the 6 or 8. These odds aren't too bad. But, if you want to lay numbers, you can forget about being a $5 bettor. You must wager more money, and the returns are small.

> ## WHAT THE CASINO ADVANTAGE REALLY MEANS
> You bet the Pass Line, where the casino has a 1.4% advantage. You wager $3,000. If the % holds true, you will lose $42. You keep betting the Big Six, where the casino has a 9.09% advantage. You wager the same amount--$3,000. If the % holds true, you will lose $273! Same action, but the loss is nearly seven times greater. Does that impress upon you that the Pass Line is a more favorable wager than the Big Six? I hope so.

147

BIG SIX OR BIG EIGHT

This is another wager which can be made or removed at any time. You can even make this wager by yourself by placing chips in the Big Six or Big Eight portion of the table layout. Your bet is won or lost in the following manner:

1) **If 6 or 8 (depending on which you bet) is rolled before 7, you win even money.**

2) **If 7 is thrown before 6 or 8, you lose.**

This is a bad bet. Here's why. 6 and 8 can each be rolled in five combinations. 7 can be rolled in six combinations. The true pay-off for this wager, which is even money, should be six to five (6:5). By paying even money the casino reaps an advantage of 9.09%!

So why would anyone still in control of his or her senses put chips on the Big 6 at a disadvantage of 9% when he or she could just as easily Place the 6 at a disadvantage of only 1.5%? Your guess is as good as mine.

Note: In Atlantic City this bet is usually paid off at seven to six, which lowers the casino advantage to 1.5%. This is much better for the player, but all bets should be made in multiples of $6.

148   HARD TEN AND HARD FOUR

These are two separate wagers which I've lumped together because the pay-offs and probabilities are the same for both numbers. There are three ways to roll a 4 (2,2) or (1,3) or (3,1) and three ways to roll a 10 (4,6) or (6,4) or (5,5). A Hard Four is the double deuce (2,2) It is called the Hard Four because there is only one way to roll a (2,2) while there are two ways to roll a (1,3). Consequently, (2,2) is the "hard" way to roll a 4. Similarly, Hard Ten is the (5,5) combination.

The person we have identified as the stickman controls this wager. Do not attempt to place chips on the Hard Four or Hard Ten section of the layout by yourself. If you've forgotten who the stickman is, refer back to Figure 1. However, the stickman is hard to miss because the stickman is the person standing opposite the boxman, who is the person sitting practically on top of all the casino's money. The stickman is also the one holding the big stick . . .the big stick used to direct the dice about the table. Anyway, you must get your money to the stickman in order to bet either the Hard Ten or the Hard Four. This can be done several different ways. You can toss, drop, or even fling your chips in front of the stickman. Don't worry about being neat. You can also toss, drop, or even fling your chips over in front of the Dealer at your end of the table, who will retrieve the chips and pass them on to the stickman. There are no "style" points awarded.

Okay, that's the first part —get the chips on the table. The second part is to announce clearly and distinctly the reason you are throwing chips onto the table. And this part is easy. I mean, how difficult it is to say, "Hard four!"?

> ## PROPOSITION BETS
> Take another look at Figure 1. Note that the wagers outlined on the right side are twins of the bets outlined on the left side. Then there are the CENTER wagers, the ones in front of the stickman which we're discussing now. Those wagers, the ones in the Center, are also known as "Proposition" wagers, probably because they should be considered "risky" propositions. From my viewpoint these wagers would more properly be called "HUNCH" bets, because most people only bet them when they have a hunch.

Or, better yet, announce both the bet you want to make, and the amount you are wagering. "Five dollar hard four!" Or, "Two dollar hard ten."

If it's the Dealer who retrieves your chips, he will identify both you and your position at the table to the stickman by saying something like "Two dollar hard four, third to your left." If the stickman is not certain who the bet came from, he will ask. Remember that the stickman is in control of the dice. The stickman will not

> ## WORTH REPEATING
> Never "hand" your chips to the stickman or the Dealers. Call (announce) your bet and either toss or drop your chips on the table, preferably within easy reach of said stickman and/or dealers.

release the dice to the shooter until all bets are accounted for. It can become quite frenzied at a Craps table, and most Dealers and stickmen do an incredible job of keeping track of all the bets.

Also important—this bet can be made or removed at any time. So, you announce your wager and make sure the stickman gets your chips. Now what? Well, if you bet the Hard Four you are wagering that the combination (2,2) will be rolled before any 7, *AND* before any other combination of 4 . . .namely (1,3) or (3,1). Same situation with the Hard Ten. If you bet the Hard Ten you are wagering that the combination (5,5) will be rolled before any 7, AND before any other combination of 10.

If you are lucky enough to win, the pay-off is 7:1. Which sounds juicy. But let's say you bet the Hard Four. Only one combination can win for you (2,2). Eight combinations will lose the bet; six combinations of 7, plus (1,3) and (3,1). The true pay-off should be 8:1, but since the casino only pays 7:1 its advantage is 11.1%!

Three reasons why people make this wager. One, more action. Two, some shooters seem to be adept at rolling numbers the "hard" way. If you note that a shooter seems to be rolling a lot of hard numbers, get on the bandwagon. Three, the pay-offs are enticing.

HARD SIX AND HARD EIGHT

These bets are also made through the stickman; they may be placed or removed before any roll. If you understood everything about the Hard Four and the Hard Ten, it shouldn't take you longer then thirteen seconds to fully grasp and understand the Hard Six and Eight. The pay-offs and probabilities are the same for both the Hard Six and the Hard Eight. If you make a bet on Hard Six you are wagering that (3,3) will be rolled before any 7, AND also before any other combination of 6. If you make a bet on Hard Eight you are wagering that (4,4) will be rolled before any 7, AND also before any other combination of 8. The pay-off is 9:1.

But Hard Six can only be rolled in one way, while there are six combinations of 7 and four others of Six: (1,5), (2,4), (4,2), and (5,1). One way can

150

> ### GOOD NEWS, BAD NEWS
> Your disadvantage with the Hard Six and Hard Eight is less than your disadvantage on the Hard Four and Hard Ten. That's the good news. The bad news is that both are terrible! Do not pursue any of these wagers with "serious" money unless you are winning. And my definition of "serious" is 5% of your original gambling stake for this session.

win, ten will lose. Ditto for the Hard Eight. The true pay-off for these bets should be 10:1, but since the casino only pays 9:1 their advantage on the Hard Six and Eight is 9.09%.

ONE ROLL BETS

Can't wait for roll after roll of the dice to determine whether you win or lose? Feel the need to have a decision on each and every roll? The casinos love impatient people like you. To my mind, these bets were all designed to allow impatient people to lose their money as fast as possible.

All of the following wagers are decided by one roll of the dice. After making these wagers, the very next roll will cause you to win or lose. With the lone exception of the Field bet, which you can easily place for yourself, all of these bets are made through the stickman. And please note that you will often hear the stickman promoting these wagers with comments like, "Yo! Cover that Yo." or "Hard ways. Any body need a hard way?" Hopefully, you don't need to be reminded that if the casino wants you to make a wager, it is probably not a good wager for any player to be making. Remember that GOOD FOR THEM IS BAD FOR US.

151

Field Bets

This bet is very popular because seven different outcomes (2, 3, 4, 9, 10, 11 or 12) can win, while only four (5, 6, 7 or 8) can cause you to lose. The pay-off is even money (1:1). Now stop for a moment and think about this. Seven numbers can win, four can lose. So, that should mean a true pay-off of 4:7, right? Think about it. Think about it again. Go back to Figure 2. There are a total of only sixteen ways that those seven winning numbers can be rolled. There are a total of twenty ways that the four losing numbers can be rolled. You have a 44.4% chance of winning and a 55.6% chance of losing. Which means the casino has an 11.2% advantage.

The odds improve when the casino pays 2:1 or 3:1 when a 2 or a 12 is rolled, but the odds are still stacked against you. You might get lucky for a few rolls, but over the long haul the casino edge will grind you down.

Any Seven

Here you are betting the next roll will be a 7. Since there are six ways to roll a 7, there are six combinations which will win for you. The other thirty possible outcomes cause you to lose. The true pay-off on this bet should be 30:6, which in its condensed form is actually 5:1. The casino only pays 4:1. The casino advantage is 16.7%. Kind of makes a bet on the Hard Four look plenty appetizing.

Any Craps

Now you're betting the next roll will be either 2, 3, or 12. 2 can be rolled in one way, 3 can be rolled in two ways, 12 can be rolled in one way. Four outcomes can win for you, the other thirty-two will cause a loss. The true pay-off on this bet should be 32:4, which in its condensed form is actually 8:1. The casino only pays 7:1, which makes its advantage on this bet 11.1%.

Two

Another poor wager. You are betting the next roll will be snake eyes (1,1). The pay-off is 30:1 which sounds very enticing.

But 2 can only be rolled in one way. Only one outcome can win for you, the other thirty-five cause a loss. The true pay-off should be 35:1, but since the casino only pays 30:1 its advantage is 13.9%.

Twelve

Same as for 2, above. Exactly the same. I mean it. The only difference is that now you are looking for box cars instead of snake eyes. And the only time you should make this bet is if you have a direct open line of communication with God and Fate and maybe even Mother Nature.

Three

Bored yet? Now you're betting the next roll will be a 3. The pay-off is 15:1. But 3 can only be rolled in two ways. Two combinations can win for you, thirty-four can lose. The true pay-off on this bet should be 34:2, which in its condensed form is actually 17:1. Your disadvantage is 11.8%.

Eleven

Same as for 3. The only change is the number.

Craps—Eleven

This one is also known as a Horn Bet, and is even worse than all the others. Here you're wagering that a 2, a 3, an 11 or a 12 will show on the very next roll. The pay-offs are as follows:

Two pays 30:1
Three pays 15:1
Eleven pays 15:1
Twelve pays 30:1

Since you're covering four numbers, you must bet four chips. From our earlier discussions, you already know that the pay-offs for all these numbers are incorrect, giving the casino an advantage of from 11.8% to 13.9%. In addition, even if you won on one of the numbers, you still lose your other three chips, which makes the casino advantage even higher. If you like these kinds of odds, perhaps you should try Russian Roulette.

153

Multiple Odds

We're done with the Hunch/Center/Proposition wagers, so now it's time to change gears and head down the home stretch by covering a few miscellaneous items. When I say "multiple odds" I am referring to the Free Odds bets which can be made in conjunction with Pass Line, Come, Don't Pass, and Don't Come wagers. Most casinos allow these Odds bets to be made in 2X or 3X the amount of your initial wager. Some allow you to go as high as 10X oddsand a few even advertise 100X odds.

> **SOMETHING TO REMEMBER**
> Place bets and Free Odds bets are always off on the Come Out roll . . . unless you tell the dealer otherwise. Simply say, "My odds are on," or "I want my odds working," or any words to that effect.

Example: You are playing at a table which offers 2X Odds. Your Pass Line bet is $10. A Point is established. You may now wager up to $20 on the associated Free Odds bet. If you were playing at a 3X Odds table, your Pass Line Odds bet could be $30. 10X would be $100, and 100X would be $1,000.

Multiple Odds reduce the casino's advantage, but don't get carried away. One bad spell of luck at a multiple odds table will quickly demolish your gambling stake.

The benefit of playing at a table which offers multiple odds, is that you can take advantage of a large wager on the Free Odds with only a minor exposure on your main wager. Let's say you are at a table which offers 10X odds. Your basic bet is $5 on the Pass Line. The point becomes 6. Six is one of the easiest numbers to roll. So you hammer the Free Odds to the tune of $50. You now have $55 wagered. $50 of it is wagered at no disadvantage . . .you're getting true odds . . .and the other $5 has only a disadvantage of 1.4%. This, folks, is about as good as it gets in a casino. Obviously, you don't need to take $50 in Free Odds. You could also bet $5 on the Pass Line and then back it up with $10, or $25 or any amount up to $50.

154

Same scenario, except now the point is 4. Pay-off is better, but it's a tougher number to roll. So, instead of $50 Free Odds, you decide to play it safe and only go with $20 in Free Odds. Your $5 Pass Line wager has to live with whatever number is rolled, but your Free Odds can fluctuate depending on the Point number. In other words, you can pick your spots with the Free Odds.

WAGERING LIMITS AND ODD AMOUNTS

Minimum wagers at most Craps tables will be either $2 or $5, with the maximum running up to $2,000 or $3,000. I suggest that you start at a $2 table until you gain confidence. Then, if you want more action, most casinos will allow you to make an Odds bet which is greater than your original Pass Line, Come, Don't Pass or Don't Come bet. I'm not talking about multiple odds, we've already covered that. I'm talking now about how some casinos will allow small adjustments in your Free Odds wagers which make the pay-offs easier to make.

Example: If your original wager is $3, your associated Free Odds bet can be $4 if the Point is 5 or 9, $5 if the Point is 6 or 8. Remember that the pay-off on the 5 or 9 is 3:2, so a $4 Free Odds bet is easier to pay off than one of $3. The correct pay-off for a $3 wager would be $4.50, and since there aren't many casinos willing to make pay-offs with quarters, you would actually only receive $4. Likewise, the pay-off on the 6 and 8 is 6:5, which would mean a pay-off of $3.60 on a $3 wager, which really means you would only receive $3 at most casinos.

Again, this is good stuff to know, so make sure certain

> ## DEALERS—TO KNOW 'EM IS TO LOVE 'EM
>
> Good dealers and stickmen are both wonderful and plentiful. I am constantly amazed at how well they can control a table, figure pay-offs, etc. and that there can be so many good ones. Tip (toke) them by making a small wager for the crew. It can be anything you want, so long as you announce that it is for them. As good as the service is, it gets even better if you make an occasional $1 Hard Way bet for the crew.

you know the exact bets allowed by the casino. All you gotta do is ask. For a lot of us, it is difficult to remember betting units, pay-offs, and how to make the proper bets to ensure accurate pay-offs without becoming bewildered.

155

COMMON BETTING STRATEGIES

PLAN 1: First, decide whether you are a Right or Wrong bettor. And don't even think about changing your mind half way through a session. If you start as a Right bettor, end as a Right bettor. If you decide you made the wrong choice, wait until your next session and then try the other way. Or try one way your first session and the other way your second. You may find that you're a Wrong bettor living in the body of a Right bettor, or vice versa.

Second, bet $5 on whichever way you're going. If you're going to be a Right bettor, place $5 on the Pass Line. If you're going to be a Wrong bettor, put $5 on Don't Pass. Then don't do anything else. Just stand there and watch what is happening. Learn. Listen and learn. Observe and learn. Soak up all the knowledge you can handle. Watch how all the bets we've discussed are handled by the dealers and stickman. Memorize the pay-offs for the various wagers and see if you can figure them out as fast as the crew. It may be quiet. Or, it may feel like you're in the middle of a riot. None of that matters. Your wager will either grow or vanish. It may take one roll, it may take dozens. You don't care because you are there to learn. You are keeping your bets simple so that you won't be distracted. Stay until you reach your Winning Goal or your Loss Limit, or until you've absorbed all you can hold for that session, or until you absolutely must eat.

PLAN 2: Do exactly the same as for Plan 1, except once a Point is established back it up with $5 in Free Odds if the Point is 4, 6, 8, or 10. Back up the Point with $6 in Free Odds if the Point is 5 or 9. If you're betting the Don't Pass, back up any Point with $6 in Free Odds. (If that doesn't make sense at first, just keep thinking about it.)

PLAN 3: This one is for Right bettors only. First, make a $5 bet on Pass. Next, back up the Point with the appropriate amount of Free Odds (as explained for Plan 2). Now we keep going another step. Make a $6 Place bet on the 6 or the 8. If 6 happens to be the Point, Place the 8. If 8 happens to be the Point, place the 6. If neither the 6 nor the 8 is the Point, choose one or the other. Now consider your exposure and your possible returns. $5 on the Pass Line + say, $5 in Free Odds + $6 Placed on the 6 or 8 = a total of $16 wagered. Your exposure is a total of $16. The amount you could profit will depend on the Point number. More on that later.

156

Now read the rest of this slowly, and don't be surprised if a small amount of confusion grabs you by the ear. You have a Point, plus either the 6 or 8. Two numbers are working for you. The idea here is keep two numbers working until a 7 is rolled. When the 7 shows up, you're going to lose whatever you have on the layout. But until that happens, you will keep two numbers working, and

CRAPS ETIQUETTE

Once you have been at the table for awhile, you will note that the dealers have set routines. They may start to the right or left, but they will settle all bets in pretty much the same pecking order every time. So there's no sense in trying to tell a dealer what you want until he is ready for you. If you are the only player at the table, it doesn't make any difference, but when there is a full table the dealers will appreciate it if you will wait your turn.

you will collect every time one of your numbers is rolled. In other words, you have greater risk, an increased chance for profits, and an elevated level of excitement. Now here comes an example. Keep reading it over and over again until you fully understand.

You start with a $5 Pass Line wager. The Come Out roll is an 11. Good. You just won $5. Collect your winnings and come right back with another $5 Pass Line wager. The next Come Out roll is a 3. Sorry, but you lost. Wave goodbye to your $5 chip and replace it with another one. This happens all the time, so get used to it. The shooter may throw several 7s or 11s, and 2s and 3s before establishing a Point. But this time we're going to say that the next Come Out roll is a 9. So your first step is to back up the Point of 9 with $6 in

You want to keep two numbers working for you at all times. Don't forget that!

Free Odds, and then immediately Place the 6 (my choice) for $6. You now have two numbers working . . .the Point 9 and the Placed 6. Your total exposure is $17. Now you hope the shooter can roll both of those numbers many times before a 7.

The very next roll is a 3. No effect on your bets. The next roll is a 10. Again, no effect on your bets. The only numbers of consequence to you are the 6, the 9, and the 7. The very next roll is a 6. Congrats. You just won $7. Now the dealer is going to look to you for instructions. The question is this: What do you want to do with that $7? (In actual practice, some dealers will give it to you automatically, others will ask.) Our answer is "Same bet." This means that you want that $7 in winnings and you also want the $6 you have on the Place 6 to remain right where it is. Now your exposure has been reduced to $10. The next roll is a 4. No effect for you. The next roll is a another 6. Wonderful. Same instructions to the dealer. Just say "Same bet". You can say it before he asks, but it is prudent to wait for him to glance your way. If the dealer forgets or ignores you, don't hesitate to speak up before the dice are passed back to the shooter. Now, guess what? You collected another $7, and your exposure just got reduced to only $3. You still have two numbers working. If the shooter can produce either on of them, you will have a profit for this round. The next roll is a 3, followed by a 4, a 5, an 8 and a 10. Again, none of those numbers have any effect on your wager. The next roll? It's a 9. The shooter rewarded your confidence. Your $5 Pass Line wager pays off even money of $5, and the Free Odds pays off $9 for your $6 wager. Another $14. Now your exposure has vanished and you have a profit of $11. Good. Now what? Well, you have several options. Choose whichever suits your style and your bankroll.

Choice#1: Wipe the slate clean. Tell the dealer to take down your Place bet on the 6 and start all over again from the beginning.

Choice #2: Leave the Placed 6 bet alone, and tell the dealer your Place bets are always "on." That means the 6 is working for you, even on the next Come Out roll. Then make another $5 bet on the Pass Line and proceed as before.

Choice #3: Leave the Placed 6 alone. Tell the dealer your Place bets are always "on." Make another $5 bet on the Pass Line. Take the Free Odds when the next Point is established. Place the 8 for $6. Remember? You already have the Placed 6 plus the Point. So, now you're going to have three numbers working for you. More exposure, more risk, greater potential return. It's up to you.

Obviously, there are a lot of other things you can do, but we're only covering the basics in this book. You could Press (double) your Pass Line wager. You could stay with the same Pass Line wager but take double Free Odds. You could begin this plan with three numbers by Placing both the 6 and 8. If either one is the Point, then Place the 6 and the 9, or the 8 and the 5, etc. You could just keep thinking about it. The possibilities are nearly endless.

PLAN 4: This one can be used for both Right and Wrong bettors. Once again, I will assume that you are a Right bettor because most people are. But the Wrong bettor can use this same plan. The basic procedure is identical. This time we start out pretty much the same. $5 on the Pass Line. Wait for a Point to be established. When it is, take the appropriate Free Odds, AND ALSO bet $5 on the Come. When a Point is established for your Come bet, take the appropriate Free Odds on that Point, AND ALSO come right back with another $5 on the Come. When a Point is established for that Come bet, take the appropriate Free Odds on that Point, too. Wheeeew! The action can be fast and furious. If all has gone well, you now have three numbers working for you, and all three of them are backed up with Free Odds. Again, we've raised the level of both risk and potential profits. Exposure? Depends on the numbers. (Just so you Wrong bettors don't get lost

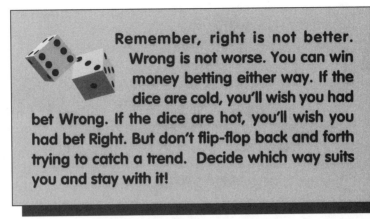

Remember, right is not better. Wrong is not worse. You can win money betting either way. If the dice are cold, you'll wish you had bet Wrong. If the dice are hot, you'll wish you had bet Right. But don't flip-flop back and forth trying to catch a trend. Decide which way suits you and stay with it!

in the shuffle, your moves would be Don't Pass + Free Odds, then Don't Come with Free Odds, and then Don't Come again with the Free Odds.)

The goal here is to have three numbers working for you. It may take three rolls to achieve this goal, it could take, literally, hundreds. It all depends on what the shooter produces. You may reach the three-number goal and then lose everything if a 7 pops up on the next roll. The three numbers may change on every roll. What? That's right. If you continue with this plan the three numbers you have working will seldom remain the same. A long example follows, so relax for a moment, make sure you are focused, and then proceed. I'm going to, by design, make this one tough to follow.

Your first move is to wager $5 on the Pass Line. Now wait and see what develops. The Come Out roll is snake eyes. Okay, you're already down $5 and you haven't really done anything yet. So start again. $5 on the Pass Line. The Come Out roll is box cars. Darn it, now you're down $10 and you still don't even have a Point established. Back again with $5 on the Pass Line. The next Come Out roll is a 4. All right. Finally. Now you're got a Point. Back it up with $5 in Free Odds AND bet $5 on Come. We want three numbers, we only have one so far. The very next roll is an 11. Good. The Come bet wins $5. Your Point of 4 is not effected by the 11. Bet $5 on the Come again. The very next roll is a 6. Another Point. The dealer takes your $5 chip out of the Come portion of the layout and moves it into one of the small boxes directly above the 6 you see in the Place boxes. To take the Free Odds on the 6, you drop $5 in front of the dealer and say, "Odds on my six, please." And then you put

DO NOT TRY THESE PLANS UNTIL YOU FULLY UNDERSTAND THEM!

Reading any of these plans over and over will help, but that's not enough. Get yourself a set of dice. Outline the Craps layout on a piece of paper. For chips, you can use paper clips, or tooth picks, nickels, dimes or pennies. Then practice. Make your bet, throw the dice, make more bets, collect profits, keep track of the losses, and keep going until it all becomes as natural as eating. Then, and only then, place yourself at a real Craps table and give it a whirl.

160

another $5 chip on the Come. You've now got two numbers working for you, the Pass Line Point of 4 and the Come Point of 6. But you're not done yet because the goal is to have three numbers working.

The next roll is a deuce. Snake eyes yet again. What is the problem with this shooter? Now you gotta fork over another $5 for your new Come bet. The next roll is a 4. Well, you've already got the 4, so what happens now? Are you kidding? Take the money. Have you forgotten that 4 is the original Point? Have you forgotten that it pays even money for the Pass Line and 2:1 for the Free Odds? Wake up! The dealer sets a $5 chip adjacent to your Pass Line wager, and two $5 chips adjacent to your Pass Line Free Odds. You won $15, but you're back to only one number, the Come Point of 6. Whataya do? Hold on for a second. Go back two sentences. Are you really down to only one number? Absolutely not. When the shooter rolled that 4 to make the Pass Line Point, you had a bet on Come. Consequently, in addition to winning your Pass Line wager, that 4 also established itself as the Point for your last Come bet. So, again, you're back to two numbers. Whataya do? Keep going. Keep plugging away. First, pick up all those chips laying by the Pass Line . . .the ones the dealer put there to pay you off for the shooter making the 4. Next, back up your Come Point of 4 with $5 in Free Odds, AND bet another $5 on the Pass Line. Remember? The 4 was made by the shooter, so now you're going to have another Pass Line Come Out roll, which means you need to have a bet on the Pass Line. Now think for a moment. In terms of exposure, where are you? Figure it out. The answer is that your total exposure, even after all these moves and up and downs, is $20. (Can't figure out how I came up with $20 worth of exposure? Here's the deal. I'm right. If you don't agree, you are temporarily lost in a fog bank. Keep figuring and calculating until your total agrees with mine. But here's a hint. Right now you've got $25 in wagers still on the layout.)

Let's get on with it. The very next roll is a 9. Place $6 behind your Pass Line bet to take the Free Odds. And, yes, you've arrived. You've got your three numbers. No more betting for now.

The next five rolls are 3, 8, 8, 11, and 5. What happens to your bets? Nothing. You're looking for a 4 because it is one of your Come bet Points. You're looking for a 6 because it is one of your Come bet Points. And you are looking for a 9 because it is

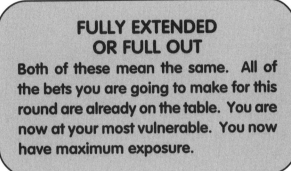

**FULLY EXTENDED
OR FULL OUT**
Both of these mean the same. All of the bets you are going to make for this round are already on the table. You are now at your most vulnerable. You now have maximum exposure.

your Pass Line Point. None of the other numbers are currently meaningful, except a 7, which would wipe you out. So what happens? No, the shooter does not roll a 7. The shooter rolls that 6 you had been looking for. Your Come 6 wins even money, the Free Odds on the Come 6 produces $6. You collect all of it, the profit and the bet, and then immediately make another Come bet. You had three numbers, now you're back down to two, and so you need to establish a third number again. The next roll is a 9. Good. The shooter made the Pass Line Point again. You're are about to receive $14. But don't forget to make your Free Odds bet on the Come Point 9, because, just as we discussed earlier with the 4, the shooter both made the Pass Line Point and also established 9 as the Point for the last Come bet. Now you must make another $5 Pass Line wager and try to get a third number working again. And again, and again. Yes, it just keeps going like this. On and on and on until the shooter rolls a 7 and kills all your bets. But I don't mean to make it sound like drudgery. If it's going on and on and on, it's because the shooter is making numbers, making Points, and providing all the Right bettors with profits. This is good. This is exciting. This is wonderful. Sooner or later that shooter will roll a 7 and the dealer will vacuum all your chips off the layout. Again, with this plan there is more of everything . . .risk, gain, and excitement.

Obviously with so many different types of wagers available to the player, there could be thousands of plans. The four I've listed here are about as good as it gets in terms of limiting the percentage working against you while at the same time keeping the game interesting. But in the final analysis you must come up with a plan of your own . . .one which makes sound financial sense without limiting your personality or your chances for profit.

MONEY MANAGEMENT

Here we are again, back to the same old thing. By now, you should have a firm understanding of the various bets. By now, perhaps you have already decided whether you will be a Wrong or Right bettor. By now, maybe you're already thinking in terms of how many units you'll need to attempt a certain method of betting. And I'm delighted that you're thinking. But now it's time for the hammer. None of that means *ANYTHING*, unless you manage your money properly. You can play as if you were born with dice in your chubby little hands, you can roll number after number after number, you can play as though directed by Fate. You can play like the greatest Craps gambler of all time and still suffer horrendous losses if you don't protect your money by using the utmost care and diligence. Let's start with elementary suggestions.

1) **Have a plan. Know what you're going to bet, how you're going to bet, the payoffs, etc. Know all of this prior to your arrival at a table. Also, know that the plan should include, as a basis, only those wagers which offer the least disadvantage to the players. Plus, make sure the plan fits your brain or personality, betting style or image. And, remember that it should be structured to compliment both your gambling stake and your ability.**

2) **Determine how much money may be required to get you through six shooters. For example. Let's say your plan is to bet $5 on the Pass Line and back up any number with double Free Odds. That's a plan which will require a maximum of $17 per shooter. I'm calling that $17 your basic unit. In order to bet the**

162

way you have planned, you'll need one unit of $17 for each shooter. Six shooters would require a maximum of 6 units x $17 = $102. I'm going to call that $102 your session money. It is the maximum amount of money you should risk during any one session. Now please go back and note that I said to determine how many units may be required. If all goes well, the first unit will light the way to riches. You may play for hours on one unit, you may lose five units in the first five minutes.

3) Determine how many sessions you want to play. You already have a plan. If you want to play once in the morning, once in the afternoon, and once in the evening, that's three times a day. Staying for three days? That's nine sessions. Nine sessions multiplied times the maximum of $102 required per session for this plan means you'll need a total bankroll of $918.

4) Never ever lose all your units at any one session. I know, I said six units. So, never ever lose more than five of them. If you lose all your units you'll feel like the name of the game.

163

5) Loss limits. No need to keep talking about this. You've already decided that you will not lose more than five units of $17 during any playing session. You've also already decided that you're willing to fund nine playing sessions. Therefore, you have also decided that you can handle a maximum loss of 5 units of $17 times 9 sessions, which = $765. If that amount causes you to choke, or if you need some of that money for a car payment, either stay home or alter the plan.

6) Winning Goal. You should set one. And please note that I said "should." If you are going to take this seriously, you must set a winning goal. If this is strictly recreational play time, you should or could set a goal, but that's not necessary. If you have the money to throw into the wind and are able to laugh when it

doesn't come back, then you don't need winning goals. The amount of your goal is entirely up to you. For some, merely retaining their gambling stake would be wonderful. Others won't be satisfied unless they double their stake. Still others will always be in pursuit of a dream . . .of breaking the bank, of emptying the money trays.

7) Part of your plan should be to know when to begin Dead Bolting. I don't mean to turn you into a robot, but when you hit X number of dollars in profit a clear bell should sound in your head telling you it is time to start getting some of those chips off the table and into your pocket.

8) Part of your plan should be to know when to make a few of the "riskier" wagers. The biggest difference between Conservative and Aggressive players in this game is that the Aggressive folks chase the high risk wagers sooner, more often, and with larger amounts than the Conservative.

9) Always quit when you arrive at your MAXIMUM LOSS LIMIT FOR ANY TWENTY-FOUR HOUR TIME PERIOD. Do not, under any circumstances, keep plugging away just because you're not tired, or simply because you don't want to take your husband to yet another show. When you're beat, admit it. Give it up. There will be another day.

Once you have finished this book, you should incorporate into your plan every idea you think may work for you in terms of Money Management and method of play. No single plan will work for all people. In the final analysis THE PLAN must be YOUR PLAN. Perhaps a plan like the one I suggest for Blackjack could be tweaked and turned into your plan for Craps. Maybe Three Card Poker has something you could incorporate here. Read it, use it. Try it. Keep what works for you and . . .no, don't discard the rest . . .keep it handy just in case you need to retool.

164

8

Casino War

et another interesting game which can be found in or adjacent to the Blackjack pit in most casinos. At least those casinos who want to take you on in a head-to-head confrontation...a no-holds-barred battle...a test of strength and endurance. Or, as viewed from a different perspective, a mindless game in which it is near impossible to determine the casino edge but is so easy to play that it requires no discernible skills, only a moderate level of intelligence, and but a modest bankroll. Yes, it's WAR, the same game you played as a child. WAR as played in the casino.

GAME REQUIREMENTS

1) **A dealer. Supplied by the casino. Controls the game, deals the cards, etc.**

2) **A shoe. Supplied by the casino. Usually contains minimum of six decks.**

3) **Chips. The same kind used at Blackjack, Craps, etc., in $1, $5, $25 and $100 denominations. Obtain them from the dealer.**

Who, by the way, in this chapter is a middle aged bald male who could make a fortune during the Christmas season posing as Santa Claus.

4) A knowledge of the ranking of cards in a standard deck. The kind of decks which contain four suits . . .Hearts, Clubs, Diamonds and Spades. The kind where the lowest card is a 2 and the highest is an Ace. The kind they use in Real Poker, Let It Ride, and 3-Card Poker. Ace is the most powerful card. Next is line is the King, then the Queen, the Jack, the 10, and so forth all the way down to the deuce.

THE BASICS

1) Make a bet. Minimum might be as low as $2 or as high as $10.

2) Each player receives one card. Cards are distributed in the same manner as in Blackjack. Dealer starts at 1st base, finishes at 3rd base, and then gives himself one card.

3) If your card is higher in rank than the dealer's card, you win even money. A bet of $8 receives a pay-off of $8, etc. If the dealer's card is higher in rank than the player's card, the player loses and forfeits the wager.

Don't even think about jumping into this game with wagers any higher than the absolute minimums required. Remember that a fool and his money are soon parted.

4) You will note on the playing surface a curvilinear section which states: TIE PAYS 10:1. Should you place a chip or chips in this "Tie" section, and should your card on the

166

very next round be of the same rank as the dealer's card, your bet on Tie will pay 10:1. If you bet $7 on Tie and actually tie the dealer, you would collect winnings of $70.

5) Dealer settles all bets in the same manner as in Blackjack. Starts at 3rd base and works back to 1st base.

6) Action is fast and furious. Game moves quickly.

7) You can win with a card as low as a 3 . . .should the dealer have a 2. You can lose with a card as high as a King . . .should the dealer have an Ace.

8) Make a bet for the dealer? Okay, but only if he 1) is contributing to the enjoyment you are experiencing, or 2) is dealing you nothing but winners. Simply place the extra wager at the top of your wagering circle.

167

GO TO WAR

Does this game sound pretty pedestrian so far? Kind of boring? Well, wake up because it's about to become more interesting. It's time to Go To War.

And, believe it or not, Going To War in the casino game is not much different from the way you might have played this game at home with your grand kids, your kids, or anyone else who wanted to play a game but didn't want a serious brain challenge. Going To War begins with a Tie. It's kinda like your front-line troops engaged the front line

TIE WAGERS—A CLARIFICATION

Don't confuse Ties with Going To War. If you bet Tie and there is one between you and the dealer, you collect 10:1 on your wager whether you Go To War or not. Going to war begins with a Tie, but Tie wagers are not dependent on Going To War.

troops of the enemy, met resistance, and were stymied. But neither you or the enemy was willing to quit. Neither of you wanted to surrender. Both of you wanted to win and carry the day. So, what to do? Bring in more troops! And hope that yours are stronger than his. Except here you do it with chips and cards, like this:

1) **Your card matches the dealers card in rank.**

2) **Declare your intent. You have two options**

3) **Option #1. You can surrender. This means you do not want to engage in further battle. It is your desire to withdraw your troops. But, naturally, you can't just slip away into the night. You gotta pay. In fact, you must donate half of your wager to the enemy. Consequently, if you decide to surrender the dealer collects half your bet.**

168

4) **Option #2. You may elect to fight on! There's no backing down. You will settle for nothing less than complete domination and victory. However, once you have decided to fight on, things get a little complicated. Just like real life. Here's the scoop:**

   A) **Extend another wager equal in value to your original. If you bet $10 before the hand was dealt, you must put up another $10 to Go To War.**
   B) **The dealer will shift your original $10 wager into the Tie section of the table layout.**
   C) **You slide your extra $10 into your betting circle.**
   D) **The dealer removes $20 worth of chips from his tray and places his chips adjacent to those of yours . . . the ones which are laying in the Tie section.**
   E) **The dealer burns three cards, then deals one to you.**
   F) **The dealer burns three more cards and gives himself one.**

G) Highest ranking card wins. If the winner is the dealer, he will collect your $20 worth of chips. If the winner is you, you get to take the dealer's $20 worth of chips.

H) If the result is another Tie between you and the dealer, you win. In fact, you may even receive a bonus . . .usually the equivalent of your original wager.

5) If more than one player Goes To War against the Dealer, the procedures remain the same as described above, but with one exception. The dealer burns three cards and then deals a card to every player who is Going To War. He then burns three more cards and deals himself a card.

STRATEGY

Strategy? Is this a joke? There is no such thing as strategy in this game. If you are lucky, if fate is sitting on your shoulder you will win. If not, it will go the other way. This is another of those YES IT CAN BE FUN TO PLAY THIS GAME BUT IT SHOULD ONLY BE PLAYED WITH "FUN" MONEY games.

Picture this scenario. You are in Las Vegas with several friends. None of them has a clue. None of them would know the difference between *en prison* and doubling down. Consequently they are 1) afraid to try anything except slot machines, 2) becoming bored, 3) looking to you for direction.

Your decision is this: Can you "teach" them all they need to know about Blackjack or Craps in the next few hours? No way. Are there any casino table games they can play which do not require in-depth knowledge or skills? Yes. Give Casino War a whirl with short money, and if that doesn't work then try Red Dog.

MONEY MANAGEMENT

Just in case you ignored what I wrote in the previous section, let me make this perfectly clear. DO NOT PLAY THIS GAME WITH ANY OF THAT PORTION OF YOUR GAMBLING STAKE WHICH WAS SUPPOSED TO BE DEVOTED

TO"SERIOUS" GAMBLING. This game should only see whatever you can afford to spend from your "fun" money. That said, remember that even though you are playing games like this for fun you should be prepared to either run or raise. By run, I mean quit the game if you are losing. By raise, I mean increase your basic betting unit if results are creating profits.

170

9

Baccarat

urely, at some point, whether it was on the Discovery Channel, or the Arts and Entertainment Network, or in your favorite magazine, or entertainment shows, or even at the library, you have read or heard about the "whales" in Las Vegas. Whales is the term used to describe the highest of the high rollers . . .the people who have more money than the Treasury . . .the people who could buy and sell both of us a thousand times over using only interest income. These people are treated by the casinos like kings and queens. They are wined and dined, supplied with the largest of the penthouse suites, assigned their own personal valets and hosts. Nearly anything they desire is theirs merely for the asking. Oh. Of course they also gamble literally millions of dollars worth of action during their stays. And the game of choice for nearly all of the whales is Baccarat. Now think about that for a few moments. These people can play any game they want. They can play at the highest of limits. Losing several million dollars during a trip is of no great concern. So, the question becomes, why Baccarat? Why not Craps or Roulette or Blackjack or Slot Machines or Video Poker? Why not good old

Texas Hold'em? As you will soon find out, Baccarat is one of the simplest of all casino games to play. It offers no serious challenge to the adventurous mind. It is tempting to call Baccarat a no-brainer game. So, again, why are the whales playing Baccarat?

Well, first, let's ask a few other exploratory questions. How did the whales become whales? Was it because they were born into wealthy families? Maybe. At least some of them. Was it because they are stupid but lucky? I doubt it. I would surmise that if we knew their histories we would find that most of them are pretty darn smart. Smart enough to start companies, or at least keep them going. Smart enough to make very wise business and personal investments. Smart enough to analyze and play the odds. And, or course, there you have it.

LIKE TO PLAY BY YOURSELF?

Yes, this is that game you see from a distance where there are only a handful of people milling about in a very large room. Look exclusive? That's by design. It's supposed to look like something you can gaze at but not touch. It's supposed to look like you gotta be somebody to gain admittance into that room.

Whales play Baccarat because the game offers the lowest disadvantage to the player. If you're going to wager $100,000 on one hand of a card game, wouldn't you like to know that you have at least an even chance of winning? Absolutely. And Baccarat does, in fact, provide the best chance for the player to win.

Think of it this way. You and me both have $5,000,000 to gamble. That's our bank roll. So, you like to play Roulette. More to the point, you like to bet individual numbers on the Roulette table. The casino advantage on single numbers is 5.26%. Which means that if you gamble your entire $5,000,000 you can expect to lose $263,000.

I've also got $5,000,000. But my game is Baccarat. I like to bet on Bankers. The casino advantage on Bankers is only about 1.2%. Which means that if I gamblemy entire $5,000,000 I can expect to lose $60,000.

You can expect to lose $263,000, I can expect to lose $60,000. Now which of us should have the best chance of actually winning money? Right. Me.

172

LET'S GET STARTED

When I said earlier that this was one of the easiest games to play, I was neither joking or exaggerating. Here's why: There are only three player options:

1) You can bet on the Banker's hand.

2) You can bet on the Player's hand.

3) You can bet on Tie.

And since a bet on Tie is a foolish wager, you can narrow down the options to only two: bet on Players or Bankers. Yes, the game really is that simple. A bet on Players pays even money. A winning bet on Bankers pays even money. A tie pays 8:1.

Yet, even though Baccarat is easy to play, most people assume that you need both millions of dollars and a superior intellect in order to play. Not so, not so.

Most every casino has at least one Baccarat table, with betting limits usually ranging anywhere from $25 to $10,000 . . .usually more for those whales. Perhaps a minimum wager of $25 scares a lot of people away from the game. I'm sure it does. But if you can afford to wager $25 on each round of play, the casino's advantage in Baccarat is only roughly 1.2 to 1.4%. Which means this game certainly merits consideration. So, here it comes.

173

DON'T BE TIMID—GET IN THE ROOM

Trudging through the casino one evening you note that one gaming area is situated off to the side, either partitioned or roped off from the rest of the gambling areas, making the activities in that room seem very private. Upon closer inspection you see men in tuxedos, lovely and glamorous-looking women in evening dresses, posh decorations. It looks beautiful, exotic, mysterious. There's even a man in a chair perched high above the action. Other spectators grouped near you are trying to watch the play, a look of awe in their eyes. But, being slightly different from the majority, you are not satisfied with watching. Even though you're dressed in denims and a cowboy shirt, you hold your head erect, jut out your chin and march into that room as if you owned the casino.

> ### PRIVATE PARTIES
> **Don't be surprised if entry to the Baccarat room is shut off by signs, guards, or Dobermans (just kidding). It is not unusual for the game to be restricted to one or two players who are wagering very high stakes. If that type of game is being conducted, the general public is not welcome.**

A few of the gamblers sitting at the table glance at you with expressionless faces as you confidently sit in the first available chair.

As with all other casino games, your first step is to purchase chips. We will assume that the table minimum is $50, so you should buy in for at least $100. I mean, you're doing this as kind of a lark, don't have a clue as to what you're about to be doing, and normally wouldn't even think about making minimum wagers of $50. So, yes, I think $100 will suffice. Okay, you're in. Now what? Well, before making any wagers, you study the table layout (see Figure 1).

Assume you're at seat number 1. Note that there are only three compartments where you can place a wager, all of which are within easy reach directly in front of your position. Two of the casino employees (dealers), both sitting on the same side of the table, are shuffling eight decks of cards. For the moment, there is nothing for you to do. You can lean back in your comfortable chair and relax. There may even be a casino shill sitting adjacent to you. Normally, the casino shills are gorgeous women, and sometimes men, so enjoy the scenery.

THE RITUAL

After a short time the dealers are finished shuffling the cards and the ritual begins. One of the dealers hands you a plain plastic card and slides all eight decks in your direction. Being astute, you quickly determine that he wants you to cut the cards. You insert the plastic card into the decks, the dealer cuts the cards at that point and then places all eight decks into a plastic shoe similar to those at the Blackjack tables. So far, so good. The other players assume that you know what you're doing.

174

Baccarat

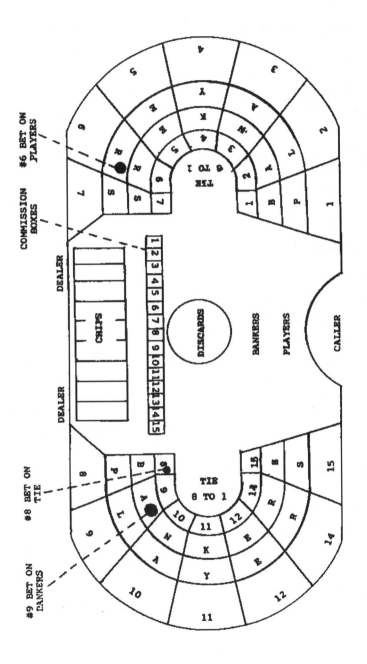

Figure 1

175

Next, the dealer removes the first card from the shoe and shows it to the players. It is a Six. You say, "Big deal," with sarcasm filling your voice. Ah, you just labeled yourself as a novice. The dealer frowns at your ignorance of Baccarat custom and then removes six more cards from the shoe, placing them in a discard slot in the middle of the table. If the first card had been a Four, four cards would have been discarded. Had the first card been a Nine, nine cards would have been discarded. Get the picture? The numbers of cards which are "burned" is determined by the first card out of the shoe. This helps prevent cheating.

You then expect the dealer to slide the cards out to the players, but something strange happens. The dealer shoves the entire plastic shoe in front of your position. You think: "My God, what now?"

Well, you've just become the Banker. And no, that does not mean you have to pay off all the winning bets when the game starts. It simply means you're going to be in control of the shoe for a while. Like a lot of other people, you have confused Baccarat with Chemin-de Fer because of the James Bond movie *Goldfinger*. In Baccarat only the casino collects and pays off, not the Banker. You issue a sigh of relief.

> The casino "banks" all the action. The banker is just another gambler. The banker makes no pay offs and does not collect chips from the other gamblers.

176

But since you're the Banker, you MUST make a bet. You can bet on Bankers or Players, but most gamblers bet on Bankers when they have the shoe. The person with the shoe is the Banker, so most Bankers bet on Bankers. Make sense? You don't have to be the Banker if you don't want to be. If you don't want to deal the cards, simply say "No thanks," or words to that effect. The shoe will then be offered to the person on your right.

Okay, you decide you want to deal, so you place the minimum wager of $25 on Bankers. For a moment, you wonder how you'll be able to deal cards to those players who are way over at the other end of the table, but another casino employee standing opposite the dealers solves the problem for you. He is the "caller," the person who directs the play of the game. He instructs you to deal him a card, then one to yourself, then another to him, then another to yourself, all face down. And, actually, just experiencing the act of distributing cards out of the shoe seems pretty cool. I mean, there might be people betting thousands of dollars on this hand, and the cards you dole out will soon determine whether they win or lose. Anyway, the first and third cards form the Player's hand, the second and fourth form the Banker's hand. Right. There are only two hands; the Banker's and the Player's.

> **SHILLS**
>
> A shill is a person hired by the casino to sit in on games and play using money provided to them by the casino. The shill returns any winnings to the casino and is not responsible for any losses. It is perfectly normal for shills to be present at Baccarat. Some players don't like to play alone. Fine. A shill or two will be available and ready to step in.

Now more ritual. The caller passes his two cards, which form the Player's hand, to a lady sitting at the far end of the table who has $2,000 wagered on the Player's hand. The reason he gave them to her is because she had the largest bet on Players. The lady turns the cards over, face up, then passes them back to the caller, who places them face up on the table in front of him. You wonder why the caller couldn't just turn the cards over by himself, but you keep quiet.

177

The caller then turns to you and directs you to turn over the Banker's hand. You do so, exposing a Six and a Nine. Because of your Blackjack experience, you assume that the hand is worth a total of 15. However, being a nov-

> **WORTH REPEATING**
>
> The Ace is worth 1 point. Two is 2. Three is 3. Four is 4. Five is 5. Six is 6. Seven is 7. Eight is 8. Nine is 9. Tens, Jacks, Queens and Kings are all 0, as in zero.

ice, you keep your mouth shut. And it's good that you didn't say anything. For, you see, it is impossible for any hand to total more than 9. Aces are counted as one. Tens, Jacks, Queens and Kings are counted as zero. All other cards are face value; for example, a Six is worth six, a Five is worth five. If the total of the cards is a two-digit number, like 15, the first digit is dropped. So 15 becomes 5. If the total were 25, the hand would still be 5.

At the caller's request, you pass the Banker's hand to him. He places the Banker's hand on the table in front of him, slightly above the Player's hand.

RIGID RULES

Did you win or lose? You don't know yet. The Banker's hand is 5, and assume that the Player's hand is 4. But, the way this game is played, the Player's hand may need another card, the Banker's hand may need another card, both may need another, or neither may need another. In any case, neither hand can have more than three cards. The beauty of Baccarat is that the decision as to whether either hand needs another card is not yours to make. The caller is in charge of the game. He will tell you if either hand needs another card, basing his decisions on the very strict rules which govern this game. You may request a copy of the printed rules and the casino will be happy to oblige you.

You need not worry about anybody at the table screwing up your hand by misplaying theirs. Those two hands you dealt out are the only hands to be played. In fact, you don't even need to worry about screwing up your own hand. Which may save you a great deal of money over the long haul.

In this case the caller says to you, "A card for Players." You deal the card face down to the caller, who places it face up adjacent to the Player's hand. The Player's hand is always acted upon before the Banker's hand. The card is a Seven, increasing the Player's hand to 11, which is really only 1. But you're not done yet.

The caller says, "A card for Bankers." You slip another card out of the shoe, face down, and pass it to the caller. He turns it over adjacent to the Banker's other two cards. It is a Three, giving the Banker's hand a total of 18, which is really just 8. Remember? You always drop the first digit of a two-digit total.

178

The caller announces, "Bankers win, eight over one." The two dealers collect the losing bets on Players and pay off the winning bets on Bankers. But as the dealer on your side of the table pays off your bet on Bankers, you notice that he is also placing a little chip in a row of boxes in front of him. More specifically, he places one of those chips in the box marked 1, which is your position. Don't be alarmed. When you bet on Bankers and win, you must pay the casino a five percent commission. The dealer is simply keeping track of how much commission you owe. He will collect the commission later, before you leave the table or after the last hand is played from the shoe. The casino does not want to slow down the game by making change in order to collect commissions.

I know, a five percent commission on winnings sounds terrible. But what you don't know yet is that the rules governing the game favor the Banker's hand. Consequently the Banker's hand wins more often than the Player's hand. Because of this, the casino must charge a commission to make any money.

Without the 5%, the casino would actually operate at a disadvantage, and you know they're not going to allow that to happen because they are in business to make profits. Had you bet on Players and won,

> ## WORTH REMEMBERING
> Each and every time you win a bet on Bankers you will need to pay a 5% commission. But that's not bad news because Bankers wins more often than Players.

179

you wouldn't have paid any commission. If you don't want to pay commissions, just bet on Players all the time. But, as I stated, Bankers wins more often than Players.

Now, does that sound like a difficult game? Of course not. The most difficult part was being the Banker (dealer), and all you had to do was follow the caller's instructions. Had you not been the Banker, you would have simply placed a bet, relaxed, and awaited the outcome.

Let's take this example a step further. You deal another hand in the same manner as the first. But this time Player's wins. All that happens is that you pass the shoe to the person on your right. The shoe changes whenever the Banker's hand loses, and travels around the table counter-clockwise. The cards are not re-shuffled, but the shoe keeps moving until the plain plastic card shows up . . .the same plastic card you inserted into the decks at the beginning. That hand is played out to completion, then the decks are either re-shuffled or eight new decks are introduced.

SETTLE THE ACCOUNT

Assume that you bet on Bankers sixteen times and won fourteen times. You bet $50 on each hand. Now it's time to pay your commission. $50 x 14 winning hands =$700. 5% of $700 = $35 Is that so terrible? Of course not, especially since the rules favor Bankers.

THE PLAYING RULES

The chart depicted below shows the rules administered by the caller, but you needn't memorize them. You have no control, anyway. You simply bet on Bankers or Players and either win or lose. While it's possible for the caller to make a mistake, that possibility is very remote. In fact, if you really want to do this right, take in your own caller. Find somebody with a great memory, have them memorize all the rules, and then take them along. Your job would be to make the bets. Their job would be to determine whether the casino caller is always correct. I'm kidding, but I bet that if you wagered like a whale the casino would allow you to bring in your own specialist.

PLAYER'S RULES

IF PLAYER'S TWO-CARD TOTAL IS:	PLAYER MUST
0, 1, 2, 3, 4, or 5	DRAW
6 or 7	STAND
8 or 9	NATURAL

Figure 2

Okay, and now that you've looked at Figure 2, you're wondering what is so hard about the rules. I mean, there's only three of them. Surely, if you're going to play much of this game, you can remember three lousy little rules. Ha! Of course the only reason I made that statement was because it's about to get a lot harder. Take a look now at Figure 3, which is the rules governing the Banker's hand.

> ## WHAT IS A "NATURAL?"
> A Natural is any two-card total of 8 or 9, either of which creates an automatic winner unless the Banker's two-card total is also 8 or 9, in which case a tie could be the result. More technically correct, there are two possible Naturals. A small one (8), and a big one (9). And big always beats small.

BANKER'S RULES

BANKER'S TWO-CARD TOTAL	DRAWS CARD IF PLAYER DRAWS A	DOES PLAYER DRAWS A
0, 1, or 2	MUST DRAW	MUST DRAW
3	0,1,2,3,4,5,6,7,9	8
4	2,3,4,5,6,7	0,1,8,9
5	4,5,6,7	0,1,2,3,8,9
6	6,7	0,1,2,3,4,5,8,9
7	MUST STAND	MUST STAND
8,9	NATURAL	NATURAL

Figure 3

181

Think you can remember all of that? Of course you can. That is, if you wanted to devote the time. Or if you had the inclination. Or if you were going to play every day. None of which is the case.

The idea of the game is to get a total of 9, or as close to 9, as possible. Whichever hand is closer to 9 is the winner. If either hand is dealt 8 or 9 on the first two cards, that hand has a Natural. If one hand has a Natural and the other doesn't, the Natural wins automatically. If one has 8, the other 9, the 9 wins the hand. Once a Natural is revealed, that round is over.

SAMPLE HANDS

Example #1. Players is dealt a Queen and a Ten. Bankers is dealt a Two and a Three. What happens now? Well, refer to the rules. The Player's two-card total is 0, so Players must draw another card. We'll say that Players receives a Six, for a final total of 6. Now what happens to the Bankers hand when Players has a total of 6? The Bankers two-card total is 5. Players has a 6, so Bankers must draw an additional card. We're going to say that Bankers draws a Seven, for a final total of 12, which is really just 2. Yes, the Bankers hand went from 5 down to 2, and loses the round. The caller says, "Players wins, six over two."

182   **Example #2.** Players receives a Six and a Five. Bankers receives a Ten and a Seven. What happens next? Again, refer to the rules. If the Player's two-card total is 1, Players must draw a card. But what does Bankers do with a two-card total of 7? Well, if Bankers has a two-card total of 7, it does not make any difference what card Players draws. The Bankers hand *must* stand on 7, regardless of what Players is showing. Even if Players draws an Eight, for a final total of 9, Bankers still can't draw another card. Yes, even though it means Bankers will lose the round. Yet, if you think about it, is standing on 7 such a bad idea? Only the Ace and Deuce can help, so there's not much chance of improving the total. But you've forgotten something. Players acts before Bankers. So in this example Bankers would already know that Players is at 9. It would be like if you could see the dealer's hole card in Blackjack. If the dealer has a total of 20, you would certainly take a hit on your 19. Almost no chance of making a hand, but you gotta try. Right? Well, not in Baccarat. If the rules say stand, you stand.

Example #3. Players two-card total is 4. Bankers two-card total is 4. Players must draw a card, does, and receives a Three for a final total of 7. And since Players drew a Three, Bankers must also draw a card.

Example 4. Again, Players and Bankers each have a total of 4. But this time the Player's hand draws a Queen, and therefore does not improve its total. Can Bankers now take another card? No. The rules clearly state that if Players draws a 0 then a Bankers two-card total of 4 cannot draw. Period. The round would end in a tie.

LET'S TALK ABOUT TIES
How often? About once every ten hands. What's the pay-off? 8:1. What is the true pay-off? 9:1. What's the disadvantage for the gambler? Over 10%. Is it a bet worth making? No, no, and then no.

Example #5. Players hand receives a King and a Jack. Bankers hand catches an Ace and a Ten. Player's two-card hand totals 20, which is really just 0. Banker's two-card hand totals 11, which is really just 1. Players must draw an additional card, does, and receives another Jack. Player's final hand is still worth only 0. You've bet on Bankers, so you think you've won the hand, 1 over 0. But, alas, any time the Banker's two-card hand has a total of 0, 1, or 2 Bankers must draw a card. In this example, Bankers could possible turn a winning hand into a losing hand by taking an additional card, but that's the rules, folks.

Now the next time you have an extra $100 in your pocket you can bounce into the Baccarat pit and make at least 2-4 bets. You can sit there and sip your drink, cast looks of disdain at the spectators on the other side of the ropes, and feel like a high roller. What the heck? Go ahead and do it at least once in your life.

Remember how simple it is. You bet on Bankers or Players. It's really that easy. Who knows? You might get lucky. Baccarat attracts many wealthy gamblers, so you can bet the minimum and watch the high rollers win or lose hundreds of thousands of dollars. Recent reports indicate that some casinos generate as much as one third of their total income from Baccarat. Next time, instead of marveling at what is happening in that small private room, join the action.

The best thing about this game is that it is entirely possible to win more than you lose, even if you pay the five percent commission. The casino's advantage on Players is about 1.4%. On Bankers (including the commission),

183

the casino's advantage is only 1.2%, which makes a bet on Bankers one of the best wagers in the casino.

Oh, yes. I forgot to tell you. That person hovering over the game from his tall, tall chair is called the ladderman. It is his job to oversee the game and watch for cheating and collusion between dealers and players. Unless you're trying to cheat, ignore him.

MINI-BACCARAT

As the term implies, Mini-Baccarat is a smaller version of the same game, It is played at a smaller table (normally found near the Blackjack tables), allows a smaller minimum wager ($5-$10), and one dealer does everything: the dealing, the exchanging of chips on wins or losses, the calling of the hands.

There are not many of these tables available, but they are a good place to start if you can find one. Play Mini-Baccarat until you gain confidence, then move on to the big table.

However, exercise some care. In Baccarat, as played on the big tables, you don't lose ties. If you bet on either Bankers or Players and the result is a tie, you don't win or lose unless you have bet on Tie. But in quite a few of the Mini-Baccarat games the casino wins all ties. This rule is bad for gamblers, so watch out for it.

Also, the minimum commission charged on a winning wager on Bankers is usually twenty-five cents. So even if you wagered only two dollars, which should mean a commission of ten cents, you still must pay twenty-five cents. Not much difference, but those nickels and dimes add up.

MONEY MANAGEMENT

Is this a joke? Money management? Humor me for a moment. Here's the bottom line regarding money management and Baccarat. When you lose all your money, leave the table. If you quadruple your original stake, stay there for a while longer. That's called keeping it simple. And I'm only half-joking.

Actually, this is one of the few games which offer a disadvantage which is low enough to provide the player a chance to win. The only reasons not to play this game are the high minimum wagers required for the real game, and some of the small twists in Mini-Baccarat which increase the casino's percentage. So, by all means, if your have the means, give this game a try. But establish some guidelines. Here's a few of mine.

1) **Have a plan.** Know what you're going to bet, how you're going to bet, the payoffs, etc. Know all of this prior to your arrival at a table. Players or Bankers. Ha! Pretty difficult to make a plan out of only two options, but at least give some thought to how you're going to play.

2) **Loss limits.** One of the most important elements of a good plan. You must set a "drop dead" number for yourself. When and if you reach that number, you quit. It's as simple as that. Let's assume for a moment that your stake is $200. Put a mental book mark in your brain of $150. Then, if you lose $150 you quit. No matter what. Save the other $50 still laying on the table in front of you. You've already lost 75% of your stake. Get while the getting is good.

185

3) **Winning Goal.** You should set one. And please note that I said "should." If you are going to take this seriously, you must set a winning goal. If this is strictly recreational play time, you should or could set a goal, but that's not necessary. If you have the money to throw into the wind and are able to laugh when it doesn't come back, then you don't need winning goals. The amount of your goal is entirely up to you. For some, merely retaining their gambling stake would be wonderful. Others won't be satisfied unless they double their stake. Still others will always be in pursuit of a dream . . .of breaking the bank, of emptying the money trays.

4) Part of your plan should be to know when to begin Dead Bolting. I don't mean to turn you into a robot, but when you hit X number of dollars in profit a clear bell should sound in your head telling

you it is time to start getting some of those chips off the table and into your pocket.

5) If you're up as many as ten units, change your unit. If your unit was $25, for example, change it to $50. When you are winning, you must push for all you can. The player most feared by the casinos is the player who gradually increases his or her bets for maximum profits. If you increase your unit and start losing, go back to your original unit. If you win another ten units, increase your unit again. But one word of caution: If you are a $25 bettor and increasing your unit to $50 or $100 makes you nervous, stay with a lower unit. I know people who play faultlessly with $5 bets, but lose control if they increase to $50 or $75 bets.

6) Part of your plan should be to know when to make the "riskier" Tie wager. The biggest difference between Conservative and Aggressive players in this game is that the Aggressive folks chase the high risk wagers sooner, more often, and with larger amounts than the Conservative.

7) Always quit when you arrive at your MAXIMUM LOSS LIMIT FOR ANY TWENTY-FOUR HOUR TIME PERIOD. Do not, under any circumstances, keep plugging away just because you're not tired, or simply because you don't want to take your wife to yet another dazzling buffet. When you're beat, admit it. Give it up. There will be another day.

Once you have finished this book, incorporate into your plan every idea you think may work for you in terms of money management and method of play. No single plan will work for all people. In the final analysis THE PLAN must be your plan. Perhaps a plan like the one I suggest for Blackjack could be tweaked and turned into your plan for Baccarat. Read it and use it. Try it. Keep what works for you and. . .no, don't discard the rest . . .keep it handy just in case you need to retool.

10

Keno: The Real Kind

kay, let's make this as clear as possible as early as possible. There's only one similarity between Keno and Bingo. Both are played with numbered balls which are drawn from a machine. Ask any gambler to describe Keno, and nine out of ten will begin by telling you that Keno is like Bingo. Wrong, wrong, and wrong again. Bingo is played with 75 numbers, Keno has 80. In Bingo, numbers are drawn until someone wins. If it takes 65 numbers to produce a winner, then 65 numbers are drawn. There is at least one winner in every game. In Keno, only *20* numbers are drawn, and it is quite possible that a game will have *no* winners. Bingo is similar to pari-mutual wagering because the pot usually consists of contributions from the crowd. The host is merely the agent. Usually a charitable organization. In Keno you are playing against the house . . .the casino . . .the bad guys.

Actually, descriptions of Keno as it relates to Bingo should be terminated once and for all. If you want to draw comparisons, here's one which is accurate. Playing Keno is like purchasing a Lottery ticket. Do odds in the millions sound familiar? Can you tolerate and/or enjoy playing against odds which run into the millions? Do you enjoy playing against a casino vig which starts at 25%?

Forgive me, because I know a lot of people who like to play Keno, but if you were down to your last dollar and had to make a gamble, and could only choose between playing Keno and a Slot Machine, and if you're wondering which offers the best shot of actually getting money back, you're better off with the Slot Machine.

Do people ever win money while playing Keno? Absolutely. I'm sure it happens every day . . .some where, some how. Could it happen to you? Of course. Could a piano fall out of the sky and squash your car? Yes. And the only difference here is that there may be a greater chance of seeing your car squashed.

If it sounds like I think this is a terrible game, you're reading correctly. It has its place, and I'll get to that in a few minutes, but this a game which should never see any of your serious money, and very little of your fun money. Consequently, this chapter will be short and not-so-sweet.

> ## KENO BOARDS
> Marques which show the numbers being drawn for each game. Also show the number of the game being played. Also usually show whether a game is closed, or whether bets are still being accepted. Usually found in all casino restaurants and some bars. Giant size edition at some Keno Lounges. Undrawn numbers remain dark, drawn numbers light up.

188

THE BASICS—STRAIGHT TICKETS

You'll Need a Ticket

Buy a Keno card (ticket). They look like the one shown in Figure 1. You will find these at the Keno counter, in the Keno lounge, and in all of the casino's bars and restaurants. The tickets are free and easily found.

How Many?

Decide on how many numbers you are going to play. In the basic games you can play up to fifteen numbers. In the gimmick games (more coming later) you can play up to forty. As to what number to select, the list is endless.

SAMPLE KENO TICKET					FIRST GAME	NO. OF GAMES		TOTAL PRICE	
					LAST GAME				
1	2	3	4	5	6	7	8	9	10	PRICE PER GAME
11	12	13	14	15	16	17	18	19	20	
21	22	23	24	25	26	27	28	29	30	
31	32	33	34	35	36	37	38	39	40	

MULTI GAME KENO FROM 2 TO 999 GAMES IN ADVANCE

41	42	43	44	45	46	47	48	49	50
51	52	53	54	55	56	57	58	59	60
61	62	63	64	65	66	67	68	69	70
71	72	73	74	75	76	77	78	79	80

WIN UP TO $200,000 OR MORE

FOR MORE DETAILED INFORMATION ASK OUR KENO SUPERVISORS

Figure 1

You could start with all the birthdays of all the people who are within reach of where you are sitting. Then you could use all the ages of the first twelve people who agree to reveal theirs. Or, you could close your eyes and point. Or, you could sit in the Keno Lounge for hour after hour and try to determine whether certain numbers or groups of numbers seem to be appearing with more frequency than others.

How Much?

Decide how much you are going to spend. It cost the same to play one number as it does to play fifteen. Pay-offs vary depending on the number of selections you make. Figure 2 shows the normal options, with pay-offs based on wagers of $1. Pay-offs may vary slightly at different casinos.

MARK	CATCH	PAY-OFF
1 NUMBER	1	$3
2 NUMBERS	2	$12
3 NUMBERS	2	$1
	3	$43
4 NUMBERS	2	$1
	3	$3
	4	$125
5 NUMBERS	3	$1
	4	$14
	5	$720
6 NUMBERS	3	$1
	4	$4
	5	$90
	6	$1,500
9 NUMBERS	5	$4
	6	$44
	7	$300
	8	$3,500
	9	$25,000
15 NUMBERS	6	$1
	7	$8
	8	$22
	9	100
	10	$300
	11	$2,600
	12	$8,000
	13	$25,000
	14	$32,000
	15	$50,000

Figure 2

Figure 2 skips from 6 numbers to 9 numbers to 15 numbers, but when you pick up a Keno brochure in the casino the pay-offs will be shown for marking 7, 8, 10, 11 numbers, etc. The more numbers selected the higher the pay-offs, with smaller pay-offs for partial success. Here's how to read Figure 2. If you mark five numbers, you must catch a minimum of three of them in order to have your bet returned. Catching 4 of your numbers would mean a pay-off of $14, and catching 5 out of 5 pays off $720.

If you were playing 15 numbers, you would need to catch 6 spots to see the return of your $1, but the top prize climbs to $50,000.

Mark the Ticket

If you decide to play a ticket with four numbers, or spots, simply draw an X through each of the numbers you select. If you decide on one number, as shown in Figure 3, the X should only cover one number. Also, use only the crayon markers provided by the casino to mark your tickets. Pencil doesn't count. Pens don't count. Magic markers don't count. Use the crayons.

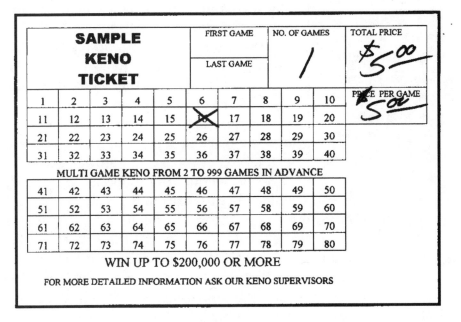

Figure 3

Fill in the Blanks

Some Keno games require that you note the amount played, how many games you are playing, the total cost of the ticket, etc. Others only require the amount you are wagering. Figure 1 is typical.

Validate Your Ticket

This is not something you can do for yourself. It must be done for you by  the people who are running the game over in the Keno Lounge. Which may pose a logistics problem. Do you want to drop what you're doing and walk, sometimes run, all the way over to the Keno counter to validate your ticket? If yes, go right ahead. Stand in line, present your ticket and money, receive your authorized copy. If no, start watching for the Keno runner, who you may now think of as being your agent. You're going to supply the ticket and the money, they are going to arrange the actual contract between you and the casino. Runners are men and women whose costume is usually similar to that of the waiters. You'll see them working various areas by calling out: "Keno?" "Keno anyone?" This is their way of asking whether you have a ticket for them to pick up. Keno runners can "sell" you a ticket. That is, they can collect your ticket, confirm the cost and the type of wager you are making, take your money and provide change. And that's wonderful. But it doesn't mean anything unless they get back to the Keno Lounge in time to validate your ticket for the very next game. And don't be surprised if the game is already underway before the Keno runner returns with your validated ticket. Remember there may be a long distance between your table at the restaurant and the Keno Lounge. Fortunately, these runners are very reliable. However, you should know that if the runner doesn't get your ticket back to the counter in time for the next game, or if they make some sort of mistake,

192

Regarding wagering limits, if you need to check on the maximums, you're either very lucky or very sick. Minimums can start as low as 50 or 70 cents for straight tickets and 25 cents for way tickets

the casino is not responsible for them. So, if you want a guarantee, do it yourself.

How Do You Win?

If some or all of your numbers are drawn from the Keno blower in the next game, you could win anything from even money to $125,000. Take another look at Figure 2. Once you've paid for your ticket and received

> ### CAN I TRUST THE KENO RUNNERS?
> Draw your own conclusion. I have a brother-in-law who has been playing Keno since 1953 and estimates he has played in excess of 5,000 games. He has always used Keno runners. He has missed one game due to a slow Keno runner. It was a game he would have lost, so he saved $5.

your authorized copy there is nothing to do but sit back and relax. You have no control over the game. Twenty ping-pong balls will decide your fate.

How Do You Know You Won?

You have the ticket. Nobody is going to watch the game for you and inform you when you win. Watch the Keno Boards. Your validated ticket has the number of your game listed prominently on the front. Your ticket, your responsibility.

How Do You Collect?

You collect by presenting the winning ticket to the people behind the counter in the Keno Lounge, or to the Keno runner. The same Keno runner who sold you the ticket can also cash it so long

> ### WORTH REPEATING
> You can fill out Keno tickets all day and night, but if they are not validated they are worthless. You pay for them and receive an authorized copy confirming your wager. Then, and only then, you have a valid ticket.

as 1) they have enough change on them and 2) the ticket does not require a signature for I.R.S. purposes. Also, be aware that one-game tickets must be collected prior to the start of the next game.

THE BASICS—WAY TICKETS

Everything is done in exactly the same way (no pun intended) as for Straight Tickets, except that now you are going to mark your ticket differently, you're going to cover more combinations of numbers, and you're going to spend more money. A way ticket is called a "way" ticket because of the multiple "ways" or combinations of numbers you can play.

This is not necessarily a better way of playing (although some people think so) . . it is just a different way of playing.

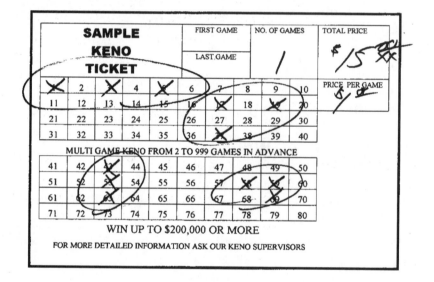

Figure 4

194

Take a look at Figure 4. What do you see? Right. Twelve different numbers with an X through them. Four circles, each drawn around a group of numbers. What's it mean? Depends on how you write your ticket. Here are the possibilities:

A) The 1, 3, and 5 form one group, or way, of three numbers.

B) The 17, 29, 37 form one group, or way, of three numbers.

C) The 43, 53, 63 form one group, or way, of three numbers.

D) The 58, 59, 69 form one group, or way, of three numbers.

Easy, so far. All of the above represent the same thing as playing four different "straight" tickets. If each way was being played for $1, the pay-offs would be the same as those shown in Figure 2. So, if you catch one number out of the 3, 4, 5 you win nada. If you catch two numbers out of that group you win $1. If you catch all three of the numbers in that "way" you win $43.00.

The same is true of each of the other ways of numbers. In group B if you catch one number, say the 29, you win nothing. Catching any two of the numbers in that group would return your bet of $1. Catching all three would pay $43.

Simple. Of course? But you're not done yet. There's a lot more ways here.

E) The 1, 3, 5, 17, 29, 37 form one group, or way, of six numbers.

F) The 1, 3, 5, 43, 53, 63 form one group, or way, of six numbers.

G) The 1, 3, 5, 58, 59, 69 form one group, or way, of six numbers.

H) The 17, 29, 37, 43, 53, 63 form one group, or way, of six numbers.

I) The 17, 29, 37 , 58, 59, 69 form one group, or way, of six numbers.

J) The 43, 53, 63, 58, 59, 69 form one group, or way, of six numbers.

Again, assuming you're playing each way for $1, the pay-offs would be the same as those shown in Figure 2. So, if you catch only one or two numbers out of Group E, the way represented by the 3, 4, 5, 19, 29, and 39, you win nada. If you catch three numbers out of that group you win $1. Should you catch four spots you would be rewarded with $4. Five spots would pay $90, and catching all six of the numbers in that "way" would pay a nice little bonanza of $1,500.

Same pay-offs would apply for the ways listed as Group F, G, H, I and J. And you're still not done yet.

K) The 1, 3, 5, 17, 29, 37, 43, 53, 63 form one group, or way, of nine numbers.

L) The 1, 3, 5, 17, 29, 37, 58, 59, 69 form one group, or way, of nine numbers.

M) The 1, 3, 5, 43, 53, 63, 58, 59, 69 form one group, or way, of nine numbers.

N) The 17, 29, 37, 43, 53, 63, 58, 59, 69 form one group, or way, of nine numbers.

196

Same deal here as before. Each of these nine-number ways wins or loses as shown in Figure 2. Let's use Group M for our example. If the 3, 5, 53, 63, and 69 are all drawn, you get back $4. If it's the 1, 3, 5, 53, 63, and 69 the pay-off climbs to $44. For any seven of the numbers it would be $300, for any eight numbers $3,500, and nine for nine is a very nice $25,000. And, you guessed it, you're not done yet.

O) The 1, 3, 5, 17, 29, 37, 43, 53, 63, 58, 59, 69 also form one way of twelve.

Figure 2 does not show the pay-offs for twelve numbers, so I'll tell you now that you must catch at least five spots for return of bet, six spots for $8, seven numbers pays $28, eight numbers would pay $200, nine numbers $600, ten numbers $1,500, eleven numbers $12,000, and all twelve would pay $40,000.

Now count'em up. How many ways could you play this ticket? There are 4 ways to make three numbers. There are six ways to make six numbers.

There are four ways to make nine numbers, and one way to make twelve. A total of fifteen ways. And if each way costs $1 the total cost of the ticket would be $15. But in this case you have several options.

1) **Do not play all the ways. There is no rule which states you must play, or purchase, all of the possible ways merely because they exist. You may buy as few or as many of the ways as you want.**

2) **When you play this many ways the casino will usually allow you to play for 50 cents per way, reducing the price to $7.50. Pay-offs would also be reduced by half. This varies by casino, but there will always be a reduced rate for way players.**

If you decide to play the groups of three and six numbers, the total cost of a $1 ticket would be $10. In this case you would show $10 at the top of the ticket, and then list the ways at the bottom: 4/3 and 6/6 tells the casino you want to play four ways of three numbers each and six ways of six numbers. If you wanted all of the possible ways, you would list 4/3 and 6/6 and 4/9 and 1/12. This, along with the amount of your bet, tells the casino you want to play four ways of three numbers, six ways of six numbers, four ways of nine numbers, and one way of twelve numbers.

197

> ## LEAVE NO ROOM FOR ERRORS OR MISUNDERSTANDING
> Do not hesitate to ask the Keno runners or ticket sellers for assistance. Always confirm that you have marked your ticket to correctly reflect your intent. Always confirm that the cost of the ticket is exactly what you expected.

WHY? WHY? WHY PLAY WAY TICKETS?

1) **It's easier to mark one ticket with all these ways than it is to make out fifteen separate tickets.**

2) What you're looking for is the big bang . . .the game where you collect multiple pay-offs. Let's say that you catch the 1, 3, 5, 43, 53, 63. Each way of three numbers (Groups A and C) would return $43, for a total of $86. Plus the six for six on the sixway (Group H) would pay $1,500. And that's not all. Keep looking at Figure 4. Keep thinking about the numbers which were drawn. How many combinations of six are affected by the 1, 3, 5? How many combinations of the six are affected by the 43, 53, 63? Catching three out of six pays $1, so that's another $5. And the nine number ways? One is a six-number winner for a pay-off of $44. The twelve way? No luck there, so the total pay-off for this $15 ticket would be $1,635. Had you bet it for 50 cent ways instead of $1, the total pay-off would be $817.

To repeat, way tickets are not a better way to play, just a different, and sometimes more convenient, way to play.

198

THE BASICS—SPECIAL TICKETS

The options are aplenty. The options are varied. The options change all the time, so what you see on this trip may be gone six months from now and then back again a year later. You still need to fill out a ticket. You still need to mark it properly. You still need to pay up. Everything else is the same. The only thing that changes with Special Tickets are the requirements for winning.

Top and Bottom

Just like it sounds. You select either all of the numbers on the top half of the ticket(1-40) or all the numbers on the bottom half (41-80). If you catch none of the numbers, you win $40,000. If you catch all twenty of the numbers, you win $40,000. If you catch eight, nine, ten, eleven or twelve numbers you get zilch. Returns start at catching 7 numbers or less, and kick in again at thirteen or more. Usually a $3 minimum.

Left and Right

Draw a line down the middle of the ticket. You'll then have five columns of eight numbers on the left side and five columns of eight numbers on the right side. Choose one side or the other. Same pay-offs as for Top and Bottom. Also usually a $3 minimum.

Sweet Sixteen

Mark any sixteen numbers. Catch none = $100. Catch one number, two numbers, three, four, five or six numbers and get back $1 to $5. Pay-off keeps climbing to a high of $125,000 for catching all sixteen spots. Usually a $5 minimum.

20 Spot Ticket

Usually a $5 ticket, but can be played for half price at some casinos. Zero catch = $1,000. From one to nine numbers pays $1 to $10. Top prize is $125,000.

When it comes to Special Tickets, the only limitation is the imagination of the inventor . . .and the blessing of the appropriate gaming commission.

199

In Keno there are three different types of tickets and three different ways to lose your money. The smallest casino advantage in this game is 25%. That's all you need to know. But I'll give you another statistic, anyway. It has been calculated that the chance of catching six numbers on a six spot ticket is ap-

ALL PAY-OFFS ARE NOT CREATED EQUAL
Always check the pay-offs before you make out your Keno tickets. What pays $25,000 at one casino may only pay $20,000 at the next. Never assume that all casinos pay at the same rate.

proximately 7,700 to 1. The pay-off at most casinos for catching six of six is approximately $1,500. The correct pay-off would be $7,700. The casino pays $1,500. And the more numbers selected, the worse it gets. When I said you have a better chance of hitting a state lottery, I was not joking.

> ## TIP THE RUNNERS
> **Win or lose. They provided service, so take care of them. It's not their fault you lost. They hustled for you, maybe even encouraged you, so give them a toke (tip).**

The attraction for Keno is the small cost, huge pay-off scenario. A $1 ticket could win $50,000! Lightning could strike. If the Chicago Cubs can win the World Series, anything can happen. What's that? The Cubs haven't won the Series? Oh, well.

Also, here's the icing on the cake. This is one of those, "you've already got me on the run and now you want me to take off my shoes?" kinds of things. All of the casinos will list in their Keno brochures the aggregate payout which is their limit. For example. If the aggregate is $125,000 it means that the total maximum payoff for all winners in any one game is $125,000. If there is more than one winner in a single game, the total payoff to **all** the winners cannot exceed $125,000. So the fact that you have a $125,000 winner does not necessarily mean you will collect $125,000.

200

MONEY MANAGEMENT

Okay, I admit I've tried to paint a black picture here. However, there is always the chance that you will get lucky, or that fate will look kindly on you, or that your astrology chart will be in alignment with all the tea leaves in China at precisely the moment when your numerology will be in consorts with both. And you just might strike it rich.

If your vacation is for three days and two nights, you'll probably eat eight meals at your hotel/casino. During the time required to eat each meat, you could play three games of Keno. At $1 per game, that's $24. If it's in your budget, do it. If it would need to come from the serious portion of your bank roll, forget it.

By yourself? With someone who doesn't care to converse? Crowded restaurant? Taking forever to get your order? Take that crayon and mark a ticket. You don't need to play for real money. Just pretend. In all probability 999 out of 1,000 times you will be happy you never actually bought the ticket. The other one time out of a thousand?

There's only one way I recommend you play this game, and it's so conservative there's almost no way to cash for big bucks. The smallest casino advantage is 25% and that's on a one-number ticket. Consequently, when you're waiting for food I suggest you purchase a $5 one-number ticket. If it loses, you're done for that meal. If it wins, parlay. The pay-off will be $15. Bet the whole $15 right back on the same number. If it loses, you're done. If it wins, you going to have $45 with which to try the parlay one more time. A win would produce $135. Now put that $135 away some where and identify it as being for Keno only. Then, the next time you have a meal repeat the process. Only the next time start with $10 instead of $5. Remember that you only need to catch one number. The trick is to do it three times in a row.

11

Roulette

203

have this wild and crazy idea for a new game. Think circular. Circular as in wheels. Think large wheel, like the ones you see in movies of the old West—the ones on the Conestoga wagons. Also, think small ball, something the size and color of a very large pearl or a medium-sized shooting marble. Now lay the wheel on its side and set it spinning. Then place the ball on the rim of the wheel and give it a shove so that it spins in exactly the opposite direction that the wheel is spinning. Got the picture? Good. Now back up for a moment. Before you set that wheel to spinning, identify the open areas within each spoke by painting a number on the rim. We'll say there's eleven spokes, so that means 10 open areas between the spokes. Now let's make a bet. The force of gravity is what is holding that little ball on the rotating rim of the wheel. However, when that wheel slows to nearly a stop, the ball is going to tumble off the rim, and since it can't possibly drop upwards (gravity), it will drop down through one of those areas between the spokes. So we'll allow that ball to decide the outcome for our wager. But what are we going to bet? Well, we have a choice of several options. We could, for example, bet on whether that ball will fall into one of the odd-numbered sections. Or, we could bet on whether that ball will fall into one of the even-numbered sections. Or we could bet on a specific number between one and ten. We could wager on whether the ball will land in one of the first five sections (rim numbers 1-5), or the last five sections (rim numbers 6-10). Certainly plenty of options. Could probably keep us engaged for several hours.

Sound too simple? I agree. Not much challenge in picking a number between one and ten. Every bet would be nothing more than a guess. If I wanted to bet that the #8 compartment was where that darn little ball would fall, I could only expect to be correct one out of every ten tries. Nah, my idea might qualify as a game which could be fun if only the two of us were playing —maybe even fun to play with our kids or grand kids, but certainly not the type of game which would attract a following. Not the type of game which people will still be playing a hundred years from now. Sure. Well, think again. The moderately expanded version of what I have just described has survived through several centuries and is still going strong. Defined in most dictionaries as a gambling game in which players bet on which compartment of a revolving wheel a small ball will come to rest in, Roulette is easy to learn, easy to play. It's also one of those games which cannot be beaten over the long haul.

204

THE BASICS

Know this right from the start. There is no such thing as a winning system for Roulette. Other games offer much less disadvantage for the player. Consequently, this is a game which should see very little of your bank roll. Can you win? Of course. You can win for a session, or a day, maybe even several days. But, like most of theother casino games, the casino percentage will eventually grind you down. The casino will play . . .hold on for a moment. Let's take a minute or two and figure this out.

TIME OUT

Assume the casino is open 24 hours each day. Assume a full year of 365 days. Hold it. There's no way the Roulette wheel will be in play for the full 24 hours every day. So, lets say the Roulette wheel is only in use 16 hours per day. 16 hours times 365 days = 5,840 hours of play every year. Okay, now lets go back to making assumptions. Assume the wheel spins out a decision every 60 seconds. I think that's fair. One per minute = 60 per hour. 60 multiplied times 5,840 hours = 350,400 spins per year. Further assume that there are an average of 4 players at the table at all times. So, 4 multiplied times 350,400 = 1,401,600 player decisions per year. One last assumption. The average wager made by each gambler is $5. I know, I know. That sounds a little low, but I'm being conservative. Now, here we go again with the mathematics. 5 times 1,401,600 = 7,008,000. And that's dollars. The minimum casino percentage held over the player in this game is 5.26%, which, when multiplied times $7,008,000, produces $368,621 per year in income for the casino, which is roughly $31,000 per month, or a little over $7,000 per week. Fine. Now why did we do this in the first place? Oh, yes. I was saying that it is definitely possible for you to win in this game . . .over the short term. It's possible that you could win for a session, for a day, even for several days. It is possible that you could win over a span of 200-300 spins, or 2,000-3,000 spins, maybe even for 20,000 or 30,000 spins. But eventually the casino percentage will overwhelm you. For, you see, while you may play for a total of 40 or 50 hours this year, the casino will play for nearly 6,000. While you may play for a total of 2,000-3,000 player decisions this year, the casino will play for over 1.4 million. I've already stated that the best player wager in Roulette carries a 5.26% disadvantage to the player. So who is in the cat-bird seat here? Would you prefer to be the entity who is playing for 3,000 spins against a vig of 5.26%, or would you rather be the entity who is playing for 1,400,000 spins with an advantage of 5.26%? Enough said.

BACK TO THE BASICS

A dealer (*croupier*) oversees the betting, makes the payoffs, rotates the wheel and spins the ball. And, incidentally, the ball was supposedly made originally of ivory, but in its present day form it will

MULTIPLE DEALERS
During play only one dealer is required to run the game. However, if a game becomes jammed with players and chips a second dealer is often inserted to keep the game moving.

most always be made of plastic. Anyway, if the ball drops into the compart-ment which houses a number covered by one of your wagers, you win. If it drops into the compartment for a number covered by somebody else, they win. If it drops into the compartment for a number covered by both you and somebody else, you both win.

There is no mystique to this game. The wheel rotates, the ball spins, you win or lose. Many betting options, but a game in which intuition is rewarded more often than intellect.

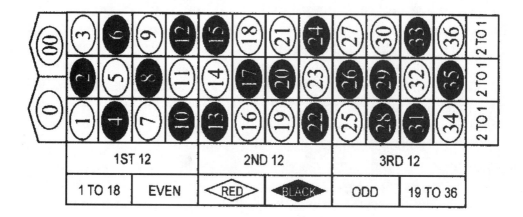

206

FIGURE 1
ROULETTE BETTING LAYOUT

I have not supplied a diagram of a Roulette wheel because I don't have one —and because a few moments observation of a real one will tell you all you need to know. The only difference between Roulette wheels is that some have one zero on the layout and others have both a zero *and a* double zero. How-ever, unless you leave the United States, all wheels will have both 0 and 00. The layouts which only have one 0 are commonly found in Europe. It wasn't until the game was imported to the United States that the layout gained a second zero. Ahhhhh, you just can't say enough about good old American ingenuity . . .or greed. All wheels in the world are the same in that they all have the numbers 1-36, eighteen of which are red, eighteen of which are black; 0 and 00 normally have a green background. The red numbers are 1, 3, 5, 7, 9, 12, 14, 16, 18, 19, 21, 23, 25, 27, 30, 32, 34 and 36. The black numbers are 2, 4, 6, 8, 10, 11, 13, 15, 17, 20, 22, 24, 26, 28, 29, 31, 33 and 35. Consequently, there are 38 compartments on each American wheel, and they are all strategically placed so that no two consecutive numbers lie adjacent to each other. According to the law of averages, each number should come up once every 38 spins. Unfortunately, while the wheel and ball have a deep and very profound understanding of the law of averages, they tend to think only in terms of millions of spins. Which means that while you are standing and watching, or sitting and playing, that wheel and ball may produce rather startling results which have no relation whatsoever to the grand law of averages.

I once spent most of an evening noting the results of each spin at a Roulette table. I did not make any wagers. I simply jotted down the outcomes of each spin. You can do the same. There are no rules against you standing alongside the table, or behind a player, so long as you do not interfere with the operation of the game. In fact, it may be a good way to start. Some casinos will even assist the players by either 1) Providing a pad upon which you can record each number as it is produced by, or, 2) stationing a marque adjacent to the table which automatically records and displays every number produced —usually the most recent number and also the past twenty or thirty numbers —in the exact order they were produced. Mentally, I was betting on number 17, but I did not actually extend a wager. How did I decide on 17? It's the date of my wedding anniversary. It's also Saint Patrick's Day. It just so happens that I was married on Saint Patrick's Day. Which means, kind of automatically, that 17 should also be one of my "lucky" numbers. Except for that particular night. For had I actually been betting on number 17, I would have lost. Number 17 was the result on the fifth spin after I arrived at the table, but it did not repeat again until the 147th spin of the wheel. Had I actually been wagering the house minimum of $2 on a single number . . .this was a long time ago . . I would have made 147 wagers. That would have been $294. I would have gotten back two pay-offs of $70 for a total of $140. I would have lost $154. That's the bad news. Here's the good news. During that same time period, 147 spins, the double zero (00) showed up twelve times, and several people at the table were all over it. One lady had, by my own count, 14 col-

PROTECTING THEIR INTERESTS

The casinos do everything within their power to ensure that each spin is completely unbiased. This means they test the table, the wheel, the balls, etc. often and with regularity. For, you see, if anything happens to fall out of perfectly balanced alignment, the numbers which are produced become biased, and any enterprising gambler can reap huge profits by calculating how the table is biased. According to legend, several casinos have experienced losses in the millions simply because they did not check their wheels often enough.

umns of chips stacked approximately 30 high. Had I wagered on 00 I would have bet $294 and won $840 for a tidy little profit of $546. But 00 was not my number. If the law of averages had held completely true, both 17 and 00 would have been the result about four times each. However, as I've already mentioned over and over again, the law of averages is not based on 38 spins. It is based on millions of spins. Consequently, it is possible to sit at a Roulette table all night without seeing your favorite number appear.

208

Conversely, it is also possible to see your favorite number appear over and over again. And that's why it's called gambling, and that's why this game sustains our interest.

Back to Basics—Again

Your first step is to purchase chips. If you already have chips from playing one of the other casino games, you can use them to make your Roulette wagers, but it is more advisable to purchase Roulette chips; in fact, you may be asked to do so. If three people each bet a red casino $5 chip and one of them wins, who does the dealer pay? How does the dealer know which chip belongs to which player? Avoid this potential problem by purchasing Roulette chips. These chips are designed especially for Roulette, so they look different, each player who buys them receives a different color, and so long as you go no lower than the casino minimum you can establish the value of your chips simply by telling the dealer what you desire.

Example: You are going to play at a table which requires a $2 minimum bet. You want to buy $20 in chips. Depending on the casino's rules, you might obtain (at your request) twenty $1 chips, forty chips worth fifty cents each, or eighty chips worth twenty-five cents each. The dealer may give you orange chips, purple chips or yellow chips, but whichever you receive, you will be the only person at the Roulette table with that color. And the dealer will mark your chips, so there will be no misunderstanding as to whether you are playing with chips worth fifty cents, twenty-five cents, or some other value. Also, when you purchase your chips take a look at the colors being used by the players in action. Unless one of them is already using your favorite color, do

Look for the signs. There is always a sign on the Roulette table which informs you of minimum wagers required and minimum chip denomination. Which, incidentally, could range from a low of ten cents all the way up to the casino maximum. You will not find ten cent Roulette chips at Mandalay Bay in Las Vegas. But you might at the El Cortez.

209

not hesitate to tell the dealer what color you want. They are nice. They will make every attempt to accommodate you.

Roulette chips can only be used at a Roulette table. You purchase them from the dealer and you sell them back to the dealer before you leave the table. *Do not* leave the table with the chips! If you try to take them from one table to another, they will not be honored by the new dealer, because the new dealer does not know what value your chips have been assigned. Also, when you exit the table the dealer will not cash your Roulette chips for real money, but will provide you with regular casino chips like those used at Blackjack and Craps.

Once you have chips, your betting options are numerous, each wager winning or losing on the very next spin of the wheel. Figure 2 is a list of the options, along with the casino's advantage for each bet.

Actual payoffs are what you actually receive if you win. True odds indicate what the payoffs *should be*. The difference between the two is the casino's advantage. As you can see, the Five Number bet is the worst you can place.

TYPE OF WAGER	ACTUAL PAYOFF	TRUE ODDS	CASINO ADVANTAGE
ONE NUMBER	35:1	37:1	5.26%
TWO NUMBERS	17:1	18:1	5.26%
THREE NUMBERS	11:1	11.7:1	5.26%
FOUR NUMBERS	8:1	8.5:1	5.26%
FIVE NUMBERS	6:1	6.6:1	7.89%
SIX NUMBERS	5:1	5.3:1	5.26%
DOZENS	2:1	2.2:1	5.26%
COLUMNS	2:1	2.2:1	5.26%
RED OR BLACK	1:1	1.1:1	5.26%
ODD OR EVEN	1:1	1.1:1	5.26%
1-18 OR 19-36	1:1	1.1:1	5.26%

Figure 2

210

Take a careful look at those numbers and percentages again. As you should know by now, there are other games which offer much less in the way of a casino advantage. True enough. However, look at the very small differences between the actual pay-offs and the true odds. I mean, get real. A bet on Red or Black pays 1:1. It should pay 1.1:1. A difference of only .1:1. That's so close nobody would ever know the difference. Right? Except that when you

> ### WORTH REPEATING
> The smallest casino advantage in Roulette is 5.26%. The highest is 7.89%. Not as good as some games, not as bad as some games. If you're playing for "fun," the percentages don't make any difference. If you're going to be playing regularly, find a different game.

figure out the percentage against you, it's still 5.26% and that's a tough vig to battle. Don't be mislead if anybody tries to tell you that the casino pay-offs are almost exactly the same as the true odds. It may seem that way, but it's not.

INSIDE BETS

Please note that the following bets can only be made on the portion of the Roulette layout which is shown in Figure 3.

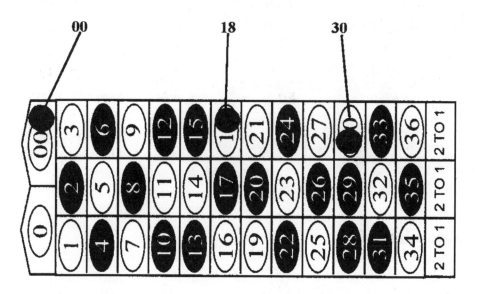

Figure 3

The reason these bets are classified as Inside bets is because the maximum amount that you can wager differs from what are known as Outside bets (described later). As stated earlier, there should be a small sign on the table which describes the minimum and maximum wagers, but if you fail to notice it, or if there is none, simple ask the dealer.

Also, some signs are ambiguous. The fact that a sign advertises a $500 maximum wager does not necessarily mean you can make a $500 bet any place you please. The amount you can wager on an Inside bet varies from casino to casino. Usually, the maximum wager on a One Number bet ranges from $25 to $50. However, a $25 bet on a single number would pay $875. Obviously, if the casino allowed $500 wagers on single numbers, where the payoff would be $17,500, a person on a lucky streak could quickly force a closing of the table.

211

BIG FISH, LITTLE FISH

When I say that the maximum wager on a single number is $25-$50, I'm referring to the wagers made by us common folk. Us little fish. If there's a big fish at your table, though that would be highly unlikely, don't be surprised to see single-number wagers in the hundreds of dollars. Highly unlikely, because big fish would normally have the table reserved only for themselves.

Also, if you are playing at a table which advertises minimum wagers of $5, you must make bets totaling $5. You are not required to wager the entire $5 on only one type of bet. If you were playing with chips worth fifty cents, you could make ten different bets. In other words, your $5 could be spread all over the betting layout. All the following are Inside bets:

One Number

Figure 3 shows three different One-Number bets (00, 18, and 30). Simply make sure your chips are clearly placed within the boundaries of the number or numbers you select. No, this does not mean that every single bet must be squarely in the middle of the boundaries for the number you have selected. But it does mean you should place your chips as close to the center of the boundaries as possible. If even a portion of your chip is covering a line, your bet could be misconstrued.

Since there are 38 numbers on the betting layout, there are 38 different ways to make this bet. You can wager on as many numbers as you like, but keep in mind that if you make $1 bets on 36 different numbers you automatically place yourself in a no-win situation because the maximum pay-off you can receive would be $35. As shown in Figure 2, the payoff for this wager is 35:1. If you bet $1 and win, the dealer would pay your $35, and you would still have the $1 bet setting on the table.

Two Number Bets

The two numbers you select must be adjacent. You could not, for example, make a Two-Number bet on 3 and 14 because those two numbers are

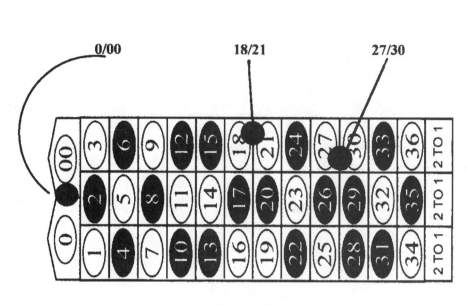

Figure 4

not adjacent. You can only make this wager on numbers which are bordered by one another. Or, put another way, you could bet on yourself and your next door neighbor, or even yourself and that old busybody who lives across the street, but you could not bet on yourself and the cute redhead who lives three streets up the hill. There are 62 different ways to place this bet. Don't believe me? Count'em for yourself. Figure 4 shows three ways, namely the 0+00, or 18+21, or 27+30. The pay-off for a Two Number wager is 17:1.

Three Number Bets

All of the bets in Figure 5 on the following page cover three numbers— .2+00+3, or 7+8+9, or 31+32+33. In all, this bet can be made in fifteen different ways and pays off at the rate of 11:1.

Four Number Bets

The three wagers shown in Figure 6 on the following page are all Four-Number bets—2+3+5+6, or 14+15+17+18, or 26+27+29+30. The pay-off for Four-Number bets is 8:1. In this example, if 5 were the result on the

213

2/00/3   **7/8/9**   **31/32/33**

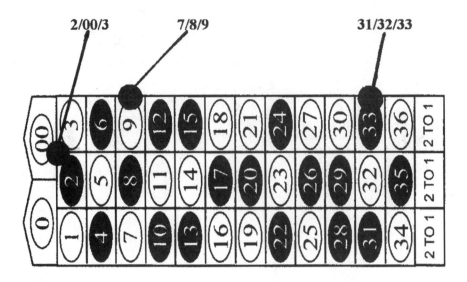

Figure 5

2/3/5/6   **14/15/17/18**   **26/27/29/30**

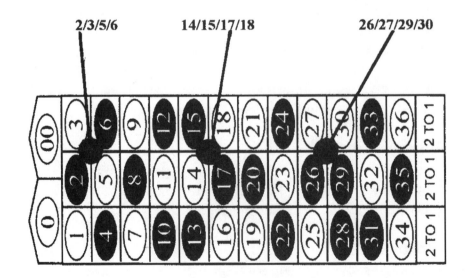

Figure 6

next spin you would be paid twice at 8:1 because 5 is covered by two different wagers. There are 22 ways to make this bet. Is it possible to cover the entire board with Four-Number bets for less than $8? Of course not. If it were possible, the casino would lose money on every spin. And, as we have discussed by now on several occasions, casinos are in business to make money. Or you could also say that casinos remain in business by always retaining an edge . . .on every bet.

Five Number Bets

There is only one Five-Number Bet. It is indicated in Figure 7 and can be made by placing your wager in either of the positions depicted. Now go back and look again at Figure 2. This is the absolute worst possible wager for the player. Winning wagers pay off at the rate of 6:1. The bet covers 0+1+2+3+00. Fine. But what happens if you're sitting way down at the end of the table by the number 35? You can't possibly reach all the way up the top of the table and make this bet. Good. Better to have it out of reach so that you are not tempted. However, if you still persist there is a way. Actually, there

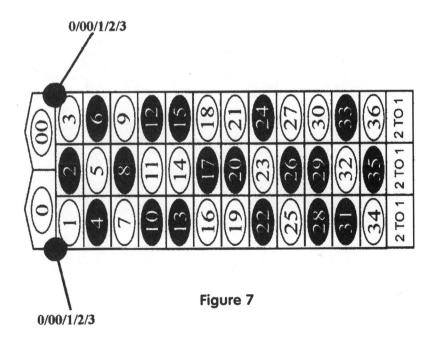

0/00/1/2/3

0/00/1/2/3

Figure 7

are usually several ways. One way is to toss a chip to the dealer along with instructions like "Gimme the five-number bet," or "Please cover zero, double zero, one, two and three with this." Better yet, you might say something like "Hey! I wanna make the five-number bet. Is there a place I can put my chips down on this end?" The answer will be yes, but I'm not going to tell you where. You shouldn't be making this bet in the first place, so if you still wanna try it you'll need to speak to the dealer.

Six Number Bets

There are eleven ways to make this bet, three of which are shown in Figure 8. The chip which you see that is down between the 1 and the 4 covers the numbers 1+2+3+4+5+6. The middle chip covers 10+11+12+13+14+15. The chip stationed furthest to the right covers 19+20+21+22+23+24. Payoff? Five chips for every one you invested, or, for those who prefer another way, 5:1.

216

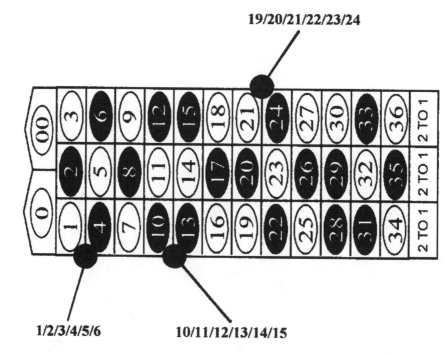

19/20/21/22/23/24

1/2/3/4/5/6   **10/11/12/13/14/15**

Figure 8

OUTSIDE BETS

Yes, yes, yes. Outside bets are all of the wagers which are not Inside bets. If you take the entire Roulette betting layout and remove all of the Inside betting options you are then left with the Outside betting options. So please don't force me to say that these bets can only be made in the portion of the betting layout shown in Figure 9. Thank you.

Half of the Outside wagers are paid off at 2:1, the other half at even money, but you can only wager the table maximum on those which pay even money.

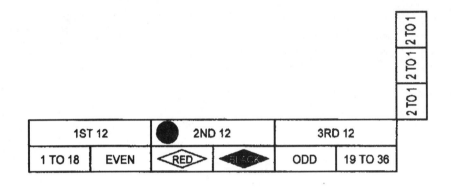

Figure 9

217

Dozens

Does the name give it away? There are only three sets of numbers which you can cover with this bet. Each of them include a total of 12 different numbers. Figure 9 shows a bet covering the dozen numbers which stretch from 13 all the way up to 24. If the bouncing ball lands in 13, 14, 15, 16, 17, 18, 19, 20, 21, 22, 23, or 24 on the next spin, you're a winner. Pay-off is 2:1. Want to think in terms of the casino edge? Well, figure it out. There are 38 total numbers on the board. You are covering 12 of them. There are 26 numbers which can beat you. True odds would be 26 divided by 12 which equals 2.166666666666. The casino pays off at 2.0000000000. So, the casino edge is only that measly little tiny .1666666666. That's the good news. The bad news is that "little" .166666666 produces a casino advantage of 5.26%.

Please note that we're back to the entire betting layout again. While the Outside bets can only be made on the outside perimeter of the betting layout, they represent every number on the board except 0 and 00. We are going to be referring back to Figure 10 several times as we continue

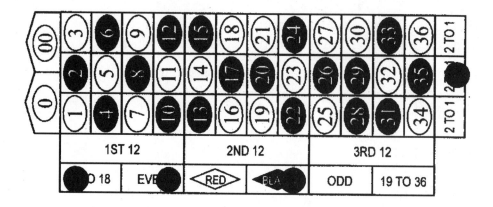

218   **Figure 10**

1-18 or 19-36

I played Roulette a few nights ago on the computer with my 10-year-old granddaughter. She figured something out. She decided that if a person wagered on 1-18 and 19-36 on every spin, that person could never lose. Every time, she explained, you would win one and lose one. She said, in her own manner with a ten-year-old vocabulary, that since there are only two ways to make this bet, and since the payoff is even money, the player cannot possibly lose. Well, the good news is that she has plenty of time to discover the error in her thinking. The bad news is that there are thousands of adults who would agree with her assessment. Unfortunately, those people forget that whenever the outcome is 0 or 00, they lose both bets. Figure 10 shows a bet on 1-18. The chips do not have to be placed exactly as shown, so long as they are well within the boundaries of the 1-18 bet. If the spin produces a 1, an 18, or any number between those two you are a winner. But keep in mind that 18 numbers can win for you, 20 create a loss, and the pay-off is even money. That's all you should need to know.

Odd or Even

Here you again have two choices, both of which pay even money. As long as the outcome of the next spin is an even number, your bet in Figure 10 would win. If the next outcome is an odd number or 0 or 00, you would lose. This is exactly the same situation as what we discussed with the last bet: 1-18 or 19-36. There are only 18 numbers which can win for you, the other 20 create a loss . . . and the pay-off is still only even money. To repeat . . .that's all you should need to know.

Red or Black

Same situation as with the last two bets. In Figure 10 you are playing Black, because that's the way you like your coffee. Does it get any more scientific than that? There are only 18 numbers which can win for you, the other 20 create a loss . . . and the pay-off is still only even money.

Column Bets

Not satisfied with playing only 2 or 3 numbers? Want, or need, more action? Here's a way to quench your number's thirst. Three choices, all of which pay 2:1. Your bet in Figure 10 would win if any of the numbers in that column--2, or 5, or 8, or 11, or 14, or 17, or 20, or 23, or 26, or 29, or 32, or 35 come up on the next spin. Twelve numbers can win for you, the other twenty-six lose. Same situation here that we had with the Dozen's bet a few paragraphs ago. In fact, Columns Bets are just another way of making a Dozens Bet. Only difference is the exact numbers being covered.

THE BOTTOM LINE

All of the betting options which we've discussed can be mixed in any combination you desire. In fact, it is not at all uncommon to see people making a Two-Number bet, a Four-Number bet, a bet on Red, and a Dozens bet all at the same time. However, there are others out there who play only one number at

WORTH REPEATING

Don't get carried away in the excitement or the heat of the moment. A person gets on a little bit of a roll, and starts scattering chips all over the layout. The result? They end up placing themselves in a situation where, even if one of their numbers comes up, they can't possibly win enough to cover all the losers. Common but costly error. Try to make it.

a time, usually the same number, over and over and over again. All of us have tried to cover important dates such as anniversaries, birthdays, age of our kids, etc. etc. etc. The options are both endless and available to all of us. We can wager as much or as little as we like. We can exercise whatever betting options we like. This game can be as elegant and reserved as you have seen in the movies, with men in tuxedos and women in evening gowns casually wagering thousands of dollars in Monte Carlo, or as loud and wild and as uninhibited as often seen in America. But the bottom line is that it is a game which cannot be beaten . . .not over the long haul. Anyone can win over the short term, but the longer you keep playing the greater the possibility that the casino edge, that 5.26%+ will grind you into powder. There are many systems on the market for winning at Roulette and I've tried most of them, either on the computer or at real wheels, with varying degrees of long-term failure. If you play Roulette you will see countless players with pads and pencils tracking the ebb and flow of each number, trying to compress a game of pure chance into something more mathematical and scientific and problematic. Literally millions of man-hours have been spent attempting to forecast the destination of that tiny sphere of plastic. You can visit a well-stocked library and discover hundreds of different betting systems which have been devised to outwit the wheel. The most popular of these would be the Martingale system, which involves both doubling the amount of your wager and adding the initial wager after each loss. It can only be utilized on even money propositions like Odd, Even, Black, Red, etc. The idea is that when you win, you always show at least the amount of your initial wager as a profit. The good news with the Martingale system is that you will always eventually be a winner. Or, not. Let's rephrase. The good news with the Martingale system is that you could always eventually be a winner if the casino would allow you to

220

escalate your bets above the maximums allowed and if your bank roll was un-limited. The bad news is that there is no such thing as a person with an unlimited bank roll, and the casinos, though they might raise the limits on occasion for a high roller, will not allow their maximums to be exceeded by regular folks like you and me. Think about it. Say you start with $5 and make eight consecutive wagers on Black. And Red shows up the first seven times. Check this out:

First wager	**$5**
Second wager	**$15 (double the $5 loss + $5)**
Third wager	**$35 (double the $15 loss + $5)**
Fourth wager	**$75 (ditto)**
Fifth wager	**$155 (ditto)**
Sixth wager	**$315 (ditto)**
Seventh wager	**$635 (ditto)**
Eighth wager	**$1,275 (ditto)**

221

On the eighth wager, the player would collect a whopping $1,275. Yeaaaaa! But here's the problem. First of all, most casinos have a limit of no more than $1,000 on outside or even-money bets. Which means the eighth bet could not be made. Secondly, look at how much money this player has already wagered before making the eighth bet. It's a total of $1,235. Now ask yourself this question: How often would I make a bet of $1,275 in order to win $40? If you are a sane person, your answer is zero times. Thirdly, how much of a bank roll would be required to bet like this through an entire session of several hours? A lot. A real very big enormous huge lot. Fourthly,and worsely . . . yes I know that worsely is not a real word but it fits here . . .what if you lost the eighth wager? Right. You don't even want to think about it. The Martingale. Don't ever let anyone convince you it will work. In fact, don't ever allow anyone to convince you that there is any kind of system which always works at Roulette because there flat out ain't no such thing. The only way to win at this game is through out-and-out blind luck.

SOMETHING TO CONSIDER

As incredible as it may sound, Roulette is the one game which may be better played in Atlantic City than in most other casinos in America, including Las Vegas. And here is why: When betting on Even, or Odd, or Red, or Black, or 1-18, or 19-36 in Atlantic City, the player has an additional option which is very favorable. This option is known as the *en prison* rule. If the player makes one of the even money bets listed above and 0 or 00 is the next outcome, the player has two choices.

1) **The player can "imprison" the bet. This means the bet stays exactly where it is. Then, if the bet wins on the next spin, the bet is returned to the player. Yes, that's two tries for the price of one, but a win on the second try results only in a return of the original wager. But that's good, because otherwise that money would already be in the casino's coffers.**

222

2) **The player may surrender half of the bet. Not bad, but why do it? If the bet was worth making in the first place, it should be worth making again.**

MORE REGARDING *EN PRISON*
Roulette is no different than other games in that if you expect to win you absolutely must make those wagers which carry the smallest casino advantage against you. If you have the option of playing Roulette with *en prison* and you don't use it, you could be rightly thought a fool. Not by me, so don't be angry. Everybody else will think you are. I won't think it, I will know it.

Think of how neat it could be to say *"en prison"* to the dealer each time you have the opportunity to use these options. You could even picture yourself as a French aristocrat and roll the words off your tongue. You might even impress somebody. But that's not why this is such a good idea. The *en prison* option lowers the casino advantage to 2.7%, which makes these bets the best on the layout.

Basically, with the *en prison* option, you're given a second chance; you're given new life. Consequently, most people never surrender half their bet, preferring instead to exercise the *en prison* option. And don't be surprised if the croupier assumes that you will always take the *en prison* option. If your desire is to surrender half your wager, speak up. Speak up clearly. Speak up and make sure you

> ### STILL MORE ON *EN PRISON*
> Why doesn't Vegas offer this option? Is there a catch? Of course. When *en prison* is offered, the betting minimum is usually higher. So, the question becomes which is better? A 5.26% disadvantage on a bet of $5, or a 2.7% disadvantage on a bet of $10? The answer? So long as your stake can handle it, a 2.7% disadvantage is better regardless of the amount wagered.

are heard. If you choose to imprison your bet, the croupier will mark whatever chips you wagered with a small plastic disc to differentiate them from the other bets on the layout. Then the very next spin of the wheel will dictate whether that bet is returned to you or whether the casino collects it.

223

Also, just to eliminate any confusion, please understand that utilizing the *en prison* option does not mean that you always need to stay with the same wager. You can bet Odd this time, await a decision, then bet Black the next, then 1-18, then back to Black, then shift to Red, etc. Simply stay with the even-money Outside Bets.

MONEY MANAGEMENT

My advice for this game is pretty much exactly the same as what I suggested for Baccarat, so what comes next is an abbreviated version of that advice. Consequently, if you already know it and understand it you may want to skip it. However, and on the other hand, you really should read it again and make certain it becomes lodged in both your conscious and unconscious beings.

1) Have a plan. Know what you're going to bet, how you're going to bet, the payoffs, etc. Know all of this prior to your arrival at a

table. There are too many betting options to let all fall to chance. Figure out which betting options you want to play and fully understand them before proceeding.

2) Loss limits. One of the most important elements of a good plan. You must set a "drop dead" number for yourself. When and if you reach that number, you quit. It's as simple as that.

3) Winning Goal. You should set one. And please note that I said "should." If you are going to take this seriously, you must set a winning goal. If this is strictly recreational play time, you should or could set a goal, but that's not necessary.

4) Part of your plan should be to know when to begin Dead Bolting. I don't mean to turn you into a robot, but when you hit X number of dollars in profit a clear bell should sound in your head telling you it is time to start getting some of those chips off the table and into your pocket.

224

5) If you're up as many as ten units, change your unit. If you unit was $10, for example, change it to $20. When you are winning, you must push for all you can. The player most feared by the casinos is the player who gradually increases his or her bets for maximum profits. If you increase your unit and start losing, go back to your original unit. If you win another ten units, increase your unit again.

6) Part of your plan should be to know when to make the "riskier" wagers . . .like the single number bets which pay off at 35:1. The biggest difference between Conservative and Aggressive players in this game is that the Aggressive folks chase the high risk wagers sooner, more often, and with larger amounts than the Conservative player.

7) Always quit when you arrive at your MAXIMUM LOSS LIMIT FOR ANY TWENTY-FOUR HOUR TIME PERIOD. When you're beat, admit it. Give it up. There will be another day.

Once you have finished this book, you should incorporate into your plan every idea you think may work for you in terms of Money Management and method of play. No single plan will work for all people. In the final analysis "the plan" must be "your plan." Perhaps a plan like the one I suggest for Blackjack could be tweaked and turned into your plan for Roulette. Maybe Three Card Poker has something you could incorporate here. Read it, use it. Try it. Keep what works for you and . . .no, don't discard the rest . . .keep it handy just in case you need to retool.

WORDS TO LIVE BY

Once you have earned a decent profit, never let'em win it all back. One of the most feared of all people in a casino is the person with enough self control to quit while they still have profits. One of the most depressed people in the casino is the person walking around with their head dragging on the carpet because they had it and lost it.

12

Slot Machines

I know there are thousands of Slot Machine junkies out there who will disagree with me, but here it is. If you want a gaming venue which can be thoroughly entertaining, which can mesmerize and tantalize, which can make you forget about the troubles at work or at home, which requires only a modicum of intelligent thought process, pick out a Slot Machine and make it your new best friend.

HOW DO THEY WORK?

The basic idea is that you give the Slot Machine money. Then, some times it gives you back some of your money. Some times it gives you back all of your money. Some times it gives you back all of your money plus donations it has collected from other gamblers. And every once in a while it gives you all that plus more money than you thought you would see in your lifetime.

Whether the machine returns any money to you is always determined by the combinations of symbols which appear on the screen, or viewing surface, or picture frame, or viewing window . . .call it what you want. Whether the "right" kind of combinations will appear is determined in a couple of different ways.

THE LURE OF SLOT MACHINES? Small investment, huge return. This is known as the Slot Machine Mentality. Why play Blackjack and receive pay-offs at odds of 1:1, when you can hit a Slot Machine jackpot and collect on odds like 200,000:1? Sound good? Well, if you can't find the fault in that kind of thinking, purchasing this book was a waste of your money. You should have been buying lottery tickets.

REEL MACHINES--THE ORIGINALS

All of the older machines found in casinos are of the reel variety. Your parents or grandparents might have played them when they were known as "One-armed bandits," but that was back when the only way to play was to insert a coin and pull a handle. Back then the first machines were actually shaped like cowboys. Comparatively speaking, that was in the ice age. Like the difference between radio and television.

On Slot Machines, reels are those things which spin and spin and then finally stop, one at a time. The symbols on the reels determine who wins, and with what regularity. Each reel is covered with many different symbols. The symbols could look like staplers, fire hydrants, or tape recorders. I've never seen any of those on a reel machine, but anything is possible. But, I digress. On the majority of reel machines currently located on Earth there are three reels. Each reel contains approximately 20 symbols. Even if you are playing a game which only displays and pays for carrot symbols, there will still be 20 symbol positions. If carrots were the only symbol, there might be 10 carrot symbols on the first reel, 5 on the second reel, and 1 on the third reel. All of the other symbol positions would be occupied by empty spaces. If the reel produces one carrot anywhere on the screen you might qualify for return of wager. Two carrots anywhere on the screen may pay 4 coins, three may pay 10 coins, etc. But the real trick is to get those carrots aligned across the center of the screen (on the Pay Line), all three of them, so you can win, say, 2,000 coins, or maybe even $150,000.

What are the odds of hitting the jackpot? 20 symbol positions on the first reel X 20 symbol positions on the second reel X 20 symbol positions on the third reel = odds of 8,000:1. Over the several million times your carrot machine is played, once in every 8,000 plays it will produce three carrots, one on each reel, perfectly aligned across the center of the viewing screen.

If a machine had four reels, the odds of hitting the jackpot would be 20 x 20 x 20 x 20 = 160,000:1. For five reels the odds would be 3,200,000:1.

Are the odds really that bad? Yes. But does that mean you would need to put 8,000 into a three-reel machine to win 4,000? No. The reasons are two-fold:

1) **When you play a three-reel slot machine you don't know if your coin is the *1st* to be inserted into that machine or the *7,999th*.**

2) **If the machine is set to pay back 80% of the money put into it, you should receive many small pay-offs before hitting the jackpot. You still might have to pull the handle 8,000 times, but it wouldn't cost you 8,000 coins.**

Let's explore this further. Assume you're playing a three-reel dollar machine. The reason you're playing that particular machine is because you saw a sign in front of the casino which stated, "Our $1 Slots Pay 97%." You inter-

229

pret the sign to mean that if you put in $100 you'll get back at least $97. Well, you could be right, you could be wrong. Your first coin could win the jackpot, your tenth coin could win the jackpot, any of your coins could win smaller payoffs, or perhaps *none* of your coins will win anything.

If this dollar machine really pays back 97%, it will return $7,760 for every $8,000 put into it. In other words, the machine will only retain

> **THEY GOTTA EARN THEIR SPOT**
> Each and every slot machine can be thought of as a casino employee. If a person failed to show up for work, was sick too often, did not produce as expected, etc. they might be terminated. Every machine must earn its spot on the casino floor. If it is expected to produce X number of dollars per month, it is held accountable. If it misses too many hours or days due to break downs or malfunctions, it is history.

$240, which doesn't sound like much profit for the casino. But you don't care about whether the casino makes profits, so your question is: Whose $240 will it retain? Yours? The next player's? Who knows? It may very well take $100 of your money and only give to play the machine, it may give back $30 for $1. There is no way to tell who the machine will pay. The machine may experience periods when it retains $3,000 before returning any money. Or, conversely, the machine may experience periods when it generates several jackpots in a matter of minutes or even seconds.

Instead of thinking about what a 97.4% machine might mean to you, think about what it means to the casino. Consider this: A moderately fast player can play fast enough to bring about a result every 7 seconds. That's 8.5 times per minute, which is 510 times per hour. Assume for a moment that the machine receives this level of play for only 8 hours each day. 365 days per month X 8 hours per day X 510 plays per hour = 1,489,200 plays per year. Even if it was only being played for $1 per spin, and even if it was set to return 95% to the players, the casino would retain $74,460 per year. If the pay-offs were set at a max of 90% the casino's take would amount to $148,920. If set at 85% it would be $223,380. At 80% it would be $297,840. Is it any wonder why casinos have so many Slot Machines?

230

> ## MINIMUM RETURNS
> States which offer legalized casino gambling have Casino Gaming Commissions which are governed by Legislatures. Consequently, there are laws. Most places, the law is that all Slot and Video machines are required to return a minimum of 75%. The only reason casinos pay more than the minimum is . . .competition.

Of course the companies which manufacture Slot Machines do not advertise the number of symbols on each reel. The total number wouldn't vary much, but the more often the symbols repeat on the same reel the more often winners are produced. More symbols = less frequent but larger jackpots. Fewer symbols = more frequent but smaller jackpots.

Example. First, you need to select a few symbols. Like footballs, basketballs, and pumpkins. The top prize will be for aligning three basketballs. Your reels will look something like this:

First reel: 9 football symbols, 6 pumpkin symbols, 5 basket-ball symbols

Second reel: 10 footballs, 7 pumpkins, 3 basketballs

Third reel: 11 footballs, 8 pumpkins, 1 basketball

Of course the lowest pay-off in this game would be for footballs because there are so many of them. You have about a 50/50 chance of seeing a football on every reel. Pumpkins are only slightly less scarce. And, for all intents and purposes, basketballs on the last reel are nearly non-existent.

In the old, old days of Slot Machines, the reels were spring loaded and if you knew a little about mechanical stuff and could play with the springs, you could alter the true nature of the results. I grew up with a 1940's era ten-cent Slot Machine in our home. It was so old it actually displayed oranges, cherries, and plums. Friends and relatives loved to play it, for fun, as the dimes were supplied by my parents. When those friends and relatives complained that they never won anything, Dad took it apart and changed the settings so it payed about five times more often than it should.

But then those same friends and relatives decided they should be able to keep some of their winnings. So Dad changed it back. Took him all of about three minutes to perform the operation.

> ## CONFIRM THE COINS INSERTED
> Make sure the machine accepts all of your coins *before* you pull any handles or press any buttons. Coins can pass through the machine and either drop in the metal catcher or be consumed by the machine. You don't want to be hitting a jackpot for two coins when you thought you inserted three. The difference in the amount of the pay-off can be staggering. This type of inattention to what is happening at your machine is the cause of many disputes in casinos. Don't let, or make it happen to you.

231

REEL MACHINES--PRESENT DAY

On the old machines, the number of symbols on each reel, when combined with the natural randomness of a spring loaded mechanism, guaranteed that jackpots and other winning combinations would be produced according to sound mathematical principles. But they could be rigged . . .to pay better, by thieves, or to pay worse, by unscrupulous casino owners. Which is why present-day Slot Machines are governed by the same kind of computer that is discussed in a later chapter on Video Poker.

In essence, a computer microchip determines which symbols will be produced, in what order, and at what time. This computer chip is commonly referred to as the RNG (Random Number Generator).

To simplify, think of the Slot Machine as a computer. It would be good to do so because that's exactly what it is. Think about the computer you have at home or the office. It is programmed to do certain chores. The basic hardware is in there, but it needs instructions in order to perform. That's why you purchase software. Same idea with a Slot Machine, except that the software is designed only for Slot Machines . . .more specifically, the software is designed for the exact Slot Machine game you are playing. The computer is programmed to generate every possible combination of symbols, over and over again. You think in terms of minutes or hours. The computer works in nanoseconds. In the time is takes for you to deposit coins or play credits, the computer may have gone through every possible combination a hundred times.

It is not necessary for any of us to understand how all of this magic occurs, but interesting nonetheless. Each symbol on each reel is represented in the computer by an icon which only computers can read and understand (sorry, but it's necessary to use "that word" here). The computer is instructed to constantly mix and churn these icons so that all combinations are random. Then, at the precise instant that you insert coins or play credits, the computer projects onto the screen one of the 8,000 or more combinations it has been churning. To the computer the icons it has been juggling may look like @&#+%. But when they appear on the screen the symbols look like bars, or cherries, or 7's. Kind of like part of the computer is a universal translator. It thinks in terms of icons but then generates the symbols in a form you can understand.

232

If you are fortunate enough to push the Bet Max Coins button or pull the handle at precisely the exact nanosecond when the RNG is generating a winning combination, you will collect a lot of money.

When these new "computer generation" machines hit the market, they almost failed to gain an audience. People simply didn't like the idea of a computer chip controlling their destiny. They preferred the older machines where the reels looked like reels. They didn't want to

TIMING IS EVERYTHING

Imagine this. In my game a person is pouring thousands of grains of sand out of a bottle. One of the grains is colored purple. If you catch that specific grain of sand someone will pay you $10,000. Only cost you $100 to play. You can only grab with your thumb and index finger, and you must close your eyes before we begin. Get the general idea? The only way you could possibly do it would be if your timing were perfect. Yet, if you keep trying over and over, sooner or later you will win the $10,000. The only question is: At What Cost?

233

watch a video representation of reels, they wanted the reel thing. Consequently, what you see now on the reel type machines is actual reels which are governed by a computer chip. In business, you would call this a win-win situation. People wanted reels, they have reels. Casinos wanted the more reliable computer chip, they got the computer chip.

LET'S PLAY

First stop, a slant top. It's a RED, WHITE, & BLUE. The colors refer to the symbols. In order to win the jackpot for this machine the symbols must be, in exact order on the pay line, RED 7 + WHITE 7 + BLUE 7. Why these colors? Because they are patriotic, and there's nothing more patriotic than playing . . .well, maybe not.

You slide into the vinyl covered swivel chair which is attached to the machine, rest your elbows on the padding which borders the front of it, and slip $20 into the currency slot. The machine racks up 80 credits because you're playing for quarters. You, wisely, take a moment to study the machine and the pay-offs. The first thing you note is that just above the padding along the front, and also just below the viewing area which displays the symbols, there are two small buttons over on the left side.

You've already played a little Video Poker, so you assume the Cash/Credit button is what to push when you're ready to cash out. Bet One Credit is fairly obvious. Then, to the right side are two more buttons which you couldn't miss if you were blind.

Both are larger than the buttons on the left.

234

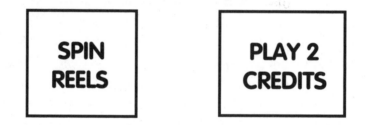

Spin Reels means exactly that. If this is a 2-coin machine, you could hit the Bet One button twice, and then engage the reels by depressing the Spin Reels button. If this was an upright machine, you could also pull or yank the handle located on the left side of the machine's armor. Should you prefer faster play, simply push the Play 2 Credits button and the machine will both deduct two credits from your total and set the reels spinning.

You then note that on the viewing screen, just to the side of the actual symbols, there are several messages printed in small type. The first says: *Machine pays up to 1,000 coins, all other wins paid by attendant.* And that's okay. You don't care how you collect the money, so long as you do collect the money. There's also a number which appears to be glued on the screen, up in the left hand corner, which says: *41178*. That's the number of this machine. It is vital to the casino's accountants, but meaningless to you unless you want to make sure you play exactly the same the next time. Then more small print: *Malfunction voids all plays and pays*. Which means that if the machine performs any action that is not part of its programming which produces a winner the casino need not honor the pay-off. This, of course, is merely a technicality. Until you play a machine which malfunctions.

The Pay Line is clearly identified across the face of the viewing screen. You can't miss it. It's in the exact middle of all those symbols, and the line is connected to the printed word, Pay Line. Then more verbiage. *Pays on center line only, only highest winner paid*. Which means that if you are playing a machine with "wild" symbols which can substitute for any needed symbol to make a winning combination, only the highest possible pay-off will be paid. This is like Video Poker in that if you hit a Royal Flush, you only get paid for a Royal Flush, even though a Royal Flush is also an Ace-high Straight Flush.

There's also a sign on the machine which identifies it as being a quarter machine. You know it's quarters because you already have money in it, but you should never insert the money until after you scope out the machine, so,

235

technically speaking, you already screwed up.

The pay-offs for all the winning combinations are printed some place on the machine. There are two columns of pay-offs because you can play either one or two coins. If there were three columns of pay-offs you would know that up to three coins at a time could be played.

The smallest pay-off is for

MY MACHINE
You play a machine for thirteen hours. You finally give up. Or, you need to visit a bathroom and there is no attendant to "watch" your machine while you're gone. You leave. You come back and somebody else is there collecting a $3,000 jackpot. You scream, "That's my machine!" Wrong. If you leave it, it is no longer "yours."

three Blank Spaces. So if you spin and no symbols show up on the Pay Line, you get back your bet. A one-coin bet returns one coin, a two-coin bet returns two coins.

Then there are a series of combinations based on whether you produce a series of single bars, double bars, or triple bars.

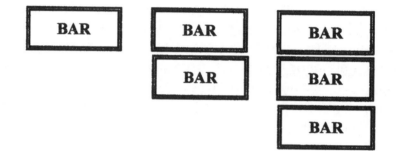

Each of the bars is black, with either red, white, or blue markings. Cross your fingers and hope that you see a lot of bars, because they generate the smaller pay-offs which are going to keep you going until you hit the jackpot. Pay-offs for various combinations of single, double, and triple bars run from 5/ 10 to 50/100. Then the 7's kick in. They look like big, bold 7's and they come in your basic red, white, and blue colors. Any three of them, regardless of color, pays 80/160. Three blue 7's all positioned exactly on the Pay Line are worth 150/300. Three white 7's pays 200/400, and three red 7's pays 250/500. To attain the jackpot, you need to line up a Red 7 + a White 7 + a Blue 7 in exact order, reading from left to right, on the Pay Line. The pay-off for one coin is 400 coins, the pay-off for 2 coins jumps to an incredible 5,000 coins.

236

> ## PLAY MAX COINS
> **Don't ever feel the need to hate yourself because you hit a jackpot with only one coin in the machine. If you can't afford two coins at a time with dollars, drop down to quarters. Or nickels. Or find a machine on which the pay-off for a two-coin jackpot is twice that of a one-coin jackpot. Jackpots happen. The next one could be yours.**

You note that all the pay-offs are in proportion to the number of coins bet, until you hit the top. One-coin jackpot = 400 coins. Two-coin jackpot = 5,000 coins. Which is meant to tell you something. If you're going to play with the idea of hitting the jackpot you had better play two coins on every attempt.

You proceed to play two credits by hammering the Play 2 Credits button, you catch a combination of bars which pays 20 coins, and you note another section of the machine, off to the right of the main screen, where there is activity. First, there is a digital tabulator which has just posted the number 20 below a sign that says "Winner Paid." That's the machine's way of confirm what you won. Also, there is another tabulator which has just climbed to 98. Next to that number it says "Credits." This is where the machine will keep a running tally of your total credits. The reason you have 98 is that you started with 80, bet 2, then won 20, which should mean your total is 98, and that's what it is so everything is copacetic. There's also another little box which says "Coins Played," which is confirmation of the number of coins or credits registered for that spin. Had there been reason to dispute the spin, or the results, or the credits, or anything else, the computer keeps a minimum of 25 spins in its memory. The casino's Service Technicians can access the chip and either prove or disprove your claim. You already know you can't fool Mother Nature, so think of the computer chip as an electronic version of her mentor.

237

PROGRESSIVES

You finally leave that Red, White, and Blue. But you truly enjoyed playing it and you've got the symbols and pay-offs pretty much memorized. And toward the end, when the machine began to eat your credits without so much as an occasional thanks, you turned your head and caught sight of yet another Red, White, and Blue. So when you finish with the first one you wander on over to check it out.

It's quarters. Apparently a twin of the one you just left. Same symbols. Identical pay-outs. Buttons are in exactly the same places. Still requires two coins for the jackpot, which is . . .the screen doesn't show an amount. On the first machine the pay-off was 400 for one coin, 5,000 for two coins. This one . . .you glance up and feel it necessary to blink because the sign is so bright. How in the world could you have missed it? There is a huge marque parked above an entire roll of these machines. You've read this book, so you immedi-

Slot Machine jackpots which never change are referred to as Fixed Jackpots. Those with a jackpot which steadily increases until hit are called Progressive Jackpots.

238

ately recognize that you are standing at a Bank or Carousel of machines. A Bank could be any number of machines lined up in a row, back-to-back. A Carousel would be a series of machines placed so that they form a race track shape. The marque is advertising that the jackpot is currently $7,456 and climbing every second. You are standing at a Bank of Progressive machines. All of them are hooked into the marque. Not all of the 12 machines in the Bank are the same, but any of them will pay the Progressive amount if you can produce a jackpot spin. Some of the machines are basic Double Diamond, there's a few Black Ties, but most of them are the Red, White, and Blues like you just left behind.

Being astute, you wonder, but only for an instant, why you weren't playing here in the first place. Same machine, same everything except that the jackpot pays over $7,000 instead of a measly 5,000 coins. Fortunately, you already know the answer. You merely needed a few seconds to focus. You know that what the casino giveth with the right hand, they taketh back with the left. You know that a Progressive doesn't pay *better*, it simply pays *differently*. Remember? Higher jackpots = fewer winning combinations. Lower jackpots = more frequent winning combinations. This Progressive reached $7,456 because? Of course. It's reached this level because no one has hit it in so long the machines may have forgotten how to produce a jackpot winner. This Red, White, and Blue that you're staring at pays exactly like the old one. So how does the jackpot get so big? The machine retains more in winnings, which it dumps into the fund which finances the huge Progressive jackpot. On the old RWB you would see bars on the center line about once every 20 spins. Now you're going to see bars about once every 45 spins. The $20 that lasted for an hour on the "normal" RWB may only last thirteen minutes at this Progressive. Or, it could win you $7,45- . . .oops, it's already increased to $7,458.

Is there a "good" time to play Progressives? Absolutely. In fact there are a couple of prime times. The first would be: You are a once-a-week regular player. You always check the Progressive jackpots. The Progressive on your RWB normally gets hit before reaching $6,000. You walk in one day and it's at $11,000. Guess what? It's time to play it. It's just like the lottery. If you play it for $1 every week when it's at $1,000,000, isn't it worth $5 when it climbs to $10,000,000? Of course it is. And the higher it gets the faster it builds, because more people play more often. Same idea with Progressives.

MULTIPLE PAY LINES

Multiple Pay Lines = Multiple Coins Deposited. Some machines have 3 Pay Lines, all horizontal. Some have 5 Pay Lines, including the 3 horizontal plus two diagonal. Some have even more. Here's another formula. Increased Number of Pay Lines does not = Increased Winnings. More winners, yes. More coins, definitely. Increased winnings? Not unless you are lucky.

The second reason for chasing that Progressive would be: You've played yournormal RWB. It was awesome. You couldn't lose. You started with $20 and hit everything on the schedule at least twice, plus the jackpot. Was it the machine, or was it you? Was it good timing, or are you "hot" today? One way to find out. Attack the Progressives. If you're hot you want to be playing for maximum pay-offs. If you're not, the machines will tell you.

239

WANT A WILD TIME?

Some machines have a symbol which is wild, meaning that symbol can substitute for any of its cousins. A good example is the Double Diamond Slot Machine. It can be played with nickels, quarters, or dollars. In exclusive VIP rooms it is common to find the $5, $25, $100, and even $500 variety. It can be found in both the two coin and three coin versions. The only difference between the two coin and three coin games is that on the three coin games the button says Play 3 Coins instead of Play 2 Coins. Lower pay-offs start with cherries. Then the pay outs move up the scale with bars (singles, doubles and

COLLECTING ON A PROGRESSIVE

Not all progressive jackpots are paid in cash. Read the fine print on the advertisements. While it is possible that the casino could provide you with $250,000 in cash or by check, it is even more likely that they will pay you in 20 equal installments of $12,500. Just like the annuities paid by most state lotteries.

triples), then up to red 7's. So, cherries, a variety of bars, and red 7's. But the key to the game is the other symbol, the one for which the game is named. It is somewhat oval in shape and twin diamonds are displayed within its boundaries. If you manage to line up three of them on the Pay Line, the pay-off is 800 for one coin, 1,600 for two coins, and 2,500 for three coins. In addition, this Double Diamond symbol serves as both a "wild" symbol and a 2X multiplier. If, for example, you had this symbol on the first reel and a pair of triple bars on the middle and right-side reels, then the machine reads it as another triple bar and you collect twice the pay out for three triple bars. If the pay-off, depending on whether you played one, two, or three coins or credits, for three triple bars is 40/80/120, then you will collect either 80 coins or 160, or 240.

Three of those big, beautiful red 7's ordinarily returns either 80, 160, or 240 coins. But if you catch them in any two of the positions and a Double Diamond in the other, you will be paid either 160, 320, or 480. And it gets even better.

Whenever you have two of the Double Diamond symbols on the center line, they are both wild, and they become a 4X multiplier. You've probably already got this figured out, but here's an example, anyway. You catch twin Double Diamonds and a double bar. Normal pay-off would be either 25, 50, or 75. But you've got three coins in and twin Double Diamonds on the Pay Line with that double bar, so your pay-out is four times the normal. You would collect 300 coins.

If you think wild cards and multipliers sound interesting, seek out the 5X and 10X machines now in vogue. Same idea as with Double Diamonds. Except that if you get a 5X symbol as part of a winning combination it increases the pay-off by five times. If the winner would have paid 50 coins without the

5X symbol it will pay 250 with it. Two 5X symbols as part of a winning combination increases the pay-off by 5 times 5 = 25X. If the winner would have paid 50 coins without the two 5X symbols it will pay 1,250 with them.

The 10X machines work exactly the same way. One 10X symbol as part of a winning combination increases the pay-off by ten times. If the winner would have paid 50 coins without the 10X symbol it will pay 500 with it. Two 10X symbols as part of a winning combination increases the pay-off by 10 times 10 = 100X. If the winner would have paid 50 coins without the two 10X symbols it will pay 5,000 with them.

VIDEO SCREENS—THE FUTURE IS NOW

Forget reels. At least real reels. Reels have a limit. Due to their size there is a limit to the number of symbols which they can exhibit. It's a physical thing. That's the first problem. As you already know, fewer symbols = more frequent pay-offs. If you own a casino and you want people chasing huge, spectacular jackpots, you must increase the number of symbols on the reels.

Second problem. If you're a Slot Machine living in, say, 1998, you've got one eye looking over your shoulder. Your main competition, those darn Video Poker machines, are gaining in popularity. They are interactive. You are not. If something is not changed, you will no longer rule the roost . . .you will soon be playing second fiddle . . .you will be (fill in your own cliche). And then in 2000 it happens. The Video Poker machines start passing you. You're in the right lane doing the posted speed limit and they are in the passing lane doing fifteen over. If your driver doesn't begin to accelerate, those Video Poker machines will soon be blips on the horizon.

Solution. Use the Video Poker concept. Provide a screen . . .like a television or a computer monitor. Dump the idea of real reels. Give'em video reels. Yes, you know this idea was not very well accepted by gamblers back in the 80's, but there's a different generation, a younger generation playing now and they were raised on computers. With video reels the possibilities are nearly infinite. Thirty symbols per reel? No effort required. Forty symbols per reel? The computer's pulse hasn't changed. Fifty symbols per reel? Causes no drain or alarm. Okay, then why not a hundred symbols per reel? Exactly, sir, why not? You want'em, you got'em.

Still, Video Poker machines are interactive. They are dynamic, Slot Machines are static. Any way to change that? Not precisely, but the computer can certainly make it more exciting.

The result? Machines which are twice as tall as the older models. Machines which display a normal view screen plus a "top box," an extension which flashes pictures or images, or even animated characters, spins like a roulette wheel, or whatever. Only three reels. Only three quarters. Basic pay-offs which are similar to the older machines, plus progressive jackpots exceeding a quarter of a million dollars. New machines which raise the player entertainment values to new levels with interactive bonus experiences. Play multi-coins and multi-lines. Forget the concept of playing up to 9 lines at a time. This computer can do 20 while providing players with a multimedia experience which includes outstanding 3D high- resolution graphics, increased sound capabilities and sound effects, better speakers, larger screens. Games which feature a larger cast of characters, all poised to dazzle the players. Innovation and technology which take Slot Machines to a new level with state-of -the-art game designs.

242

Coins striking a metal catcher are intended to be loud so that fellow gamblers know somebody is collecting. Jackpot music, lights and sirens are intended to notify the rest of the casino that somebody is winning a lot of money!

Interactive? Perhaps an exaggeration. More interesting? No question. All of these games work pretty much the same way, so let's consider one of the first: Wheel of Fortune. For the first four feet up from the floor, this game is identical to every other Slot Machine you ever saw. But it has another 3 feet built onto the top. That part is called the top box. In the Wheel of Fortune game the top box houses, literally, a Wheel of Fortune. It is a wheel which spins in certain circumstances just like the one on the very popular television game show. The lower game plays just like normal. There are little pay-offs for certain symbols, large pay-offs for other symbols, but every time a SPIN symbol appears, lights flash, music sounds, and you qualify for a bonus. You hit the SPIN symbol which is found on the machine's chest, which sets the Wheel Of Fortune spending. But there is no Lose A Turn, or Bankrupt. The Wheel of Fortune is all about awards. There is no down side. When it stops, you will win from 20 to 1,000 coins. In other words, it's a Slot Machine inside a Slot Machine. You still need three of the Wheel of Fortune symbols to qualify for the jackpot, but the bonus SPINS can keep you playing for hours. The music becomes slightly tedious after the first fifty or sixty times you hear it, but fun nonetheless.

Another "interactive" game is Wild Cherry Pie. But now a task must be performed in order for you to qualify for a bonus. They are usually found in both quarters and dollars, and require three-coin deposits to qualify for bonuses and jackpots. The top box shows a small screen which is filled with the picture of a pie. Every time a Cherry appears in the lower game, a Cherry is added to the Pie. When the pie is full the very next Cherry ignites the pie and provides the player several hundred coins. Best time to play? When the pie is over half full. In addition, there is a Cherry basket also shown on the mini-screen. It sets off yet another bonus when full of Cherries.

There are also games like Empire Deluxe, where a certain symbol provides the players with the opportunity to help a gorilla climb up the side of the Empire State Building. When the gorilla reaches the 70th floor it pays a bonus of 20 coins. At the 90th floor it's 40 coins, at the 110th floor 100 coins. There is a time limit once the gorilla begins to climb, and the player must provide assistance for the gorilla, so "interactive" becomes a more justifiable description. Like the others, you can play all day without achieving any bonuses, or you can play for ten minutes and spend nine of them climbing the Empire State Building.

WHEN ARE NICKELS NO LONGER NICKELS?

The answer? When you play 45 of them on each round. That's $2.25. That's called TURNING NICKEL PLAYERS INTO DOLLAR PLAYERS, and it is by far the fastest growing segment of Slot Machines. For fiscal 1999, Nevada casinos won over $1,000,000,000 from people who were playing nickels. Nickel play represented 38% of the casinos total Slot and Video Poker play. Nickels! The kind where it takes 20 of them to equal a dollar. A nickel is only 20% of a quarter, is only 5% of a dollar, yet nickels represented 38% of the total Slot revenue.

White Tiger, The Gambler, Wild Africa, The Enchanted Forest. They are all the same. Minor tweaks, but the basics are identical. Numerous symbols, all of which are produced by a computer. No real reels. There are reels, but they are of the video graphics variety. There are 9 different Pay Lines, you can play up to 5 coins per line, for a total of 45 coins. You can also play one coin per game and cover one Play Line, but there's no excitement in that.

Sample game. White Tiger. A combination of White Tigers, Elephants, Cobras, a Prince, the Taj Mahal, a Princess, a King, a Queen, A Joker/Jester, a 9 and a 10. The trick is to get at least three of them aligned on a Pay Line. There are 5 columns. I don't want to call them reels because they aren't real. White Tigers are wild and 5 of them on a Pay Line create the largest pay-off. Three White Tigers in the correct positions would pay 500 coins, four would pay 1,000 coins, and all five pays 5,000 coins. But remember what you learned earlier in this chapter. If each of the five columns contains only 20 symbols (no chance), the odds of lining up all five of the same symbol on any Pay Line would be 3,200,000:1. Also, don't forget that one of the reason these machines were invented was because they could produce more symbols per column.

Some of these games offer semi-interactive bonuses, some don't. Yes, it's possible to win $1,250 jackpots playing for nickels. But not one nickel. Many nickels. Many, many nickels. And so many winning combinations, on so many Pay Lines it is bewildering. Worth playing? Absolutely. So long as you are winning. But that advice should come as no surprise.

"MANIA"

Specifically, Nickelmania or Quartermania. Banks or Carousels of machines which are tied electronically to thousands of other machines throughout your city or state. Progressive jackpot. Seldom less than $150,000. Played on normal machines like Double Blackjack, Red-White-Blue, Triple Diamonds, Double Diamond, etc. One Pay Line. One or two coins. A Mini-Mania (small jackpot) paid for certain symbols, a huge Progressive jackpot for certain symbols. There are usually wild symbols, there are usually multipliers. Remember this: bigger jackpots = less frequent small pay-offs. Remember this: What the casino giveth with the left hand they retrieveth with the right hand.

The advanced form of Nickelmania and Quartermania is MegaBucks. Same idea except that now you're playing for a top prize of millions of dollars instead of hundreds of thousands of dollars.

The most interesting thing about the Mania and Bucks promotions: You see it in the papers all the time. MAN COLLECTS $7,000,000,000! WOMAN RECEIVES $500,000! Read the stories. It's usually pretty much the same. Person puts in two coins, and Bingo! Person plays for two minutes and Bingo! Person decides to drop in a few coins while waiting for better half to get out of the bathroom, and Bingo! The similarity is that none of these winners is ever a person who fought those machines for 27 straight hours, or days, or whatever. They are never won by people who put $3,000 into them. They are always won by people who invested less than $20.

WHY MONEY EVAPORATES

You play a machine which is set to return 90% of every dollar put into it. You may win a lot, you may lose a lot, but if you play it long enough, here is a synopsis of what happens to the money you insert.

You put in $100. You might play even more, but the $100 represents your entire gambling bankroll. You have winners, you have losers, you may play all day. But the bottom line is that you cash out with $90. You take a break. You visit the snack bar. Then you begin all over again. You put in the $90 you still have and get back $81. You put in $81 and get back $73. Notice that your bankroll is deteriorating. Over the long term this is precisely what is intended to happen. If you start with $100 and play once a week, it would take over thirty weeks to lose the entire $100. There may be weeks when you will be up $1,000, but if you continue to play that 90% return machine you should be out of money in a little over thirty weeks. That's the bad news. The good news is that if it takes that long for you to lose $100 you should count your blessings. Had you joined the casino's Slot Club you would have earned more than $100 in free cash or food.

HABITS AND SUPERSTITIONS

You see some of this at other games. A Blackjack player may carry a talisman of some sort. A Craps player may only want to stand at one position on the end. The lady playing Baccarat won't allow anyone to sit on either side of her. A Roulette gambler plays red only when the sun is shining, black only after midnight, and would never consider placing a chip on 13. Slot Machine players? They take the proverbial cake.

Like the lady who won't gamble unless she has her stool situated precisely between the two machines she is playing.

The person who always closes his eyes every time he pulls the handle. The person who hits the Play 2 Credits button, then pivots in a circle which lands him back face to face with the machine just in time to see the last reel come to a stop. The person who refuses to use the currency acceptor and will only purchase coins from Janet.

The man who progresses from outlandish to just flat stupid. Always uses the Play 2 Credits button exclusively. Nothing silly about that. In the early rounds he depresses the button by striking it softly with thumb. If he is winning, he continues to use the thumb. If he is losing, he switches from his thumb to the palm of his hand. Still okay. If he continues to lose the progression includes his elbow, then his nose, and then his forehead. Wacky? Fortunately, he plays at the same casino all the time and they are accustomed to his unusual habits. Still, when he gets to the nose stage the security folks are soon at his side. Which, I discovered, was for the casino's protection as well as his own. Seems he got carried away one time while using his forehead and bloodied the machine so bad they had to disinfect it.

> ### WORTH NOTING
>
> If you ever have the good fortune to hit a jackpot, *do not* play the machine again until *after* you have received your total prize. The machines are supposed to "freeze" until an attendant pays you off and releases it, but why take any chances? Also, if you hit a jackpot *do not* leave the machine. Call for an attendant, scream for help, yell until you're hoarse, but do not leave the machine. The casino won't try to cheat you, but other gamblers might.

Another lady plays uprights, and slumps her head over the base of the machine so that the symbols are hidden from her view. She plays by using the Bet Max Credits button on her favorite machine. She assumes the position and never raises her head until notified by the machine that she has a winning combination. On larger pay-offs her machine starts playing "You're In The Money" and the digital tabulator noisily adds credits to her total. On smaller pay-offs there's no noise but the digital tabulator still makes a racket when it adds the credits.

An older gentleman only plays while wearing white gloves . . .on the wrong hands. Left glove on right hand, and vice versa. Usually totes five or six pair, but stays with any pair of gloves which is helping provide winners. I've seen him toss away perfectly clean gloves after losing less than $20. And when he spins to riches, he turns to anyone standing nearby, thrusts out his hands showing the palms, like a song and dance man, and says, "It's all in the hands! I've got magic hands!"

Another man shoots pretend six-shooters into the air to celebrate even the smallest of pay-offs. Of course he also provides his own sound effects.

The man who buys in for $100 worth of quarters, dumps them all into a coin cup, then starts at one end of the casino and plugs two or three coins into every quarter machine he can find. One try per machine, win or lose. Stays on the move with this frantic look on his face, like he's afraid he'll run out of machines before he runs out of quarters.

> ## DON'T TOUCH IT!!!!
> When you have the good fortune to hit a jackpot, do not play the machine again until you have been paid. The machines are designed to "freeze" the symbols when a jackpot is produced, but why take any chances on screwing it up? Also, do not leave the machine until you are paid. Call for an attendant, scream for help, yell until you're hoarse, but do not leave the machine. The casino won't try to cheat you, but other gamblers might.

247

An older lady says, "This one is from me" on all odd-numbered insertions of coins, and "This one is from George" on all even-numbered insertions. If her coins produce a winner, she takes full credit by saying something like,

"That's mine. That's all mine." She doesn't turn her head, so I can only assume she is speaking to the machine. Naturally, as you might expect, if a pay-off shows up on one of George's insertions she usually says something like, "There you go again, George! Don't be so greedy. That should've been mine."

STRATEGY

There is no such thing as Strategy when playing Slot Machines. Well, almost none. There are a couple of things you can do prior to your arrival at the casino. One, decide whether there are specific types of machines you will be seeking. Two, decide whether you will be playing for jackpots, which means always playing max coins, which means your bank roll may not last as long as you would like. The reel strategy for Slot Machines is all about money management. So keep reading.

248

MONEY MANAGEMENT

Would any intelligent person play a game in which the casino's advantage could be 25% or more? Remember Baccarat? A bet on Banker's gives the casino an advantage of only 1.2%. If you compare Slot Machines against a bet on Bankers, your chances of winning are nearly seventeen times greater in Baccarat. A bet on the Pass Line in Craps has a fourteen times greater chance of winning than a bet in a Slot Machine. So, the question becomes, why do people play Slot Machines?

You know the answer as well as I do. People play Slot Machines because they are fun, addictive, and offer huge payoffs. Even though you know it's unlikely that you'll win, there is still the outside chance for riches. Or maybe you'll become addicted to the graphics, or the sound of coins being dropped into a metal catcher, or

Tournament play is low cost to enter, fun, great prizes, free food and/or even rooms. The bad news: Designed to get you in the casino and keep you there.

the overwhelmed sensation which can be ignited by ringing bells, flashing lights and even blaring sirens. Or, worse yet, maybe you're one of those super-competitive people who just won't quit until they've beaten the unbeatable.

The best money management advice is not to exceed your limits, but I realize that's too basic. So, here's more food for thought.

Form a Plan. This could be part of your Strategy, but whether it is or isn't is not important. What is important is that you analyze all the dynamics which will be at work. Think about how long you're going to be in the casino. Will it be for a few hours or for several days? What will be the length of your gambling sessions? How many gambling sessions will time permit? How much will your bank roll allow per session? What specific types of machines will you be playing? How much are you willing to risk, per machine? Is your preference to play one machine for as long as possible, even when you are losing? Will you have a Winning Goal, or are you merely playing for the enjoyment derived from it?

Earlier in this book, I suggested the idea of separating your bank roll into "fun" money and "serious" money. Twenty years ago I would have also suggested that no more than half of your 'fun' money be used at Slot Machines. But times have changed. There are now hundreds of thousands of gamblers who play nothing **but** Slot Machines. There is more competition in the casino business. The percentage return on machines is inching ever upwards. Overall, you have a better chance of winning while playing Slot Machines than you did in years past. However, you still must exercise self control and you still must manage your money effectively.

So what's the financial strategy? Remember the guy who started at one end of the casino and deposited two or three coins into every quarter machine he could find? If you take my advice you'll be more like him than you might have thought.

First, let's clarify. You will only be playing machines which require three coins or less to hit the jackpot. You will always play with maximum coins. You will begin by playing only those machines which offer a Fixed Jackpot. You will only be playing those machines whose jackpot is less than $1,500. In other words, you will be positioned so that you give yourself as much chance as possible to play for as long as possible.

249

Now, as preposterous as it may sound, my advice is that you never stay at any one machine longer than the time it takes the machine to eat:

$5 if you are playing nickels.
$10 if you are playing quarters.
$20 if you are playing dollars.

Think about it. $5 worth of nickels is 100 of them. If you're playing a machine which requires 3 coins, you can try it 33 times before moving on. And that's if you have no winners whatsoever. But don't be surprised if you can't locate a 2 or 3 coin nickel machine. And if you want to play those 45-coin video specials, we'll get to you, later.

$10 worth of quarters is 40 of them. At a 2-coin machine that's 20 pulls or pushes. If 20 attempts doesn't get you going, move on.

$20 in dollar tokens provides 10 tries at a 2-coin machine. Not many, but if you follow my advice you'll find out it's plenty. Dollars normally pay back at a higher percentage than quarters or nickels. You should see winning combinations sooner and with more regularity.

Whether nickels, quarters, dollars or higher, stay at any machine which allows you to do so. You're going to leave if you lose your $5, $10, or $20. If you're not losing, stay.

As soon as you reach your first winning goal, Dead Bolt half of it. Keep playing. If you reach your secondary goal, then either remain at the machine which is paying-off or move up to the next level. However, you must define the next level for yourself. Will you move up from quarters to dollars? Or does moving up mean remaining at quarters and initiating an attack on the Progressives?

If you are losing, continue to move from machine to machine until either of two events occur.

1) **You connect with a machine which allows you to play. In which case you continue to play until or unless the machine changes its mind and drives you away.**

2) **You lose half of your stake. In which case you drop down one level. Dollars drop to quarters. Quarters drop to nickels. Nickels continue to play until 90% of the stake is gone (never let'em take all the money). If you are forced to drop, begin anew. For example. You start with $100 as your stake. You play dollars. You lose $50. You drop to quarters. You start fresh. You begin with a "new" stake of $50 and continue as before. Ditto for quarters. If you continue to lose, quarters drop to nickels and continue playing until 90% of the original stake is gone.**

Obviously, if you start with dollars and need to drop to nickels you will be at least mildly depressed. But you'll still be playing and there is always the chance for a turnaround.

Sound too conservative for your tastes? Too bad. If anything, my plan might be too aggressive. For example. I did not suggest that you always leave a machine which has recouped 50% of what it has given out. What if you stick in your $20, and run it up to $100? If you were conservative, you would keep playing that machine unless the credits decreased to, say, $60, then leave. The aggressive player might keep playing until the machine had reduced them all the way down to the original $20.

If your original stake for this particular session is $100, that's 2,000 nickels! It is also 400 quarters. With 400 quarters you can "test" 10 different machines. If you do so and can't find a way to win, you must be prepared to acknowledge that it just might not be your day. Or, if testing 10 different machines doesn't sound like enough, then start with a larger stake. Ditto for dollars.

Another informal survey result. What did all Slot players feel was the most common mistake they made? They all agreed, nearly 90% of them, winners and losers, that the most common mistake was staying at a machine too long. It was not knowing when to quit. If you follow the plan, you'll know. The hard part is being able to exercise enough self control to actually do it.

Last and least. If you insist on playing those 45-coin video specials, plan on a stake of about $400. Sound like too much? Think about it. If you play for

251

45 nickels for, say, 15 attempts, that's 675 nickels, which is $33.75. If you want to test 10 different machines, or try the same one ten times, you'll need a stake of $337.50. And since you never want to lose your entire stake, figure that $337.50 is 90% of $375. So make it about $400. Other than that, the same rules apply. Leave if losing, stay if winning, Dead Bolt when possible, etc.

13

Video Poker

question. Between approximately 1980 and 1998, what was the
fastest growing gambling venue in America? Here's a small hint.
Look at the title for this chapter. The same casino which had two
Video Poker machines on its casino floor in 1978, now has 100. Casinos which
were large enough to support 20 machines back in the 70's now has on hand
over 500. There hasn't just been growth in Video Poker machines, there has
been an explosion. As we begin the year 2000, Video Poker is the King, Queen,
and Court of gaming venues for the masses.

Why did Video Poker make such gigantic leaps in popularity? Read and
believe.

A) **The only knowledge required to play is a basic understanding of
the rankings of poker hands.**

B) **You can play for small stakes. Nickel machines are plentiful and
every bit as fun to play as quarters or dollars.**

253

C) **The games are interactive. Unlike a Slot Machine, you don't merely push a button or pull a handle. Decisions must be made. Challenges must be overcome. The game requires you to think. There are dynamics at work here.**

D) **It's a little like watching television and the buttons are the remote control.**

E) **No one else can affect your hand. You are in total control of how the machine will be played.**

F) **You are alone. No need to socialize. No need to smile, or laugh at jokes.**

G) **Your mind is completely focused on the machine, which means it is not thinking about problems at work or home.**

254

H) **The top pay-offs are large enough to entice most everyone, particularly when compared to the amount wagered. A bet of 5 measly nickels could return over 8,000 of them. A winning wager on the Pass Line in Craps pays off $1 for every $1 bet. In Video Poker, a wager of five quarters could win over $1,000.**

Sound interesting? Sound tempting? Is there a down side? Yes, yes, and yes.

UNDERSTANDING THE NATURE OF THE GAME

In games like Blackjack, the casino vig can be attacked and even turned in your favor in certain situations. In games like Craps and Baccarat, you're fighting a casino advantage of less than 2% on the prime betting options. With Video Poker you will be up against a disadvantage which could be as little as 0% or as much as 25%. Consider the following.

A hundred people decide to play Video Poker. They all play the same machine. Over several days or weeks each of them deposits $100. That's a total of $10,000.

Fifty of these fine folks lose every penny. They experience winning hands, some large, some small, but they bet back the winners and keep doing it until all the money is gone. Maybe they played for hours or even days, maybe their play time could be counted in minutes.

Forty of this same group walk away from the machines with $50. They leave after losing half of their investment.

Five people enjoy moderate success. They each cash out for $200. They doubled their stake. Good for them.

That leaves only six people. And five out of the six do very well, thank you. Each of them collects $500. Wow! Started with only a hundred and ran it up to five hundred. Wonderful. Time to celebrate.

The Video Poker machines are interactive. You must think, react, calculate, etc. If your brain is dead, stay away.

255

So, now we've covered ninety-nine out of the one hundred people who played,which leaves only one. And how did that person fare? That person won $4,000. That person started with the same $100 as everybody else and played exactly the same machine, but perhaps that person was smarter, luckier, or a combination of the two. All in all, the same as with most games. Lots of losers and a handful of winners.

Now, how about that machine? Consider that $10,000 was put into it and $9,500 was returned to the players. The machine returned 95% of every dollar put into it. It did exactly and precisely what it was programmed to do. Some people caught hands because

YOU AND THE CASINO VIG

How you play the various and myriad hands which will appear directly impacts the casino advantage. Ignorant play = giant sized casino edge. Perfect play = 1/2% in your favor for some games.

they made mistakes; others lost hands due to ignorance or misplays. Most of the big winners were people who made intelligent choices on each and every hand. The machine didn't care. All the machine knew was that it was supposed to give back 95 cents for every dollar it received and it did exactly that. Had it been programmed to return 71.375 cents for every dollar, it could have done that, also. Because it is a machine. It does not get tired. It does not make errors. It goes on, and on, and on, twenty-four hours every day of the year. It's total shut-down time for the year may not exceed an hour. All it needs is electricity and a tiny fan to cool its circuitry . . .it's computer chips. You can beat it over the short term, you may even beat it for several years, but you cannot beat it forever. Sooner or later it will take more of your money than it gives back.

In essence, Video Poker is the same as all the other games. The casino has an advantage. You try to overcome it with skill, intelligence, or luck.

RANDOM NUMBER GENERATOR

256

A microchip has a great impact on whether you will be a winner or loser. The manner in which you play your hands is also of importance, but it is the computer chip commonly referred to as the RNG (Random Number Generator) which provides the opportunity for you to either make the intelligent play or botch the attempt.

You don't need to know what is going on inside the machine. It doesn't make any difference if it's being run by software or miniature elves. Interesting, maybe, but not necessary in order to play.

To simplify, think of the Video Poker machine as a computer. It would be good to do so because that's exactly what it is. Think about the computer you have at home or the office. It is programmed to do certain chores. The basic hardware is in there, but it needs instructions in order to perform. That's why you purchase software. Within certain parameters, the computer will do whatever you ask. You can open one program, let it run, then open another one without interfering with the work of the first. When you print a document, the computer sends the appropriate information to the printer, then continues to work. It does not need to wait until the printer is finished. Same idea with the Video Poker machine, except that the software is designed only for that particular Video Poker game. The computer is programmed to generate every possible poker hand, over and over again. You think in terms of minutes or hours. The computer works in nanoseconds. In the time is takes for you to request a hand, the computer may have gone through every possible combination a hundred times.

It is not necessary for any of us to understand how all of this magic occurs, but interesting nonetheless. Each card of the deck is represented in the computer by a symbol. The computer is instructed to constantly mix and churn the symbols so that all combinations are random. Then, at the precise instant that you make a specific request (like hit the space bar on the keyboard), the computer flashes whatever symbols it is juggling at that moment onto your video screen. To the computer the symbols which represent cards may look like @&#+%. But when they appear on the screen the symbols look like the Ace of Hearts, the Ten of Hearts, the Jack of Diamonds, the Queen of Spades, and the Three of Clubs. Kind of like part of the computer is a universal translator. It generates the symbols in Videopokerese, but displays them as pictures of specific cards that we humans can understand.

If you are fortunate enough to request a hand at precisely the exact nanosecond when a great one is being created, you will be an automatic winner. Or, the computer may supply you with several alternatives . . .it may provide you with cards which create a multiple choice question, the answer to which could be a, b, c, d, or none of the above.

THE BASICS—THE VERY BASICS

You'll know when you see one. In terms of physical shape and form, there are basically three types of Video Poker machines. All look the same in one respect . . .all look like small televisions encased in fancy metal boxes. The most common form is the upright model, and they are usually about 24 inches wide and 48 inches high. Most are propped atop a platform which is about two

> ### SIZE COUNTS
> Quarter machines have openings which will accept nothing larger than a quarter. Dollars are designed specifically for dollar tokens, etc. You might get a nickel or dime into a quarter machine, but the machine will ignore it and you'll never get it back. Same is true for dropping quarters or half dollars into a dollar machine.

feet high. To play this variety you will need a chair or stool and you will be looking directly ahead. Sorta like setting in front of that 13" television you have in the kitchen. The next type is the slant-top version. Usually wider and deeper than the stand-ups. You can sit in a chair and rest your elbows on the front of the machine. You look down at the screen. And the last is the bar-top variety. These are built right into the top of the bar. You sit on a bar stool and look down at the top of the bar.

Whichever you decide to play, here are the common elements.

258

1) All V.P. games have a screen. Call it a television or a computer monitor. It displays the cards and confirms your decisions.

2) There will be, usually on the right side of the machine, a handy slot where you deposit your coins or currency.

3) A pay schedule will be printed somewhere on the front of the machine, or one will be displayed on the screen.

4) There will be several buttons directly beneath the screen. Normally, the furthest over on the left and the one immediately adjacent to it will look like this:

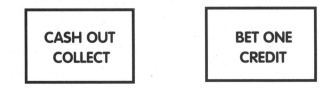

Cash Out is the button you push when you're ready to quit playing. If, that is, you still have any money in the machine. Bet One Credit means exactly what it says. But it could also mean bet two credits, three, four or five. In other words, you may utilize the Bet One Credit button to play from a minimum of one all the way up to the maximum coins. The buttons are usually plastic and lighted from the back so that you can continue to play should all the other lights in the casino go off. Just kidding. They are lighted so that you can see them clearly.

The next five buttons to the right of Bet One Credit are the ones you will use to execute your playing decisions. They look like this:

These buttons correspond to the cards which will flash on the screen above them. If the button over on the left has the Ace of Diamonds stationed above it, and you want to keep it on the screen when you draw, simply hit the Hold/Discard button. If you don't want to retain a card, simply ignore its button. So "Hold" should make sense. But what about "Discard"? Well, go back to the Ace of Diamonds. You want it in your hand. You hit the Hold button. Then you realize that retaining the Ace of Diamonds is not the best way to play the hand. So to let the machine know you've changed your mind, you hit the "Discard" button. That tells the machine you want to trash the Ace of Diamonds and re-

259

> ## CHECK IT OUT
> Game designers like to be creative. So, while the overwhelming majority of Video Poker machines exhibit the exact buttons described on these pages, don't be surprised when you see something different. Cash Out may be on the right. Play Max Coins may be on the left, etc. Ten seconds of observation will tell you all you need to know.

place it with another card. Yes, Hold and Discard are the same button. One holds, one allows you to change your mind.

The last two buttons are usually found over on the right side of the row and look like this:

PLAY MAX COINS	DEAL DRAW

If you are playing a machine which allows you to wager up to five coins per hand(the standard), striking the Play Max Coins button will play five coins immediately, so long as your credit with the machine is good. More on that, later. If the maximum allowable wager is seventeen coins (never heard of it), hitting the Play Max Coins button would prompt the machine to play seventeen coins immediately. The Deal/Draw button is used in a couple of different ways. When you play maximum coins,

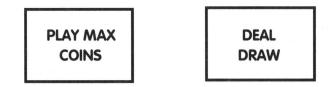

The Play Max Coins button could also read Play Max Credits, or Play 5 Coins. All mean the same thing. The casino, and the machine, want you to be playing for maximum allowable wagers on every hand.

the computer deals the hand as soon as the last coin registers. However, if you play less than maximum coins the computer does not know when you want the hand to be dealt, so you must tell it. If your desire is to play three coins, then insert them and then hit the Deal/Draw button. That's the "Deal" part of Deal/Draw. The "Draw" function of this button is used on nearly every hand. Once your initial cards are dealt, and you've touched the Hold/Discard button under the cards you want to keep, the machine must be told that you are ready to finish the round. You inform it by pushing the Deal/Draw button. And that's the "Draw" portion of the Deal/Draw button.

260

The screen serves many functions. In a manner of speaking, it communicates with you. When you hit the Hold/Discard button, the word Hold appears at the top or bottom of the card you have selected. That's the machine's way of communicating with you. You give it commands, it verifies and then acts out your wishes.

The machine is a prompter. It will tell notify you whenever you have cards worthy of pay-offs by flashing a message onto the screen. Got two pair? Two Pair will be exhibited across the screen in script too bold to miss.

The machine will inform you when the hand is over by posting "Game Over" some where on the screen.

The machine is an inducer. Hand over? The machine will immediately display a sign suggesting you play maximum coins.

The machine will tell you if it needs help. Perhaps a coin is jammed, perhaps there is a malfunction, perhaps it has a circuit which is overheating, etc.

PLAYING WITH CREDITS

Create your own banking account. Provide yourself with immediate access to a line of credit . . .one which comes out of your pocket prior to the beginning of play. Hate having messy, dirty, even filthy hands? Then don't touch the coins. These machines/computers are awesome, but their cleanliness habits leave a lot to be desired. On the outside of the machines people spill drinks and drop cigarette ashes into the coin catchers. On the inside the hoppers (where the money is deposited) are metal and mechanical, which means lubricants and dust. If the coins aren't already dirty when they enter the hopper, they will be on the way out. Play coins for fifteen minutes. Then look at your fingers. Some people actually wear gloves when they play.

Also, even though an experienced coin feeder can load five coins into the machine in three or four seconds, the machine can play five credits in less than one.

So, there are two reasons to play with credits. One, because you don't want to be handling those dirty coins all the time. Two, because you can play faster.

Instead of purchasing coins to play, which was the only option for many years, you can now play with currency. Simply slip your $5 bill, or $10 or $20,

261

CREDITS

Credits are always displayed prominently on the screen, usually in the lower right or left corner. The numbers roll up when you have winning hands, and shrink every time you ask for a new game. Though your computer banker seldom makes errors, it is always a good idea to keep one eye on the tabulator to confirm that your balance is receiving the correct deposits when you have winning hands.

into the bill feeder which is always prominently displayed somewhere on the front or side of the machine. The computer will read the currency and load up your account with whatever credits are appropriate. If, for example, you insert $20 and it's a nickel machine, the computer will post 400 credits. The same $20 in a quarter machine would buy you 80 credits, for dollars it would register 20 credits.

You are establishing a bank account from which you may make withdrawals and into which you can make deposits.

262

Every time you play a game (hand of poker) the computer will withdraw whatever coins you want to play. If you tell it to play one coin on each hand, one coin will be deducted prior to each new deal. Same holds true if you decide to play one credit this hand, four the next, and then three after that. And every time you register a winning hand, the computer will add the appropriate amount to your account.

Want to know how your fellow gamblers are faring? Check out their credits. These days most everybody plays with credits instead of coins. Even those people who begin with coins usually make the switch after their original stake has been deposited. For example, you purchase $20 in quarters. You insert all eighty of them into the machine. Those coins may produce hundreds or thousands of credits, or they may produce none, but usually it's somewhere in between.

So after all the coins are in, you continue to play, but instead of purchasing more coins or cashing out, you utilize the credits which are in your "account."

DEAL THE CARDS

Ready to play? Okay. All the time you've been standing in front of this machine, or monster, or whatever you want to call it, the computer inside of it has been churning through, literally, tens of thousands of possible poker hands. And it's not going to deal a hand until 1) you deposit max coins or 2) you play max credits or 3) you hit the Deal/Draw button after depositing coins or credits. The instant you take any of these actions, it will hurl five cards onto the screen. Some machines are set to play so fast the speed can startle you. Others are set so slow you can become bored.

Now back up. Before you leap into the skirmish, ask yourself a question. Are you sure this is a machine you want to play? There are many different types. Most of the games are played with a standard 52 card deck. A few add Jokers. The pay schedules may fluctuate wildly for the same basic games. Are there certain types you should learn on, others better to tackle after graduation? Depends on what you're after.

In the section which follows you will find descriptions of many types of Video Poker games. Then, later on, you will be provided with basic strategy suggestions. Combine the two. Within certain limitations there are no "right" or "wrong" kinds of machines. Once you're shown the options of the types of games available and have a firm understanding of how to play, the choice is yours.

263

After you decide whether a specific machine is worth your efforts, it's time to deposit money. It's time to begin exercising your options. It's time to activate your brain. It's time to initiate the strategy you plan on utilizing. It's time to win or lose.

All games are the same in that you receive five cards, Hold the ones you want to keep, then Draw additional cards. Whether you win or lose depends on the minimum requirement posted for that particular game. The amount you win depends on the pay schedule. Different games = different pay schedules. We'll start with the "base" game, the one which started it all.

Pay schedules are also called pay tables or pay-out tables.

JACKS OR BETTER DRAW POKER

Royal Flush	250	4,000 coins/credits
Straight Flush	50	250
Four of a Kind	25	125
Full House	9	45
Flush	6	30
Straight	4	20
Three of a Kind	3	15
Two Pair	2	10
Pair of Jacks or Better	1	5

Pay-Offs as shown are based on 1-coin wagers and 5-coin wagers.

Quick perusal of the pay table should tell you why this game is known as Jacks or Better. The minimum requirement for a winning hand is a Pair of Jacks. Pay-offs are shown for one coin because the pay-off shown is the mul-

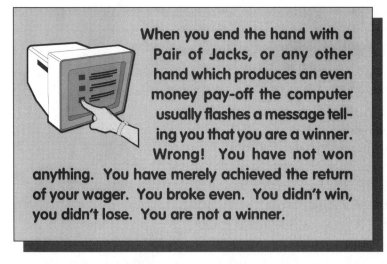

When you end the hand with a Pair of Jacks, or any other hand which produces an even money pay-off the computer usually flashes a message telling you that you are a winner. Wrong! You have not won anything. You have merely achieved the return of your wager. You broke even. You didn't win, you didn't lose. You are not a winner.

tiplier for that hand. In other words, a Straight with one coin played pays 4 coins. A Straight with two coins played pays 8 coins. Three coins would pay 12, four coins pays 16, and, as shown, five coins returns 20. Pay-offs are also shown for five-coins for two reasons. Note that you cannot achieve the maximum pay-off unless you play five coins, or credits. A Royal Flush

264

pays 250 coins if only one is inserted, 500 for two coins or credits, 1,000 for three coins, 1,500 for four coins, and then 4,000 for five coins. If you hit a Royal Flush, that fifth coin is worth another 2,500 on the pay schedule! All of the other hands pay in equal proportion.

Also, I recommend that, generally speaking, you always play max coins. You should always be playing to win the top prize. If you can't afford to play dollars, play quarters. If you can't afford to play quarters, play nickels. Don't cheat yourself out of a full-pay jackpot by wagering with cheap money.

The pay table you see listed is referred to as a 9/6 machine. Spoken, it would be ninety six. Which means that a Full House returns 9 coins per each invested, and

9/6 MACHINE
A 9/6 machine set to return 80% will drive you away faster than a 6/5 machine set to return 95%. Unfortunately, the percentage return is not listed on each machine. So we're back to that same old tale. This is why it's called Gambling. Pay your money, take your chances.

a Flush pays out 6. Focusing on this portion of a pay schedule is an excellent way to determine what you're up against. Don't be surprised to find Jacks or Better games which return as little as 6/5 or as much as 10/7.

Is it always better to play a 9/6 machine instead of a 8/5 or a 6/5? On the surface it would seem so, and all the experts will tell you to never play anything less than a 9/6. And I agree . . .so long as you are playing Video Poker for five or six hours a day, at least one day a week all year long. If you're only going to be playing for a few hours over a long weekend, luck will be such a large deciding factor in winning or losing that the type of machine isn't going to make a lot of difference. Also, what good is a 9/6 machine if you never see a Full House? How good is a 6/5 machine if Flushes are a common occurrence? Would you rather play a 9/6 machine which produces a Full House every 95 hands, or a 6/5 machine which gives you a Full House every 60 hands? Figure it out for yourself. My suggestion? Play them all. Keep playing the ones which provide value for your investment. Avoid the ones that don't.

Fine. Jacks or Better is a nice little game. It kept most of us occupied in the 70's. Then what? What came next to grab and hold our attention?

JACKS OR BETTER BONUS POKER

Royal Flush	250	4,000 coins/credits
Four Aces	80	400
Straight Flush	50	250
Four 2's, 3's, or 4's	50	250
Four 5's to Kings	25	125
Full House	8	40
Flush	5	25
Straight	4	20
Three of a Kind	3	15
Two Pair	2	10
Pair of Jacks or Better	1	5

Pay-Offs as shown are based on 1-coin wagers and 5-coin wagers.

266

Same game. Or, is it? When you played the basic Jacks or Better, the top prize for five coins was 4,000. Same here. The pay-off for a Full House change to 8/40 and for a Flush it's now 5/25, which makes this a eighty-five (8/5) machine, but it could just as easily be a 9/6 or 7/5. The real difference is the addition of two pay outs . . .for Four 2's, 3's, or 4's and also for Four Aces. Either pay more than any other Four of a Kind. Why the change? You. You're the answer. You and people just like you wanted the additional prizes. The basic game was getting old. It needed a little more punch and vitality. Which is the same reason the next two games were invented.

DEUCES WILD

Royal Flush	250	4,000 coins/credits
Four Deuces	200	1,000
Royal Flush w/Deuces	25	125
Five of a Kind	15	75

Straight Flush	9	45
Four of a Kind	4	20
Full House	4	20
Flush	3	15
Straight	2	10
Three of a Kind	1	5

Pay-Offs as shown are based on 1-coin wagers and 5-coin wagers and this is the last time I'm going to tell you!

There are four wild cards in the game, which makes for a lot of changes, the biggest of which is the minimum qualifier. Now you need at least Three of a Kind to get any money back. Full Houses and Flushes don't seem to be worth the effort. But don't forget you're going to see more of them because of the wild cards. There is also a slight variance in the rankings. You can have Five of a Kind. Four of a Kind can pay more than Five of a Kind if they are Deuces. Royal Flushes don't mean all that much unless they are made without the benefit of wild cards.

As is the case with other games, the pay out schedules can and will fluctuate. Both between different casinos and even within the same casino. A Full House may pay 4 coins here, 5 over there, and even 6 down the street. Also note that the paytable offers spectacular returns for the top two hands but then drops off significantly.

267

> **"WILD" CARD**
> A card which can be used as whatever rank and suit you want or desire. If you need a King of Spades to complete a good hand, then the wild card becomes the King of Spades. Need an Ace? If it's a game with wild cards you really need *either* an Ace or a wild card.

Wild cards can make for interesting games. The strategy changes. In fact, the strategy for playing with wild cards is so different that most people prefer to play one or the other exclusively.

JOKER'S WILD—aka—JOKER POKER

Royal Flush	250	4,000 coins/credits
Five of a Kind	200	1,000
Royal Flush with Joker	100	500
Straight Flush	50	250
Four of a Kind	20	100
Full House	7	35
Flush	5	25
Straight	3	15
Three of a Kind	2	10
Two Pairs	1	5
Pair of Kings or Better	1	5

Only one wild card. Bad news is that you won't be seeing Five of a Kind very often. Good news is that you'll be seeing more Straights and Flushes and Full Houses, but you gotta have at least a Pair of Kings or Better for return of wager. Earlier I noted that some people prefer to play wild games exclusively. Here's what can go wrong if you jump back and forth between wild and basic. You play Jacks or Better for two hours. Then you decide to try Joker Poker. You're dealt a hand which contains nothing except one face card—a Queen. You hold the Queen. Wrong! It takes Kings or Better to win. You are no longer playing the basic game. You must change your thinking and your strategy. Now back to the basics . . .the "new and improved" basics.

JACKS OR BETTER DOUBLE BONUS POKER

Royal Flush	250	4,000 coins/credits
Four Aces	160	800
Four 2's, 3's, or 4's	80	400
Straight Flush	50	250
Four 5's to Kings	50	250

Full House	9	45
Flush	7	35
Straight	5	25
Three of a Kind	3	15
Two Pair	1	5
Pair of Jacks or Better	1	5

Increased pay-offs for different types of hands. Meaningful? Only if you are drawing the meaningful hands. When last we saw Jacks or Better it was a Bonus game. Now it's Double Bonus. That's original. I suppose the next progression would be to Double Double Bonus. Well, what can I say. That's exactly the situation.

DOUBLE DOUBLE BONUS POKER

Royal Flush	250	4,000 credits
Four Aces w/2, 3, or 4	400	2,000
Four Aces	200	800
Four 2's, 3's, or 4's w/Ace, 2, 3, or 4	200	800
Four 2's, 3's or 4's	80	400
Straight Flush	50	250
Four 5's to Kings	50	250
Full House	9	45
Flush	6	30
Straight	4	20
Three of a Kind	3	15
Pair	2	10
Pair of Jacks or Better	1	5

Remember what I said about more at the top meaning less at the bottom? Even more true here. The greater the potential glory, the greater the chance for disaster.

STRATEGY

Before we start, please note the following. If you are playing Jacks or Better Video Poker, here are two sets of calculations which you must acknowledge. The first column shows how often you can expect to see each hand, the second shows the same number as a percentage. Both are approximate because even a game of Jacks or Better can vary somewhat.

	Odds to 1	Hit Frequency
Royal Flush	40,0000	0.0025
Straight Flush	10,000	0.0100
Four of a Kind	420	0.2400
Full House	90	1.1500
Flush	95	1.0700
Straight	85	1.1800
Three of a Kind	13	7.5000
Two Pair	8	13.000
Pair of Jacks or Better	5	22.0000

270

Here's how to read this. You can expect to see a Full House about once in every ninety hands, which represents a frequency of a little over 1%. You can anticipate seeing Two Pair about once every 8 hands, or about 13% of the time.

When you move up to Bonus, and Double Bonus, and especially Double Double Bonus games the figures at the bottom end go down because the payoffs are loaded at the top end.

Also, note that a Flush is more difficult to achieve than a Full House, yet still pays less. The reason? I have no clue.

Knowing what to expect when you play should be vital in terms of your planning and your strategy. If a machine does not produce as expected, you may be wasting your time.

Now for strategy. Keep it simple. First, decide how aggressive you want to be. Next, analyze each hand. Finally, execute your decisions. No, I don't mean kill them. I mean Hold the appropriate cards and then hit the Deal/Draw button. Keep in mind that if you play Video Poker regularly, it is actually possible to win consistently. Not every day or every week, but for the month or year. Winning requires perfect play, but perfect play isn't all that difficult to achieve. What you're about to see here will set you on the right path. For more detailed strategies, purchase a book which covers them in greater detail.

> ## READ AND REMEMBER
> Study the pay tables before you play. One of the most important questions to be answered is whether 2-Pairs pay more than 1-Pair. Also, what is the minimum required for return of wager? Knowing the answers to only these two questions can greatly effect your playing strategy.

The strategy which follows applies only to Jacks or Better Poker. The format I'm utilizing has no top or bottom. It does not start with smallest hand and work up, or vice versa in exact order. The question is always Whataya do if? As in whataya do if you've got a Pair of ? but also three to a Flush and four to a Straight? The cards will offer options, you must decide which is the best. Now let's see how far we can get into the alphabet.

271

> ## WINNING WHEN WRONG LOSING WHEN RIGHT
> Selecting the correct option will not always make you a winner, screwing up will not always make you a loser. Perfect play will help over the long term, but does not guarantee perfect results. However, proper play will help you last longer on less money.

A) **Whataya do when none of your first 5 cards match, and none is higher than a 10? Draw all five. Unless you are a madman. Under the guise of being super aggressive in trying to nail the Royal Flush some people would Hold a 10 if there was nothing else in the hand.**

B) Whataya do when none of your first 5 cards match, but one is a face card? Hold the face card and draw the other four.

C) Whataya do if two of your first 5 cards match and there are no other possibilities? Hold the Pair and draw three new cards.

D) Two low Pair in the first 5 cards? Hold both of the Pairs and draw one card. Unless you want to be real aggressive. If so, Hold one Pair and hope you fall into Four of a Kind. Nutsy and bordering on insanity, but aggressive. Get the point so far? I hope so because I'm going to quit referring to the first 5 cards. You always start with five cards. Also, get out a deck of cards as you will probably need one. Deal yourself these hands so you can see exactly what I'm suggesting, and why.

272

HOLE IN THE STRAIGHT

The hole is simply the missing card. If it is some where in the middle of the succession of cards, it is referred to as an Inside Straight possibility. If it's on either end of the succession it's referred to as an Outside Straight possibility. Outside Straights are easier to fill than Inside Straights because there are more cards which can help.

E) Four cards to a Straight with the hole some where in the middle, and no more than two of any suit. Like, 6 C + 7 H + 9 D + 10 S + 3 H. Dump'em all. Draw five new ones.

F) Four cards to a Straight with the hole on either end, and no more than two of any suit. Like, 6 C + 7 H + 8 D + 9 S + King S. Conservative? Hang on to the King. Aggressive? Hold the four to a Straight and draw one card.

G) Four cards to a Flush. Hold all four.

H) Four cards to a Flush along with a Pair of 9's. Like 6 S + 9 S + Jack D + 2 S + 9 H. Conservative? Kill the 9's and go for the Flush. Aggressive? Kill the 9's and go for the Flush.

I) Four cards to a Flush along with a Pair of Queens. Like 6 S + 9 S + Queen D + Queen S + 4 S. Conservative? Hold the Pair of Queens. Aggressive? Kill the Queens and go for the Flush.

J) Four cards to an Inside Straight along with a Pair of 8's. Conservative = Hold the 8's. Aggressive = Hold the 8's.

K) Four cards to an Inside Straight along with a Pair of Jacks. Conservative = Hold the Jacks. Aggressive = Hold the Jacks.

L) Three cards to a Flush, no Pairs, no face cards. Conservative = Discard all five. Aggressive = Hold the three to the Flush.

M) Three cards to a Straight Flush, no Pairs, no face cards. Go for it.

N) Three cards to a Straight Flush and a Pair of 9's. Conservative = Hold the 9's. Aggressive = Hold the three to the Straight Flush.

O) Four cards to an Inside Straight Flush and no Pairs. Go for it.

P) Four cards to an Inside Straight Flush and a Pair of Kings.

Q) Three to a Royal Flush and a high Pair. Like, Jack H + Queen H + King H + King D + 7 S. Conservative = Hold the Kings. Aggressive = Kill the Kings and try for the Royal.

R) Three of a Kind and three to a Royal. Jack D + Jack H + Jack C + King C + 10 C. Conservative = Hold the Jacks. Aggressive = Hold the Jacks. I never said the Aggressive player was stupid.

S) Four to a Royal and a Pair of Faces. 10 D + Jack D + Queen D + King D + King S. Conservative = Kill the Kings and Hold four to the Royal. I never said the Conservative player was stupid, either. Aggressive = you know what.

T) Two Pair. 6's and 8's + a trash card. Conservative = Hold both Pair. Two Pair represents a profit, and there is the chance of filling the Full House. Aggressive = Ditto.

U) Two Pair. 6's and Jack's + a trash card. Conservative = Hold both Pair. Two Pair represents a profit, and there is the chance of filling the Full House. Aggressive = Ditto. Super Aggressive = Hold the Jack's and Draw three cards. Jack's guarantee no loss of money and this player is looking for Four of a Kind.

V) You're dealt a Straight. Hold all five cards.

274

W) You're dealt a Straight which consists of 4 D + 5 D + 6 D + 7 D + 8 C. Conservative Holds all five. Aggressive kills the 8 C and tries for the Straight Flush.

X) Consider this hand. 6 D + Ace C + Ace D + Jack D + Queen D. Analyze. The Pair of Aces represent a pat hand. You can't lose. But you also have four to a Flush. And you also have four to a Royal Flush. The conservative player may keep the Aces. The aggressive would kill the Ace of Clubs and try for the Flush. The super aggressive would kill both the Ace of Clubs and the 6 of Diamonds and try for the Royal.

Y) Same hand as #X. But now you have more information. You started with 80 credits. You've built it up to 300. Same responses? I don't think so.

Z) **Same hand with additional information. You're playing dollars and it's a Progressive Jackpot which is up to $7,555. Same responses? Are you nuts? If you're too conservative to go for the Royal now, you may want to reconsider your strategy and game plan.**

Z1) **You're still playing dollars, the jackpot is still up to $7,555. Now you're dealt 9 S + 10 S + Jack S + Queen S + King S. That's worth $250 if you hold all five. Do you?**

It is not my intent to provide you with answers for every possible situation. All I'm asking is that you think, consider and analyze before acting. If you decide to play Video Poker on a regular basis sit down some night and deal yourself hundreds of 5-card hands. Or buy one of the hand-held games. Or purchase a Video Poker software program for your home computer. Over time, your plays will become automatic. Over time you may be able to distill your strategy into ten or fifteen ironclad rules. You can also purchase several of the books which are devoted solely to Video Poker. Take and use what makes sense. Whatever strategy you use must make sense to you. It's your money, your risk, etc.

Also, adjust your strategy for the game you are playing. Take another look at #X. What if you were dealt that hand while playing Double Double Bonus Poker, where four Aces could be worth up to $2,000. Would that change your thinking?

Go back to "U." If you were playing any of the Bonus Poker games you would never consider keeping both Pair. You would always keep the Jacks and try for Four of a Kind because the pay-off makes it worthwhile to do so.

For Deuces Wild of Joker's Wild, structure a strategy which fits the pay table. If you need two more Kings to make a hand in Deuces Wild, don't forget that there are still two Kings and four Deuces which could help. Consider what you need and whether the cards remaining in the deck provide a decent opportunity. Again, the strategy you utilize should be structured to fit the game you are playing, your philosophy, and your bankroll.

If I'm waiting in line to cash my coins, and the person in front of or behind me has several buckets of dollars, I'll say something like "Wow! Looks like you did great." And all too often what I hear back is something like, "Well, I had it going for awhile. I had it up to over $1,000 but then I played it back down to $500."

I just shake my head in wonderment. First of all, anybody who puts five hundred dollars into a quarter Video Poker machine is deranged. Think about it. They didn't start off by inserting $500. They played a little, lost, dug deeper, lost, dug deeper, maybe won a little and then lost it back, dug deeper, etc. They sat there and let that little computer-driven monster suck them dry. And that's pure insanity. Obviously these kind of people have no sense of Money Management, never had a plan, have never heard of Dead Bolting profits, or setting Losing Limits or Winning Goals.

> ## MONEY MANAGEMENT
> I developed a habit a long time ago. If I'm walking past a quarter machine and I notice the person playing has racked up, say, 1,000 credits, and if I can speak to that person without disturbing them, I'll make a statement like "Tell me you only started with ten coins." I do this for a reason. First, I'm eager to witness success stories. Second, I want to see how many times I will hear a response like "Nah, I've got five hundred dollars in this stupid machine."

The second example is even worse. The person who had the machine up to $1,000 and then played it down to $500 is at least as incompetent as the first person. They actually had winnings and dumped most of them back into the machine. You could make a case for them by saying they were smart enough to walk away with profits, but they exercised no control by staying long enough to allow the machine to recover so much of its losses.

There are no secrets here. If you have read other chapters in this book you recognize and hopefully have accepted ideas like Dead Bolting, etc. Those suggestions work for all the various gaming venues, including Video Poker.

276

1) **Have a plan.**

2) **Establish your Loss Limit. Doesn't make any difference whether you are a recreational player who will only be in the casino for two hours, or if you play every day. You must know what portion of your bankroll you're willing to risk.**

3) **Set a Winning Goal. If you reach it, start Dead Bolting.**

4) **Once you get ahead, never allow the machine to take it back. If that means quitting dollars and going to quarters, do it. If it means quitting quarters and going to nickels, do it. If it means leaving the casino, do it.**

5) **If you're there for an extended stay, determine how many times you will be playing. Each of these times is a session. Divide the total sessions into your total bankroll. If you do this you will have an automatic Loss Limit.**

277

6) **Take it one machine at a time. You sit down with the idea in mind that if that machine takes as much as X dollars of your money you are moving. There are lots of machines. Never assume that a cold machine will suddenly turn around and start producing winning hands. It could be hours or even days before that happens. Move on. And keep moving until you find one who is more friendly.**

TEST YOUR IMAGINATION

If you play a lot of video poker, which I do, and if you like to play at the bars in the casinos, which I do, you are bound to encounter machines called Game Makers. What fun. I don't mean to imply that you will only find them at bars, but that happens to be where I've found most of them. These guys offer several of the normal games which we've already discussed . . .games like Jacks or

Better Draw Poker, Deuces Wild, Bonus Poker and Double Bonus Poker. They even offer video versions of games like Blackjack, Let It Ride, and Keno. But what we're gonna talk about now is the other Video Poker games . . .the games which go fishing every day in an attempt to reel one of us humans into their lair. No, the games aren't rigged or set at lower percentages, they are simply different. And interesting. And sometimes appealing. And sometimes drop dead addictive.

"POKER PLUS—WIN UP TO 2,000 COINS!"

That's the hook, just like you see it printed above. Win up to 2,000 coins! Win up to 2,000 coins, that is, for any Four of a Kind. The game is similar to Jacks or Better, and played in the same manner. You are dealt a hand, you hold what you want to keep, discard the rest, and then hit the Deal/Draw button. Here's the payoff schedule for five coins or credits.

278

Royal Flush	4,000 coins
Straight Flush	250
4 of a Kind	125
Full House	30
Flush	25
Straight	20
3 of a Kind	15
2 Pair	10
Jacks or better	5

Look familiar? Exactly like Jacks or Better Draw Poker, right? Yes. So how is it different? Here's the skinny. When a Four of a Kind is made, whether the machine flat-out deals it to you or whether you have to Draw and pray for it, the five cards making up this very nice winning hand are reshuffled and dealt face down on the screen. This is the big difference. This is the Plus in Poker Plus. The cards are reshuffled and dealt face down because now you're going to get a chance to take that one hundred and twenty-five credits and run it all the way up to two thousand. At no additional charge. At no risk to the one hundred and twenty-five you've already won. Is this great, or what? All you need to do is find each card as instructed by the machine, in the exact order requested by the machine. Each card correctly selected doubles the payoff. You can go from 125 to 250 to 500 to 1,000 to 2,000.

Let's take it one step at a time. You're dealt five completely worthless cards, so you draw all five cards and end up with a hand consisting of the Jack H + Jack C + Jack S + Jack D + 3 H. Congrats--you're won 125 coins. What? You don't believe it's possible to discard all five cards from the original deal and then draw Four of a Kind? Hey, it happens every day. Yes, it has happened to me, and more than once. Anyway, I digress. You've got this beautiful 4 of a Kind. And then the machine automatically reshuffles that exact same winning hand, all four of the Jacks plus the 3 H, and deals all five cards out yet again, face down. Then it asks you to locate the Jack of Spades. Of course you have no idea where the Jack of Spades might be, so this is a complete guessing game. Yet, remember, you've already won 125 coins, and you're not going to lose anything. So, directed solely by the hand of God, you touch one of the cards on the screen or press the corresponding

Progressives grow with each coin deposited into that "bank" or "carousel" of machines. For Bonusgames, there could be multiple progressive pots, such as one for the Royal Flush, another for Four Aces, etc.

Hold buttons, and up jumps the Jack of Spades. Can you believe your good fortune? You have just increased your payoff from 125 to 250. And you get to go again. The machine requests the Jack of Diamonds. You select one of the cards which is still face down, and, unbelievable as it may seem, you correctly pick the Jack of Diamonds. Your payoff races to 500 coins. And now you're thinking you might just go all the way. I mean, now there's only three cards left face down, so your chances are improving. I mean, the hard part is already over. Right? Well, the machine now requests the Three of Hearts. You've got three cards to choose from. Can you do it? Of course. You nail that Three of Hearts and the credits climb to 1,000.

Only two cards left. You've got a fifty-fifty chance of collecting 2,000 coins. The machine requests the Jack of Hearts. Only two face down cards to choose from. One is worth nothing, one is worth another 1,000 coins. If you're playing quarters, that's $250 for being right, or a grand total of $500. You're down $375.00 for the day. One more correct guess and all of a sudden you're up $125. What a come back that would be. Your head is dancing with enthusiasm, fueled by adrenaline and dreams of success. You're certain this is going to happen. Darn it, you're going to select the right card. So you touch the one on the left and ...try not to feel bad because it was only a guess ...and the Jack of Clubs is revealed. C'mon, deep down you never believed you could pick 4 in a roll. I mean, what are the odds of doing that? Well, since you asked, the answer is actually a smaller number than you might think; 120:1. On the first card, your chances were one out of five, on the second card one of four, then one out of three and one out of 2, which total 120 possibilities. Anyway, you still collected 1,000 coins for what began as a 125-coin payoff, and that's wonderful.

280

WORTH NOTING & REMEMBERING

On most of the newer machines, particularly those that require multiple bets like Triple-Play Video Poker, you only need to hit the Bet Max Coins button once. After the first hand is played you can make the same bet again by hitting the Deal/Draw button or by touching the Deal/Draw symbol on the screen. So long as you want to make bets of the same quantity as the hand before, simple hit/touch Deal/Draw. This is called making a re-bet. The credits are subtracted in a flash from your total and the cards are dealt immediately, so the game moves along much faster. Of course if you're going to keep changing the amounts on your bets, then continue using the Bet One Coin button/symbol; push it once for each coin you want to bet, then touch the Deal/Draw button/symbol to receive your cards.

But now the hardest question. What's your chances of coming up with Four of a Kind? I'm sure you can figure out the answer to that one for your-self.

Nobody but the manufacturer knows the exact odds, but we know this much for certain: Increased payoffs and bonuses for any kind of special hand means reduced pay-offs somewhere else. The pay table is accurate and gives no hints as to how the machine is going to accumulate these extra coins to use for the 4 of a Kind bonus, so you can only assume you will have fewer winning hands than normal. Either that, or we may seldom see a 4 of a Kind. Yes, this game can be fun to play. No, it is not worth the extra $10 or $20 or, don't even think about it, $50 to find out what might happen if you could just get a couple of Four of a Kinds.

SECOND CHANCE POKER

Here's another twist. It's looks like normal, well-adjusted basic poker game, but beneath the exterior lies a game which offers intriguing possibilities, a greater chance to use your brain, and a lot of frustration. Here's what the pay table looks like with max coins wagered:

Royal Flush	**4,000 coins/credits**
Straight Flush	250
4 of a Kind	125
Full House	40
Flush	25
Straight	20
3 of a Kind	15
2 Pair	10
1 Pair	5

You deposit coins, you are dealt a hand, you play the hand in the nor-mal manner. You Hold a few cards, you replace a few cards. Hopefully you have a winner. But whether you have a winner or not, you may receive a Second Chance opportunity. Second Chance Play is offered any time the addition of a sixth card can improve the original poker hand to a Straight or better. The sixth card is taken from the cards which still remain in the deck after the original hand has been played. A mini-screen appears in the upper left hand corner of the main screen. It informs you as to what the pay-offs will be should the sixth card option make a better hand. If you elect to accept the Second Chance offer, push the Second Chance button. It you elect not to accept the Second Chance offer, push the Decline button. Should you elect to exercise the Second Chance Option, another wager must be placed. You can make this wager by hitting the Bet One button from one to five times. The size of the wager is up to you. If your intent is to play five coins or credits, simply push the Bet Max button for an automatic 5-coin wager. The Second Chance option is, in reality, a totally separate bet from your first wager. Remember what I said. A mini-screen within the screen pops up in the left hand upper corner. If you have picture-in-picture capability on your home television, you know exactly what I mean when I say a small screen appears on the big one. That mini-screen explains what you will win if this wager proves successful.

282

Your original bet is not effected by the Second Chance opportunity. If it was a winning hand, it will still be a winning hand and you will be paid as shown in the pay table. Again, the Second Chance opportunity is a separate wager and can be thought of as playing the nephew of the original hand.

So you decide to try it. You want to see that sixth card. And, by the way, the sixth card is already on the screen, usually in the upper right side of the screen, separate from your 5-card hand, but it's face down. You touch the Second Chance button. You hit the Bet Max button because you firmly believe that anything worth playing is worth playing at maximum coins. And on that issue you won't get any argument from me. So, option selected, money in, now either press the Deal button or touch the sixth card. Walla! The sixth card either helps, in which case you collect the Second Chance payoff and the credits from your original hand, or the sixth card is worthless and you collect only the credits from your original hand. But remember that your original hand might not have been a winner. Again, you don't need a winning hand to qualify for the Second Chance option. You don't need a losing hand to qualify for the Second Hand option, either. What you need is a hand that could improve to a Straight or better with the addition of a 6th card.

Here are some examples.

You are dealt a Pair of 6's and three junk cards. You hold the 6's and catch a Pair of Kings + one card which is worthless. You now have two pair. Congratulations. You have a winning hand. You're about to collect ten credits. Whether or not you decided to pursue the Second Chance option has no effect on those ten credits. You're going to collect them regardless of what else happens. You have won ten credits, so stop worrying about them. They are yours. Period.

Now, a question arises. Can a hand consisting of a Pair of 6's and a Pair of Kings be improved to a Straight or better with the addition of a sixth card? Actually, you don't even need to think about the question, because the machine will do it for you. In this case the answer is an obvious yes, because you could improve to a Full House with the addition of another King or another 6. But is the payoff worth it? A quick glance at the Second Chance Bonus payoffs should answer that question. A Full House is worth 55 credits. Is it worth it to try for the Full House? Think about it. You've already won 10 credits. You bet 5 coins to win the 10. If you bet another 5 coins your total risk is 10 coins, or credits, and you've already won that much, so you can't possibly lose. So, why not go for it? Well that reasoning is sound, especially for you aggressive players. You can turn this into a formula. Can't lose + might win = Go For It! And I wouldn't fault your thinking or argue with your reasoning. Particularly if you're up a few credits and therefore have a little "cushion" in your bankroll. On the other hand, the more conservative player may be thinking of a different formula, one like this: Credits In Hand + Will Probably Lose = Take The Money And Play Another New Hand. It's the age-old question of risk versus potential gain.

283

In our example, let's say you went for it and caught a King. Now you collect the 10 credits from your original two pair + another 55 credits for filling the Full House, for a total of 65 credits.

> ## HERE'S A TIP
> When you want to Decline the Second Chance option: In addition to pressing the Decline button, you can also touch the Deal button. This action automatically ensures that you will decline the Second Chance option and launch into the next hand.

One more example. Here's your hand: 4 D + 5 D + 6 D + 7 D + 8 S. You've won 20 coins because you have a Straight. The Second Chance option appears. Is it worth it? You glance at the Second Chance pay-offs and note that a Straight Flush is worth 220 coins. A regular old Flush is still worth 20. Are you gonna go for it? Are you nuts? This is a no brainer! The worst case scenario is that you wager a total of ten credits and collect twenty. The next scenario is that you catch the Flush, in which case you wager a total of ten and collect forty. The best scenario is that you wager ten and collect two hundred and forty. Don't dawdle. Just do it!

Don't forget, when you elect the Second Chance option, you are not required to bet the max of five coins. You may wager one, two, three, four or five. Also remember that the Second Chance option is a separate wager and does not effect any pay-offs you have qualified for on your original hand.

284

The synopsis on this game? Can be fun . . .can be dangerous. If you're one of those people who will elect the Second Chance option every time you have four cards to a Straight or Flush, this game could drain you. If you are one of those people capable of weighing pros and cons and making intelligent decisions, this game can be very interesting . . .more so than normal Jacks or Better Video Poker. In other words, it's a game worth experimentation so long as you don't let it pound your bankroll into oblivion.

PICK'EM POKER

I have never had any success with this game, but I still enjoy playing it and that's as dangerous as it gets in a casino.

Why would anyone play a game like this one? Because some of us are stupid? No, that's not it. Because it's a challenge? No, it's not at all difficult to play; in fact it's pretty simple. Because we're competitive? Absolutely! We hate to lose, and we are convinced we can beat'em, whether "them" is another team, a crossword puzzle or a game of chance. Consequently, even though we've tried numerous times without success, even though this game keeps nibbling at our bankroll, we just won't give it up. For some of us the game might be Craps, for others Baccarat. For me it's Pick'em Poker. Recognizing that this is not my best game, I have managed to both establish and ruthlessly implement

> ## WARNING! WARNING!
> Whatever you do, don't fall in love with a game which destroys your bankroll faster than steaming water melts ice cubes. You can be the world's top expert at any particular game, but if that same game keeps beating you down you gotta give it up. No matter how much you love it, no matter how much fun you have playing it. Give it up before it hurts you! I repeat: Give it up!

limits. In fact, the only positive here is that this game is a test of my self control, and the game may win the little conflict over money, but I am winning the campaign to determine which of us has the most control. For, you see, I only play Pick'em Poker for a max of $20 per confrontation, and I never dig for more when the first $20 is gone. Fortunately, $20 represents such a small percentage of my bankroll it is insignificant. But, as you've said so very often, it's the principal of the thing. Yes, I've met many people who have experienced success playing this same game. And one of these days one of those people will be me.

Same routine here as with the other Video Poker games. Insert your five coins or slip in paper money and play five credits. And therein lies the last of the similarities between this and all of the other video poker games. From here on, all is strange and eerie.

When the deal is exposed, you will be viewing four cards which are face up. On the left side of the screen are two cards which are a permanent fixture in this hand. (This is another case where actually seeing the hand will be of benefit, so I suggest you deal this out for yourself.) If those two cards are the Queen D (occupying the far left position on the screen) and the King S (which is depicted immediately to the right of the Queen of Spades, or what you might want to call the second card from the left), they are there until the end. You also then have two cards exposed on the right side of the screen. Both of those

285

VERY IMPORTANT!

All this talk about credits. Play credits, cash credits, build credits. Credits, credits, credits. We see the word on the face of the machines, both video poker and slots, so much that we tend to forget that credits = coins or tokens = real money. Which is easier? Wagering 20 credits or $20.00? Credits directly reflect your bankroll. Don't treat them as play things. Don't let them lose their value. Don't ever forget that credits mean money. Otherwise all is lost.

cards have stacked below them two additional cards which are face down and thus out of our view. We'll say that the one all the way to the right is the Queen H, and the second from the right is the 5 C. Again, both of these cards are on the top of their respective piles. Each has two additional cards layered below them. You can see that clearly on the screen. And here's where the name comes from. You must select...Pick or Pick'em . . . one of those piles of cards. You can choose the pile that has the Queen H on top, or the pile headed by the 5 C. When you make that decision, either by touching the screen or a corresponding Hold/Cancel button, the two hidden cards will be revealed to provide you with a five-card poker hand. Here's the pay table for five-coin bets. Note that pay-offs are higher than normal, which means you can expect to see them less often.

Royal Flush	6,000 coins/credits
Straight Flush	1,199
4 of a Kind	600
Full House	90
Flush	75
Straight	55
3 of a Kind	25
2 Pair	15
Nines or Better	10

Note that to achieve a return of your bet all you need is a puny pair of 9's. If you had the hand listed above, your choice would be very simple. You would choose the pile headed by the Queen of Hearts because that would give you a sure pair of Queens. And you hope that the Queen of Hearts is hiding something which would really give your hand a boost; like another pair of Queens, a King, a pair of Kings, etc. For example's sake, play this out. Your hand consists of, reading from left to right as you view the screen, the Queen D + King S + a pile of three cards which is topped by the Queen H + another pile of three cards which is topped by the Five C. You know and understand that if you choose the pile topped by the Queen of Hearts you cannot lose, so that is the pile you select. As soon as you do so, the pile headed by the Five of Clubs disappears from the screen and the two hidden cards which were below and behind the Queen of Hearts are revealed. In this case those two hidden cards turn out to be the 6 S and the 9 H, so all you have is the Pair of Queens. You never find out what was hidden under the 5 of Clubs. You can only wonder.

So what have you got? First, a game which is only partially like real draw poker. Second, a game where your decision a majority of the hands is going to be nothing more than a guess. Which leads you to what conclusion? Exactly. If you want to fool around for a few hands some night when you've already won all the money in the casino, and you merely want to kill a few minutes while your wife is spending part of it in the gift shop, go ahead and give it a try. Or if you're like me, just keep on playing this stupid, ridiculous, asinine, absurd game for small stakes until you can beat it and feel like a real winner.

REVERSIBLE ROYALS & RICOCHET ROYALS

Most Royal Flushes pay a minimum of 4,000 coins. Progressive Jackpots can easily reach 10,000. With Reversible Royals and Ricochet Royals it gets even better.

Both of these games are the same. The first trick here is to hit the Royal Flush. The second is to have a Royal Flush which reads in exact order of rank from either left to right, or right to left. Like, Ace H + King H + Queen H + Jack H + 10 H. Or, like 10 D + Jack D + Queen D + King D + Ace D. And what's the big deal if you should hit a Royal which lays out as depicted? If you are playing quarters instead of receiving 4,000 coins you will receive 50,000 to

100,000. If you are playing dollars, instead of receiving $4,000 you will receive at least $50,000. Which is wonderful. So, like, if you can expect to see a Royal Flush in the basic Jacks or Better game about every 40,000 hands, how often do you think that Royal will appear with the cards in exact order of rank? Figure it out for yourself.

Ricochet Royals and Reversible Royals are usually basic Jacks or Better Bonus or Double-Double Bonus games.

DOUBLE DOWN STUD

Truly unique and enticing. Very simple to play. Usually a quarter game, but dollars can be found. You only see five cards, total. Insert your five coins, receive a hand. The first four cards, from left to right, are face up. The last card, the one all the way over to the right side of the screen, is face down. You need make only one decision. Would you care to double your wager before that face-down card is revealed? Total of 5 cards, a chance to double, a card which is face down. Hence the name, Double Down Stud. Here's a typical pay table. Pay-offs are shown for 5 coins and 10 coins.

288

Royal Flush	4,000	Progressive
Straight Flush	1,000	2,000
4 of a Kind	250	500
Full House	60	120
Flush	45	90
Straight	30	60
3 of a Kind	20	40
2 Pair	15	30
Pair of Jacks-Aces	10	20
Pair of 6's-10's	5	10

You'll seldom see a Progressive Jackpot of less than $7,000 and I've seen them over $20,000. Except for the Progressive Royal, all the pay-offs are in proportion. All it takes is a little, itty bitty Pair of 6's to win. Excuse me. All it takes is a little, itty bitty Pair of 6's to qualify for return of wager. The pay table looks attractive. Now find the chapter in this book on Caribbean Stud and take a look at Figure 5. In a game of 5-Card Stud you can expect to see a Royal Flush once every 648,700 hands. In a game of basic Jacks or Better Draw Poker you should see the Royal about every 40,000 hands. Enough said.

The strategy is simple. Hit the Double Down button every time:

A) You have a Pair of Sixes or better
B) You have four to a Flush
C) You have four to an Outside Straight

When you double down two events take place. One, you must deposit five additional coins/credits, and two, the face down card is revealed. If you are already playing with credits, the machine takes the extra five off your total. If you win, you will be paid based on the 10-coin pay table. If you don't see any of the above, simply hit the Deal/Draw button and the face down card will still be exposed. You will then either lose and move on to the next hand, or win and be paid per the 5-coin pay table.

Careful with this game. Due to the pay-offs you can accumulate credits so quickly you'll think you're on the verge of financial independence. Unfortunately, these machines can go dead faster than a rattlesnake living at the North Pole.

TRIPLE PLAY

The single most popular game, whether Video Poker or Slot Machine, to hit the market in the last twenty years. Quite a statement? Quite a game. The basics are quite simple. You are playing three hands instead of one. Or, maybe I should say you are playing one hand but paying and collecting based on three. Here's what I mean.

Same deal as with all the other Video Poker games. You must insert coins or develop credits with cash or winnings. Physically, the game is larger than all the other Video Poker machines. Bigger case, bigger screen, etc. Taller and wider. The main screen will exhibit a menu. You can ordinarily choose from five games:

Deuces Wild
Jacks or Better
Bonus Jacks or Better
Double Bonus Jacks or Better
Double Double Bonus Jacks or Better

If you take a moment to observe, second nature for me, you will note that nearly 100% of all the players have elected to play Double Double Bonus. Why? Go back and take a look at the pay tables printed earlier in this chapter. Double Double Bonus provides more of the "Jackpot" size pay-offs.

People dump and dump and dump into this game because they know they can hit those Four Aces with a kicker for 2,000 coins at any time and bail out all or most of their losses. Bigger pay-offs, increased risk, seems to be the most popular carrot for the majority of gamblers.

These games are usually quarters, dollars are scarce, and nickels are plentiful. You can play from 1 to 15 coins. Which, for quarters, means anywhere from 25 cents to $3.75. Which is why this game was invented. For, you see, the marketers realized that the same person who would never consider playing dollar Video Poker because $5 is too much to risk on a hand of V.P. is the very same person who will play 15 quarters. Correct. This game is a way to get the quarter players to play more money faster.

First, select your game by touching the screen. No buttons required. They are present, but you can do everything by touching the screen in the proper locations. Next, look for the little icon on the screen which represents speed. You can adjust the speed of the game to fit your level of skill, your eyesight, or whatever. Want the cards coming at you at the speed of light? Set it for fast. Want to see every individual card as it is revealed? Set it for slow. Want more info? Select the Help menu.

290

Jackpots are never paid by the machine. An attendant will verify that the pay-off is correct, take your IRS info if necessary, and pay you with currency or, if it's a really large number or if you request it, by check.

Second, do the coin/credit thing. The number of hands which will appear depends on the number of coins deposited. If you only insert/play one coin, only one hand will appear. You get two for two, and three for three. If you play 4 coins, the first two will be applied to the bottom hand on the screen, with the upper two hands receiving one coin each. In other words, the computer/machine applies the coins/wagers to each of the three hands depending on how many coins were wagered. If you bet 12 coins, that would be 4 coins for each of the three rows of cards. 11 coins would be 4 for the bottom, 4 for the middle hand, and 3 for the top.

We'll assume you played all 15 coins. The machine deals out fifteen cards. What

HOW TO PLAY CREDITS

There is a Bet One button. There is also a Play Max button. There is also a Deal/Draw button. With these machines, the Deal/Draw button will automatically bet whatever you bet on the previous hand. If you bet 10 coins on the last hand, hit the Deal/Draw to bet 10 again. No need to hit the Bet One button ten times. This works whether your previous wager was 1 coin or 15. However, should you want to change the amount of your wager, use either the Bet One or Play Max buttons.

291

you see on the screen is one row of exposed cards across the bottom, plus a row of face down cards above those, plus another row face down about those. One hand exposed, two hidden. Play the bottom hand. Hold and Draw exactly as you would for a single game. For the moment, forget about the other two hands. Concentrate only on what you can see. Hold by either touching buttons or touching the screen. Whatever card positions are held in the bottom hand are also held in the other two. For example. The first two cards on the screen, on the left side, are the Queen of Clubs and the Queen of Hearts. You Hold them. When you do so, the second and third hands reveal precisely the same cards in precisely the same positions. In other words, you started with the Queen of Clubs on the bottom row of cards all the way to the left. The Queen of Hearts was immediately adjacent to the Queen of Clubs. You could not see any cards in the second and third hands. You Hold the Pair of Queens. As soon as you Touch/Hold the Queen of Clubs another one shows up in the second hand in exactly the same position. Same is true for the Queen of Hearts. As soon as you Hold/Touch it, another one shows up in the second and third hands in exactly the same position. On the screen, it will look like this:

Queen Clubs + Queen Hearts + ?   **+?**   **+?**

Queen Clubs + Queen Hearts + ?   **+?**   **+?**

Queen Clubs + Queen Hearts + X   **+X**   **+X**

Draw by touching the screen or a button. Each of the three hands will be treated as individuals. The computer has a separate deck of cards for each hand. When you draw cards, the computer deals to each hand from it's own deck. You will not receive nine cards from one deck. You will receive three from deck 1, three from deck 2, and three from deck 3.

Whether you win depends on the game you are playing and what you draw. The pay tables are pretty much identical to those listed earlier in this chapter.

In our example you could draw out to Four Queens on all three lines, or you could draw no help, or nearly anything in between. Each line pays per the pay table. Assume you are playing Double Double Bonus. Assume the hand ends like this.

Queen Clubs + Queen Hearts + Queen Diamonds + King Hearts + King Clubs

Queen Clubs + Queen Hearts + Jack Clubs + Ten Spades + King Clubs

Queen Clubs + Queen Hearts + Queen Spades + King Hearts + Queen Spades

On the bottom, you caught the 4 Queens. That's 250 coins/credits. The middle hand showed no improvement, so its Pair of Queens pays 5 coins. And the top hand caught a Pair of Kings to make a Full House, which pays 45. That's a total of 300 coins, and you collect all 300.

Don't worry about figuring out what you have because the computer will help. It will tell you if you have Jacks or Better in the bottom hand. It will tell you the value of each hand after you draw. It will tell you how much you won on each hand. It will run up your credits. It will do everything except kiss you.

HAND PAYS

Read the small print on the front of your Video Poker machine. Note that some advise that quarter machines only pay 1,000 coins, dollars only pay 400. Any amounts higher than those must me paid by an attendant. If you are playing quarters and you rack up 1,500, and then try to cash out, don't be surprised if the computer informs you that an attendant is needed. A light will flash on the top of the machine. You'll get your money, but you may need to wait a few minutes for the cash.

293

TOO MUCH

This may give you a hint of where Video Poker is headed. During my last stay in Las Vegas I found a Triple Play machine at the Fiesta which offered nine different games. They were/are:

Jack or Better
Bonus Jacks or Better
Bonus Deluxe
Deuces Wild
Double Bonus
Double Double Bonus
Super Double Bonus
Triple Double Bonus
Super Aces Bonus

During the same trip I discovered a 10-Play Video Poker machine at Sunset Station. It was only a nickel machine, but try to imagine ten hands all displayed on the same screen. Even when set on the slowest speed the cards flash up so quickly no human can possibly read them until the hand is over. Though only nickels, the same idea is used here as for quarters in Triple Play. Under ordinary circumstances a nickel player would never consider playing $2.50 on a hand of Video Poker. But with 10-Play that's exactly what happens. Five coins per hand x 10 hands = 50 coins = $2.50. So, how long do you think it will be before we see 10-Play games for quarters or dollars?

There are many other Video Poker games. Games like White Hot Aces, Sneak-A-Peak, Loose Deuces Wild, Deuces Wild Double Down Stud, several forms of Jacks or Better which offer the player to go for double or nothing on winning hands . . .the list could go on and on. All are variations on a theme. All are some form of good old basic Jacks or Better Draw Poker. Any time you see something new and different read the pay tables and determine for yourself whether it is worth trying. And don't forget thatwhat they giveth with the right hand they usually retrieveth with the left hand.

294

14

Software & Cyberspace

Y ou're two thousand miles from the nearest casino. Or, you can't schedule a vacation, or a quick weekend trip to Vegas, or even a mini-junket because, well, you know, just too many other commitments. Yet you've really got the bug. You are in great need of action. Of the casino variety. So, whataya do? Actually there are a three choices, two of which require a computer.

The first option is for you to visit your local drug store, department store, Wal-Mart or Target. Buy one or more of the hand-held electronic games. You might want one for Blackjack and another for Video Poker or Slot Machines. None of them cost more than $20. They even come with batteries already installed. They fit in the palm of your hand. You can take them anywhere, carry them in your pocket or purse. The games are played just like in a casino. You start with X number of credits and either win or lose. If you win, the game will retain your credit total so that you can play indefinitely. If you lose? If you go broke? No problem. Hit a button and get more credits. Surely you have seen these games by now. People play them in airports, at the grocery store, in their automobiles . . .wherever they happen to be when the opportunity to play is presented. If you haven't seen them, go buy one.

Enough said about "toys." Time to get on with the title of this chapter. Time to get on with what we are really here to discuss. Software and cyberspace. The good news is that there's a way to play without buying a toy. The bad news

> **WORTH REPEATING**
> Those $4.95 games can provide all the enjoyment and practice you need. Poor graphics, sounds, etc., but still worthy.

is that in order to use either of the other options you must have a computer. If you don't, you can stop reading right now. And, actually, if you don't own a computer don't feel bad. Those little hand-held toys mentioned earlier can provide all of the practice you need. They may not wet your appetite for the real thing, but they are much less expensive than the other options.

Play and practice. That's the point. Whether by utilizing a hand-held toy or software, you need to play and practice the games. Toys and software allow you to do just that. Cyberspace and the Internet provide play and practice, but also add another dimension. On the Internet you can gamble for real money.

So, here's the deal. If you have gambling fever and cannot get to a live casino, try to pacify yourself by playing "pretend" casino games. The pretend games are accurate in every way except one: no real money changes hands. Or, if that's not good enough for you, if making pretend wagers doesn't cut it, just doesn't get the adrenaline pumping, then your only other option is to become a web surfer. The preference should be to satisfy yourself in the pretend manner, so that's where we'll begin.

SOFTWARE

First, the disclaimer. If you have no computer exposure or experience you're about to be left behind. This is not a computer book. This is a gambling book. I'm not here to explain software, hardware, or the difference between DOS and Windows 98. This section is all about software games which can be played on a computer. Casino gambling games. Rich graphics, interactive characters, excellent sound, the chance to gamble your way to riches without risking a penny of your own money. These games can be purchased anywhere computer games are sold. Comp USA, Best Buy, Media Play, or whoever offers the best availability and pricing in your town. Or, for those of you already connected to the Net, direct yourself to places like Amazon.com. Most of the games sell for less than $30. Some cover all casino venues, some specialize. Some offer expert advice as you play. Some are better than others, but I say that only as a generality because I've never seen a bad one. If your game is Video Poker, you might

Here's the good news and the bad news about software. Good: great practice, no chance of losing real money. Bad: no risk—no excitement—no thrill—no fulfillment.

start with one of the games which offers all of the gaming venues, and then move on to more specialized software as your expertise and level of comfort improve. Ditto if you enjoy Slot Machines.

Spending hours in front of a cathode ray tube while casino gambling is no different than planting yourself in the same spot and playing Space Invaders. Same idea, different games.

Older games are loaded onto 3.5 inch floppy disks, newer ones on compact disks. And while there's nothing wrong with some of the older games . . .I, for example, have an excellent one on video poker . . .don't buy games which are only on floppies. Given a choice between buying an older game on a floppy disk for $7.98 or a brand new one on CD for $24.99, spend the extra $17.

You will find the difference to be night and day. Like, would you buy a record player which only produces monaural sound when for slightly more you could have a stereo with surround sound? Yes, the difference could be that great.

Here's what typically happens with the newer software games when you load them. First, music blares but in moderation. However, if you usually have your speakers turned up you might be startled. A cover page identifies the game and announces that you'll be able to choose from 7 different venues. Then several backgrounds are depicted, a Craps table for example, with the technical information overlaid. If you want to know the names of the de-

> ## PLAY IT STRAIGHT
> Pretend that the credits are not pretend credits. Pretend they are very real. Pretend that they are precious. Elsewise, practice hands carry no validity.

signers, the art directors, the technology director, the voice talents, the team which created the graphics, etc., this is where you'll find that information. If you want to skip past all of that, simply hit your Escape key. All of the technical information is followed by a picture of a hotel lobby. A clerk is standing behind the check-in counter, which is situated adjacent to an elevator. There is a pop-up menu asking whether you choose to return to a previous game (select Load), or begin a new one (select New). Of course you can also Exit, but why?

You select New. A voice says "Welcome to Casino DeLuxe."

It's the first time you've played, so now you wait, and wait, and wait. Nothing happens. So, it's either read the directions, which of course is an absolute last resort, or check out the options at the top of the screen. Options like File, Sound, Speech, Speed, Game Options, and Go to Elevator.

The file menu contains options for New Game, Load Game, Save Game, and Exit. Under Sound are options for turning the music on or off, and setting levels. You enjoy the sound, so you choose the On option at max levels.

Under Speech the options are for a Male voice, a Female voice, or Off.

Speed can be set for Slow, Medium, or Fast.

Game Options are to turn the Animations On or Off, and also to view previous high scores.

Go to Elevator tells you nothing, but maybe you've played enough games to know that you must move the mouse pointer somewhere, and so you head for the elevator and double click.

Voila! All of a sudden you're inside the elevator. Again, music plays. Soft andmellow, like elevator music. And all of the floor selections are keyed to gaming venues. Blackjack is on the 3rd floor, Pai Gow Poker on the 7th floor, etc. There are also symbols for opening and closing the doors which look just like the ones you see on real elevators, but clicking on them doesn't do anything. Decor only. However, a click on a bell shaped symbol provides a loud and obnoxious ringing. Obviously the emergency button. Don't do that again. Not ever.

Time to choose a floor. Roulette is on the 4th, so let's start there. The floor button lights up, the floor indicator begins to climb, and in the blink of several eyes a Roulette layout appears. A voice says, "Place your bets." A sign at the bottom of the screen tells you to do the same thing: Please Place Your Bets. Fine. How? There's a picture of a Roman Nobleman on the right side of the screen. He is standing atop a pedestal. At the base of the pedestal are six stacks of casino chips ranging in value from $1 to $1,000. Above the Roman stiff is a tabulator. It says your bankroll is currently 4,999 coins and your bet is one. Okay. You click on the number 25 on the layout and, in a flash, a $1 chip is deposited on that number. It's so easy you keep clicking. A couple of chips on Black, four on the 1st 12, and seven on Odd. Every time you click, a chip is added to that wager. When you get up to five on Odd, the chips change from white to red, and then another two white are added. Just like in a casino. Red chips, highest value, on the bottom, lesser value chips on top. Each time you make a wager the appropriate chips are deducted from your total credits. The amount of the current, or last, wager is also shown.

The same person who wouldn't think of betting $10 in a game of Roulette in a real casino will bet $1,000 in a pretend game. No harm done? It depends. If this is really practice, then practice exactly like you would play. If this is for fun, bet the ranch.

299

But what about all those other piles of chips? There are $100 chips over there. Maybe you've never played a $100 chip in your life. So, go for it. You click on the chips, then move to the layout and click again at the intersection of the 4, 7, 5, and 8 to cover all four numbers. The $100 chip drops in place exactly as you intended.

Keep betting? Hey, you've already wagered $113. Don't get carried away. There's a Spin button at the bottom of the screen, so click on it. A full sized picture of a Roulette Wheel appears. You can see the entire wheel plus the ball. The ball is projected, the wheel spins. The actual sound of a ball rotating around a wheel is played and it sounds so much like a real ball you are amazed. At the precise moment when the ball lands on a number, the view changes to a close-up shot of the specific section of the wheel where the ball is about to land. The outcome is 00. A voice says, "Double zero."

> **REASONS TO BUY SOFTWARE GAMES**
> 1) to get better at the game you love the most. 2) to learn more about the games you don't understand.

The view then switches back to the layout and that voice says, "Place your bets," again. You do. But this time you pick up one of those $500 chips by clicking on it, and then click again on Black. $500 on Black? You're very brave. But then, you can't really lose because you're not playing for real money.

You click on Spin. The wheel turns, you hear the ball, the ball drops into a number and the voice says, "Thirty-two, red, even." You lose, but before you can even become disappointed the layout is back on the screen and the voice is saying "Bets, please." And this time you note that there is another button on the screen which states, "Repeat Bets." You correctly infer that if you want to repeat the last bet, make exactly the same wager for the same amount of money, you should click here. You do so and everything changes. The money is gone from your account in a flash, the wheel spins, the ball rattles, and you win or lose.

You place a bet on #32, then change your mind, but there doesn't appear to be a way to remove it, so you spin again, and again, and . . .whoa! Look at your tabulator. You're down to $3,000. You've already lost $2,000. Time for two actions. First, tone down those bets. Second, move on. Try a different game. And how do you do that? Well, when you began playing Roulette another drop-down menu option appeared at the top of the screen which states Leave Game. You click there and, like magic, you are transported back inside the elevator. Time to choose another game. You decide on Video Poker. It's on the 2nd floor.

It's standard Jacks or Better. No other options. Just the basic game. You check the screen, click here and there, and in only a few moments you've

300

figured out how to play. But then you change your mind and dash back to the elevator. For some reason Pai Gow Poker flashes in your mind, so you climb to the 7th floor.

Same idea here as with the rest of the games. Stacks of chips, a tabulator which has carried forward your total credits, a voice telling you to make a wager, a sign asking you to place your bets, etc. There's a Pai Gow layout, but it only shows your hand and the dealers. You play once, win, and then your telephone rings. It's the next door neighbor. You forgot that you were supposed to be somewhere. So it's time to get out of the casino, or game, and you do so by clicking on the File menu, then selecting Exit. A mini-screen appears requesting that you type in your name. Apparently you've qualified for the high-score list. You type "Lost Puppy" in the box, and the mini-screen produces a list which shows that Lost Puppy is in 8th place on the all-time list of high rollers. You hit Okay, and the game disappears.

The second generation version of this game is similar to the original but adds more game options, improved graphics, and a Help menu. When the help menu is selected, you have a choice

> **WORTH REMEMBERING**
> If the software game you purchase does not offer all the options of a real game, take it back. No sense practicing darts if you're trying to improve your abilities at chess.

of games. Whatever game you select, a message board pops up with printed information, and a voice is heard reading the same. You can also check the history of the game and recommended strategy.

Also, the arrow representing the mouse is changed into a hand. Point it where you want to go and it will notify you if you've chosen the wrong path.

Most games are pretty much the same. And of course to some extent they must be. Rules for Blackjack should be standard. Ditto for all the other games. So the flexible part of software casino games is in the setting (are you in the desert or on an ocean liner), the voices (from announcers only, or even from other players), the graphics, the screen layouts, etc.

What you need to find is the very best game on the market for whatever your specialty. For example, in the description above you couldn't remove a bet from Roulette. Maybe a better game will allow you to change your mind, just like you would in real life. Perhaps a Craps game's programming will not allow you to take Free Odds, whether on the Pass Line or on the Come. If the game does not allow you to play exactly like you would be playing at a real casino, then you need to keep looking for better alternatives.

CYBERSPACE

In terms of the manner in which the games are played, there is little if any difference between gambling on the Internet, gambling On Line, and playing with those software games you might have purchased. On your computer screen you can see little difference in the actual games. The screen will look different because there will be advertisements and all kinds of links to other web sites. But, in essence, the games will be the same.

You already have a computer. You already have a service provider. You already have a browser. If none of this means anything to you, get ready to spend, at the minimum, several hundred dollars. On the other hand, if you have the computer, service provider and browser, you're ready for gambling in cyberspace. You have the equipment. That's the starting point. Of course you could borrow somebody else's, or even go down to the library. Well, no, you can't go to most libraries and connect to casino gaming sites.

> ### NEVER HEARD OF YA
> Most online casinos are owned by corporations which did not exist until a few weeks before their sites were opened. But don't be alarmed. If all of the Internet companies which are owned by corporations with fewer than two years of existence were shut down, there would not be much of an Internet.

Don't know where to start? Do a search. Doesn't make much difference which vehicle you choose. Simply type in CASINO GAMBLING, or ONLINE CASINO GAMING, or nearly any words to that effect. You will be inundated with options. Thousands and thousands of options. They won't all be on your screen at once, but one leads to another, which leads to another, which leads to . . .anybody who has ever done a search knows of what I speak.

302

If you have not been referred to a specific site by a friend, relative or acquaintance, or if you have seen none advertised, or if you have no clue, then you probably need to seek out one of the portals. A portal web site is one which offers directory options. It can point you down a path. It can lead you to where you need to be. The portal is where you will find the link which will take you to sites like "5,000 Top Online Casinos," or "Top 40 Online Casinos As Rated by the American Society of Head Stone Carvers," or even "Top 100 Online Casinos by Prairie Dog Casino Publications." Portals are supported by advertisements, so don't be surprised if you're enticed by any number of them. At most portals you can also register for free stuff. Like Blackjack strategies, or Craps betting secrets, and that sort of thing. You're required to provide your e-mail address in order to receive most

> The risk with Internet or with online casino gambling does not lie in going to jail. The risk is in having someone drain your credit card.

303

of the freebies, so don't be surprised if you hear from them down the road. The Portal site is also one which might offer travel guides, free casino games, free screen savers, chatrooms, a message board, free newsletters, articles on how to improve your game, etc.

You'll need to keep moving and checking and investigating until you find the portal site, and then you'll need to keep moving and checking until you

> ### I.G.C.
> I.G.C. stands for Interactive Gaming Council, a self-governing organization invented to assure gamblers there is somebody out there trying to watch out for their best interests. Hasn't much power, but nice to know they are trying.

find an online casino which catches your interest. But don't get the impression that it will be difficult to find one. Once you begin surfing, you will see them advertised virtually everywhere. Finding one is not difficult. Finding many is not difficult. Selecting one can be tough, because you won't know whether they meet your criteria until after you've signed on. But stick with it. You may need to investigate several. You'll find online casinos which are portrayed as being in outer space, on cruise ships, in the Antarctic, on railroad trains . . .if you can think of it, there's probably an online casino using it as a theme.

Once you spot one that looks appealing, knock on their door by clicking on the link which will take you there. Here's what will happen.

The fact that an online casino might have a name like Denver Casino does not mean they are located in the United States. None of them are within U.S. borders. They are located in places like Australia, Costa Rica, the Bahamas, the Commonwealth of Dominca, and the Island of Curacao, Netherlands Antilles.

304

You will be connected to the casino's home page. A welcome message will greet you. Numerous options will be shown on the screen. Some-where, in fairly large type, will be a note worded to the effect that: "As members of the Interactive Gaming Council (IGC), this casino takes pride in their position of trust within the online gaming industry. Our members are assured a safe online experience. Flexible payment and collection devices guarantee that the players are always in control of their money. All types of wagers are easy to place, and all transactions are confirmed by e-mail for complete peace of mind." A good way to start.

What you're seeking on this first cyberspace trip is a site which allows you to play for fun. No way you want to risk real money your first time out. Fortunately, most sites can be visited as a guest. If your desire is to play for free, that can be arranged.

However, before you are allowed to play, identification is necessary. But don't be alarmed. All they want to know is your first and last name, e-mail address, and the name of your country. No big deal.

Now, remember the software discussed in the early portion of this chapter? You gotta have software to play. And each online casino has its own software. In order to play in their virtual casino, you must have their software.

This means you'll need to download their programs. Which could take 20 minutes and be sent to your hard drive, or could take 10 minutes and happen right on your screen. So relax for a few minutes.

Software loaded, time to play. You select Blackjack, and when the game pops up on the screen you are semi-amazed because the game is nearly identical to the one on which you practice. There is an overhead view of a Blackjack table showing your player position and that of the dealer. There's a tabulator which is starting you out with 100 pretend credits. You can only bet a max of $25, but that's by choice. Your other option was $25 to $250, and even though it was going to be pretend money you didn't want to develop any bad habits. Good thinking.

Please do not download anything from web sites unless you have virus protection software on your computer.

Software is software. You wonder if the person or team which created this specific Blackjack software was the same one who developed the one you bought for $19.95. The game plays a little slower than your own game, but that's all right. There's no rush. You win with a 15, lose with a 20, catch a Natural Blackjack and then lose a Double Down. Same rules as usual. Dealer has to hit any 17, and that's good. Ah! There's a difference. You can only Double Down on 10 or 11. But, still, pretty good rules. You also take a break for a couple of minutes to see what lies behind the field which is advertised as "Recent Winners." What you find is a list of ten names posted under a heading which is for February, 2000. The first name and last initial are shown, along with the person's location, and then an amount. And it's interesting. The top person is a gal named Nancy who apparently listed Montreal as her home. According to the stats, she won $6,780 in February. Holy Smoke! You wonder what she was playing, but the list doesn't say. The guy down in tenth place didn't do so bad, either. He's Eddie from Chicago and his total win was $975. And, believe it or not, some guy from Moscow is on the list, in fifth place with $3,560. Moscow? Well, don't forget this is the World Wide Web. Americans aren't the only people on Earth with computers which can access the Internet.

305

Back to the game. It's decision time. Are you going to continue wagering pretend dollars, or are you ready to try it with some of your own? You click on the top of the screen, up where it says Open An Account. While there, you take note of another message which you had previously overlooked. It says you are in FakeBet mode. The online casino was confirming that your bets did not count as real money. But, too late for that now, anyway. You're going for the real thing. And what you will see next is pretty much the same thing you'll see from any online entity from whom you are about to make a purchase.

> ## WEB BROWSER
> **Don't be surprised if your web browser complicates matters by interrupting and issuing warnings as you open your account with the online casino. It is programmed to do so. It does not like encrypted data.**

The web site already has your first name, last name, and e-mail address. Now they want more. And of course that was to be expected.

You are provided with four choices. First, you may place a credit card deposit. If you choose the credit card option and also intend to establish an account in excess of $500, you'll need to fill out a special form, but you've already decided on $100 so that would not apply to you. There is also a disclaimer. It doesn't make you feel any better, but you kind of knew what you were getting into before you started out, so it comes as no surprise. It looks something like this:

Online gambling may be illegal in the jurisdiction where you are located. This includes locations within the United States. Visa cards can only be used for legal transactions. The fact that an online casino may display a payment card logo from an online merchant does not mean that Internet gambling transactions are lawful in any or all of the jurisdictions in which the cardholder is located.

Many of the same sites which offer casino games also offer Sports Wagering. Some sites are devoted solely to Sports Wagering. Basics are the same,

306

open an account, deposit money, etc. Scare you a little? Are you positive you want to continue? It's not too late to change your mind.

The second choice is to arrange for a bank-to-bank wire transfer. The casino pays a bonus of 5% if you deposit a minimum of $500.

The third choice is to send your deposit via Federal Express. If you select this option, only cashier's checks are acceptable. Again, bonuses are available depending on the amount you deposit.

The fourth choice is to send money via Western Union. Again, bonuses are available.

Also, for Western Union, Federal Express, and bank-to-bank transfers, the casino picks up the costs.

You elect to use your credit card.

Now the really scary stuff appears. Legalese. Two or three pages of legal details. Employees of the casino are not eligible to participate. You can't enter the casino unless you are of legal age. You acknowledge that the games are for entertainment only. You become a party to all the rules. You . . .it goes on and on. And, of course, you ignore all of it and click on the icon which states that you accept all of the terms and conditions.

The next screen tells you that all transactions are in U.S. dollars. It also informs you that a special encryption program is used to protect your information. Visa and MasterCard are the only credit cards which can be used.

Next, fill in the blanks.

Name on Credit Card:_____

Zip Code: _____

Credit Card Number: _____

Expiration Date: _____

Amount: _____

Everything filled in? Click on Submit. Wait a few seconds. You're about to receive confirmation that your deposit has cleared. Now you are ready to play for real. Or, are you?

Yet another screen appears to request even more information. Again, fill in the blanks:

307

Age:_____

Work/Day Phone:_____

Home/Evening Phone:_____

Address:_____

City:_____

State/Province_____

Zip Code:_____

How did you hear about us:

Insert characters to create your account number:_____

Insert a password

Confirm the password

Now you're set. Now you can play. No more requests. Pull up the Black-jack game. But this time verify the rules before you begin. The casino supplies all you need to see. In fact, in the real game you can Double Down on any first two cards. Even better than the FakeBet game.

You play.

You win a few, you lose a few, but that's not what is important. What counts is that you are no longer worried about whether you should be doing this. You're into the game. You were planning on counting cards but dispose of that idea when you confirm a suspicion. Two Aces show up on the first hand and three more on the next, so the cards are being shuffled after each

> **VIRTUAL CASINOS**
>
> Same as online casino. A casino existing only in cyberspace. A casino which attempts to make you think you are in a real one.

round. Nothing really out of the ordinary happens. The online casino was very careful about the way they set up your account. As if they were afraid of cheaters as much as you. As if they were totally legitimate. You are also encouraged by the fact that the toll free 800 number for the casino's customer service department is listed on every page you've seen, and there's even a link to Gamblers Anonymous.

At one point your game is interrupted so that you can be notified you have just accumulated your first comp point. You decide that cyberspace comps sound good, so you take a few minutes to look around until you find the full information. When you locate the comp page you are astounded because your comp points can earn gift certificates for web-based catalog outlets. Great! So keep going.

You play for several hours. At one point you leave Blackjack to play a few hands of Video Poker, then return. When you are ready to quit you click on the field for Account Activity. In order to access your account information, you need to supply your account number and password, so it is hoped you remember them. You then confirm you've lost $15. Which means they still have $85 of your deposit. You actually fared better than expected. But how hard will it be to get back that $85? Or, would you rather leave it on account? Will you play again? Probably. But since you've never done this before you'd better see how it works when you want money back. So you click on Withdrawal. More questions, but easy.

How much do you want back:_____
How do you want it sent:_____
    a) via your credit card
    b) check via Federal Express
    c) check via regular mail

309

You select credit card, then click on Submit. A few seconds later another screen pops with notification that you have a transaction confirmation number, that the amount withdrawn is $85. It also confirms your credit card number and the name listed on the account. Time to exit.

Should you return to this site, you won't need to go through this whole process again. You'll merely log on, make your deposit, and play. Had you left that $85 on account, you could simply log on and begin playing.

Was it fulfilling? Would you do it again? Questions only you can answer.

I don't care whether or not you gamble for real money. But I do want you to continue cruising the Web. There's interesting stuff in cyberspace. And a ton of it is information associated with casino gambling. In fact, there is enough information spread throughout the World Wide Web pertaining to casino gambling that if you started at age 18 and saw something new every day until you were 80 you would never see it all.

Now You **<u>Can</u>** Know It All...

Fell's Official Know-It-All Guide™

Check out these exciting titles in our Know-It-All series, available at your favorite bookstore:

- ❏ Fell's Official Know-It-All Guide™ to Advanced Hypnotism
- ❏ Fell's Official Know-It-All Guide™ to Advanced Magic
- ❏ Fell's Official Know-It-All Guide™ to Budget Weddings
- ❏ Fell's Official Know-It-All Guide™ to Bridge
- ❏ Fell's Official Know-It-All Guide™ to Career Planning
- ❏ Fell's Official Know-It-All Guide™ to Coins: 2001
- ❏ Fell's Official Know-It-All Guide™ to Defensive Divorce
- ❏ Fell's Official Know-It-All Guide™ to ESP Power
- ❏ Fell's Official Know-It-All Guide™ to Getting Rich & Staying Rich
- ❏ Fell's Official Know-It-All Guide™ to Health & Wellness
- ❏ Fell's Official Know-It-All Guide™ to Hypnotism
- ❏ Fell's Official Know-It-All Guide™ to Knots
- ❏ Fell's Official Know-It-All Guide™ to Magic for Beginners
- ❏ Fell's Official Know-It-All Guide™ to The Mortgage Maze
- ❏ Fell's Official Know-It-All Guide™ to Online Investing
- ❏ Fell's Official Know-It-All Guide™ to Palm Reading
- ❏ Fell's Official Know-It-All Guide™ to Secrets of Mind Power
- ❏ Fell's Official Know-It-All Guide™ • Super Power Memory
- ❏ Fell's Official Know-It-All Guide™ • Wedding Planner
- ❏ Fell's Official Know-It-All Guide™ to Writing Bestsellers

FREDERICK FELL PUBLISHERS, INC.
Email: fellpub@aol.com
Visit our web site at www.fellpub.com